**COMMUNITY COLLEGE OF
PHILADELPHIA**
Philadelphia, Pennsylvania

GAYLORD S

# Hezbollah

# Hezbollah

## The Changing Face of Terrorism

*Judith Palmer Harik*

I.B. TAURIS
LONDON · NEW YORK

Published in 2004 by I.B.Tauris & Co Ltd
6 Salem Road, London W2 4BU
175 Fifth Avenue, New York NY 10010
www.ibtauris.com

In the United States of America and in Canada distributed by
Palgrave Macmillan, a division of St Martin's Press
175 Fifth Avenue, New York NY 10010

ISBN 1 86064 893 2

A full CIP record for this book is available from the British Library
A full CIP record for this book is available from the Library of Congress

Library of Congress catalog card: available

Typeset in Melior by Steve Tribe, Andover
Printed and bound in Great Britain by MPG Books Ltd, Bodmin

# Contents

*Preface*                                                                        ix

*Acknowledgements*                                                               xi

*Maps*                                                                          xiii

Introduction                                                                      1

**Chapter One**   **Hezbollah's Version of Political Islam**                       7

    Islam in Perspective                                        7

    The Islamic Resurgence of the 1970s                        9

    The Crisis of Secularism and Fundamentalist Reactions     11

    Government Corruption and the Purification of Society      20

    Colonialism and its Discontents                           23

**Chapter Two**   **Hezbollah and the Outside World**                            29

    Anti-Imperialism and Common Cause                         29

    Syria's Problems with the West                            29

    Imperialism and the Iranian Experience                    31

    Lebanon: An Arena for Foreign Battles                     34

    Iran Enters the Battle for West Beirut                    35

    Damascus and Tehran Strike a Deal                         38

    Hezbollah: The Only Choice                                39

**Chapter Three**   **The Mechanics of Hezbollah's Transformation
from Radical Militia to Mainstream Party**                                       43

    Syria Gains the Upper Hand in Lebanon                     43

    Guaranteeing Jihad                                        46

The State/Resistance Deal    47

Public Reaction to Hezbollah's New Face    48

**Chapter Four**    **Managing the 'True Believers'**    53

Islam or the System: The Internal Debate    53

Rationalizing Compromise from an Islamic Perspective    57

Convincing the Grassroots    60

An Eminent Clergyman Lends His Authority    60

**Chapter Five**    **Squaring Jihad with the General Public**    63

The Political Effects of Hezbollah's Violent Emergence    64

The Party of God Tries to Calm the Waters    66

Islamist Discourse and Integration: Jihad in a
     National Context    69

*Infitah*: Securing Christian Understanding and Support    73

Political Networking with Christians and Others    75

**Chapter Six**    **Serving the *Umma* – Hezbollah as Employer and
Welfare Organization**    81

The Effect of Lebanon's Civil War on Public and
     Social Services    82

Service Delivery in the *Dahiyeh*    83

Rural Services and Programmes    86

Speaking for the 'Abandoned'    89

Jihad al-Binaa (RC) as a Model Rural Development Agency    90

Hezbollah's 'Good Works': The Prognosis for Growth    93

**Chapter Seven**    **The Grass Roots Speak – The 1998 Municipal Elections**    95

The Struggle over Election 'Rules'    96

Hezbollah Plays the Democracy Card    98

Beirut Campaigns and Elections    99

The *Dahiyeh* Decides    101

The Electoral Struggle in the South    105

Hezbollah's Bekaa Coup    107

**Chapter Eight**    **The Mechanics of Military Jihad**    111

Beirut's Priority: Extending Control over the South    112

Incipient Tensions between the Lebanese Government
     and Hezbollah    113

The Imperatives and Rules of Syria's Two-Track
Resistance Policy     114

'Grapes of Wrath' and the Dynamics of Syrian Foreign
Policy     117

Policy Pay-offs     122

Post-'Victory' Frictions     123

**Chapter Nine**     **The Collapse of the 'Security Zone'**     125

Israel's 'Security Zone' Begins to Shrink     126

High-Tech, Low-Tech Jihad Pays Off     130

Guerrilla Warfare in the Communications Age     133

Diplomacy and the Israeli Withdrawal     134

The End of the 'Security Zone'     136

Resistance Challenges and Their Resolution     139

**Chapter Ten**     **Hezbollah's Standing After the Collapse of the
'Security Zone'**     147

Parliamentary Election Pay-offs     148

The South and the Bekaa Reward Hezbollah     149

Elections in the Capital     150

The Guns vs. Butter Clash     151

New Resistance Opportunities     155

All the Way to Jerusalem?     160

**Chapter Eleven**     **The Terrorism vs. Resistance Controversy**     163

Lebanon, Syria and Iran: Willing Partners in the
Anti-Terrorism Coalition?     164

Beirut's Position on Hezbollah as a Resistance Force     165

The US-Israeli Position: Hezbollah as Terrorist
Organization     169

**Chapter Twelve**     **America's Half-hearted War Against Terrorism**     177

The Anti-Terrorism Campaign in Lebanon     178

Lebanon's Response     179

Hezbollah's Developing Resistance Role     183

The Party of God and the Intifada     185

Guarding the Lebanese-Israeli Frontier     189

**Chapter Thirteen Conclusions and Implications**     193

*Notes*                                         203

*Select Bibliography*                           221

*Index*                                         235

# Preface

I was a new professor of political science at the American University of Beirut in 1982 when Israeli military forces that had already occupied a strip of southern Lebanon since 1978 drove all the way to the capital in pursuit of 'Arab terrorists'. As had been the case four years earlier, the Israeli government said it was determined to end cross-border attacks by the Palestine Liberation Organization, but this time the operation was on a far more massive scale. The expanded Israeli presence had many repercussions, one of which was the rise of Hezbollah (Party of God), the Shiite fundamentalist organization that has been on the US State Department's list of terrorist groups since the 1980s.

Like all Americans living and working in Beirut at the time, I was deeply affected by acts of terrorism said to have been ordered by the Islamic Republic of Iran and carried out by locals about whom very little was known. Since I lived near the US Embassy at the time, I was among the first on the scene when a suicide bomber drove an explosives-laden car into the building on 18 April 1983, killing 63 people. A close friend of mine had dropped by to see her husband, who worked for the US Agency for International Development, when the blast occurred, she survived a face full of glass shards, but her husband was killed.

October of the same year saw the second tremendous explosion to hit American personnel in Lebanon when a reportedly relaxed and smiling man crashed through a barricade and drove his truck straight at the concrete building at the Beirut International Airport that was housing US Marines who had come to help evacuate members of the PLO. The massive structure came down on top of the soldiers leaving 243 dead and many wounded. My husband, who rushed to the scene to help bulldozers enter the compound and begin the rescue operation, suffered a broken leg when a heavy piece of rubble struck him. He managed to drive to the American University of Beirut Hospital, where I met him.

My daughter was already there with fellow teenage volunteers from the American Community School, trying to comfort dazed, crying and dying Marines lined up in the emergency section on gurneys. Some of the kids were extracting impacted sand from the soldiers' ears while they waited for medical assistance.

Then, as the kidnapping of several close colleagues at the American University of Beirut followed – an administrator, an electrical engineer and a dean of agriculture – Americans were evacuated from Beirut. I acquired a personal bodyguard – a member of one of the Shiite factions – to accompany me to the university and wherever else I went. The thinking behind this was that since the number of American men available for kidnapping was running low, women might be next.

Like so many others at the time, I wondered who the perpetrators were. Then a Shiite fundamentalist organization emerged, backed by Iran and Syria, that was accused by Washington of the above acts as well as having hijacked a TWA flight in 1985 and murdering an American serviceman who was on board. Fundamentalist leaders denied these accusations but did not hide their opinions that the acts in question were legitimate within the context of the struggle against Israel and its major backer, the United States of America.

This situation and the reaction of Lebanese friends to all these events peaked my interest and it was thus that I began a 20-year period of close observation and documentation of Hezbollah's behaviour, following the organization from the shadows to the Lebanese limelight as it changed its terrorist face and became a deeply respected resistance movement. In this book I relate how and why this transformation took place and what effect it had on the Party of God's capacity to make itself a less likely target for Washington's global war on terrorism.

# Acknowledgements

I owe a great deal to my husband, Antun F. Harik, whose knowledge of regional politics and interest in my research led him to contribute valuable information and ideas as this book took shape. My daughter, Vaira, also contributed to the book by critiquing some parts of it and lending her encouragement throughout the writing process. Turi Munthe, Commissioning Editor at I. B. Tauris, deserves thanks for encouraging the book's development along lines that would make it more accessible to a general readership, and so do Marc Sirois and Steve Tribe for the editorial assistance they rendered.

*I had hoped to have the satisfaction of placing a published copy of this book in the hands of my Mother and greatest fan, Amy G. Palmer. Words cannot describe the impact of her presence in Lebanon with me during good and bad times, nor the importance of her unflagging support for this and all my other 'ventures'. To the memory of the hardiest of us all, I dedicate this book.*

## Map 1: PRACTICAL LINE OF WITHDRAWAL

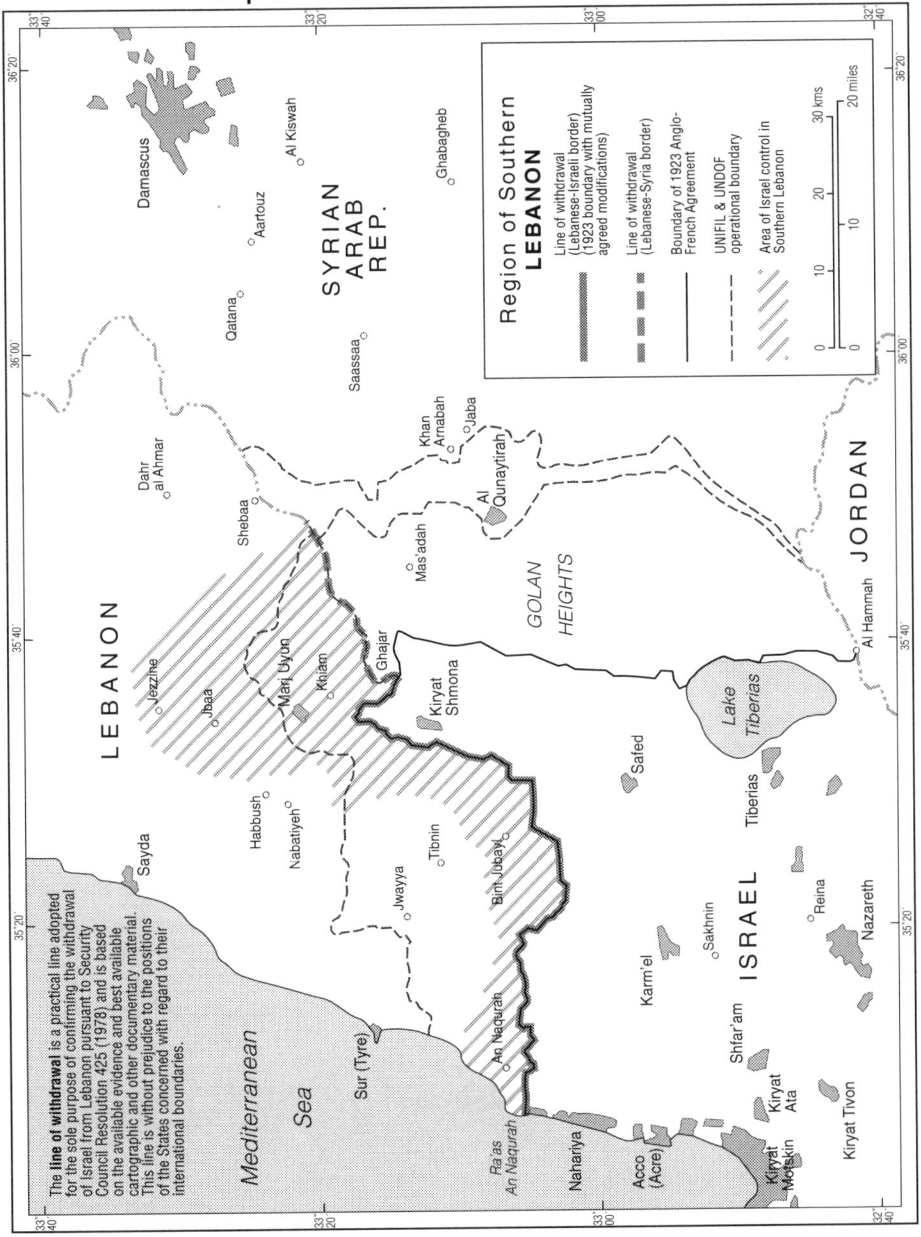
The line of withdrawal is a practical line adopted for the sole purpose of confirming the withdrawal of Israel from Lebanon pursuant to Security Council Resolution 425 (1978) and is based on the available evidence and best available cartographic and other documentary material. This line is without prejudice to the positions of the States concerned with regard to their international boundaries.
Region of Southern LEBANON
Line of withdrawal (Lebanese-Israeli border) (1923 boundary with mutually agreed modifications)
Line of withdrawal (Lebanese-Syria border)
Boundary of 1923 Anglo-French Agreement
UNIFIL & UNDOF operational boundary
Area of Israel control in Southern Lebanon
0 10 20 30 kms
0 10 20 miles
Mediterranean Sea
LEBANON
SYRIAN ARAB REP.
ISRAEL
JORDAN
GOLAN HEIGHTS
Lake Tiberias
Damascus
Al Kiswah
Ghabagheb
Aartouz
Qatana
Saassaa
Khan Arnabah
Jaba
Dahr al Ahmar
Shebaa
Al Qunaytirah
Mas'adah
Al Hammah
Ghajar
Kiryat Shmona
Khiam
Marj Uyun
Jbaa
Jezzine
Habbush
Nabatiyeh
Sayda
Tibnin
Bint Jubayl
Jwayya
Sur (Tyre)
An Naqurah
Ra'as An Naqurah
Nahariya
Acco (Acre)
Kiryat Motskin
Kiryat Ata
Kiryat Tivon
Shfar'am
Karm'el
Sakhnin
Reina
Nazareth
Tiberias
Safed
33°40'
33°20'
33°00'
32°40'
35°20'
35°40'
36°00'
36°20'

# Map 2: THE JORDAN BASIN

# Introduction

Hezbollah, the Shiite Muslim 'Party of God', has transformed itself from a radical, clandestine militia to a moderate, mainstream political party with a resistance wing in the 17 years since its activities against the Israelis began. Underlying all of Hezbollah's actions are its claims of deep faith and a literal interpretation of God's words as expressed in the Koran. This has resulted in the pursuit of objectives 'sanctioned' by Islam such as waging war against the usurpers of Muslim lands and serving the public and their community, and has made Hezbollah a formidable opponent on the battlefield and in the political arena. Yet Hezbollah's successes on both fronts still clash with the terrorist label that has been applied to it by its adversaries – most notably Israel and the United States of America. *Hezbollah: The Changing Face of Terrorism* is specifically concerned with the dynamics and outcomes of the terrorist/resistance controversy and whether American anti-terrorist policies will succeed in settling old scores with the Party of God and tipping the strategic balance at the Lebanese/Israeli frontier in favour of its ally.

Ever since the heavy loss of American lives in Beirut in the 1980s through car and truck bombs and an airplane hijacking, the Iranian-backed Shiite fundamentalist organization, Hezbollah, has denied involvement and tried to distance itself from those events, attempting to cast off the terrorist label imposed upon it by the USA and its allies at that time. In fact, fracturing the 'terrorist myth', as Hezbollah leaders call it, was considered vital to the leadership's plans to continue and develop the *jihad*[1] against Israel after its troops invaded Lebanon in 1982.

As events showed, allegations of Hezbollah's use of violence against Israeli troops who had occupied a strip of Lebanese territory were used several times to provide Tel Aviv with a rationale for marshalling international pressure and raining considerable destruction on Lebanon to halt the Shiite fundamentalists' military operations.

Today, two decades after the Israeli invasion and over 12 years after Hezbollah transformed itself from a radical, clandestine militia to a moderate, mainstream political party with a resistance wing; the country Hezbollah called 'an abomination' in 1985 – the USA – has renewed terrorist charges against it and given them teeth. As part of its war against global terrorism, the USA has threatened Lebanon with economic sanctions if the party's bank accounts are not frozen, and hinted at more 'direct action' to enforce its anti-terrorist campaign against Hezbollah.

The world's only superpower thus seems determined to shut Hezbollah's military operation down and remove its forces from the volatile Lebanese/Israeli frontier once and for all. Hezbollah leaders therefore have their hands full defending their organization against this serious American initiative.

In this book, I examine the struggle between Hezbollah and the American administration over whether the former is a terrorist group or a resistance force fighting Israeli occupation. Since these terms are politically loaded I weigh each side's argument against facts I have been able to uncover as a result of my research into this controversy.

My thesis is that Hezbollah developed two major strategies to combat these charges and that the deliberate implementation of those strategies during the past decade has allowed the party to change its terrorist face. This being the case, present United States foreign policy toward the Party of God therefore is not driven by an effort to halt terrorist acts against the Israelis as purported, but is rather an attempt by the American administration to settle old scores and relieve pressure on its ally as it grapples with the ongoing Palestinian uprising.

This thesis is supported in various ways. During the course of Hezbollah's 17-year struggle with Israel along the Lebanese/Israeli frontier in southern Lebanon, it has never been established by any party directly involved (including the United Nations contingent on the ground) that the Party of God has perpetrated a single terrorist attack against Israeli civilians. Highly conscious of the fact that accusations of terrorism would be used by the Israelis to try to halt the war of attrition being waged against them, Hezbollah leaders adopted and pursued a military strategy against Israeli military forces inside Lebanon's borders in which attacks against civilians meant to demoralize the government – a common definition of terrorism – had no place. Instead, guerrilla warfare techniques were used by the Party of God to achieve its primary mission – the removal of an illegal occupation. This strategy significantly undercut Israel's capacity to generate outrage against Hezbollah as a terrorist organization, while its successes elevated the Party of God to almost heroic status in Lebanon and throughout the Arab and Muslim worlds. This has prompted the USA to think twice about any 'direct action' against the Party of God it may have had in mind.

The military strategy used against Israel, however, could not succeed on its own. It required the development of an interrelated political strategy that would sustain popular support during the lengthy period when Hezbollah's hit-and-run missions were slowly taking their toll and beginning to provoke massive retaliations from Israel. This popular support was vital in terms of countering Hezbollah's terrorist image, which was also founded on its links with Iran and Syria. Since a certain section of the Lebanese population opposed Syrian influences in their country after the civil war ended and feared Iran's influence on Hezbollah, the Shiite leaders recognized that something like a sustained public relations campaign would have to accompany the ongoing confrontation in South Lebanon. In fact, the Lebanese population would have to be persuaded that Hezbollah was no longer a radical Islamic militia that might try to replace the state with an Islamic republic if given any leeway. Hezbollah would therefore have to take every opportunity to prove that its transformation into a mainstream Lebanese party was authentic rather than opportunistic. Since this was a difficult undertaking in a country with a large Christian population, where secularism was well advanced among religious groups, Hezbollah's integration process required careful management to overcome the obstacles in its way.

I argue that this process was aided by various factors. First, Hezbollah's transformation and integration advanced the foreign policy goals of Iran, Syria, and Lebanon and therefore the Party of God received a great deal of support of varying kinds from these governments. However, that support was not sufficient to effect the party's thorough integration into Lebanese society, since many Lebanese were unhappy about the arrangement between their government and Syria or were fearful of a fundamentalist group in their midst that might try to change their country's secular status.

Second, Hezbollah leaders tried to overcome this hurdle by developing simultaneous strategies and tactics of accommodation with the Lebanese authorities and other Lebanese groups, and militancy toward Israel. This approach was helped by the fact that Hezbollah leaders chose to use considerable ideological flexibility to allay the suspicions of the liberal component of Lebanese society, by presenting their organization as a moderate, national party while still retaining its Islamic appeal and pious supporters. Moreover, projection of Arab and Lebanese identities and goals in addition to Islamic ones attracted new and diverse sympathizers, while deeply religious convictions, acts and Islamic discourse retained the loyalty of core constituents.

Third, pragmatic Hezbollah leaders were also able to adapt their organization to Lebanese political traditions and exploit the realities that imposed themselves after the 1989 Document of National Reconciliation achieved peace.

Fourth, the adoption of modern political techniques and new technologies to spread their message and expand their reach in many domains of national life and on the battlefield suited the psychological and material needs of the varying constituencies Hezbollah wished to mobilize. This eventually earned the party tolerance and respect.

Fifth, Hezbollah's development of a Media Department and satellite-connected television channel allowed it to constantly beam its message of resistance in Lebanon and throughout the Muslim and Arab worlds, where popular support for its fight against Israel was needed to insulate it from terrorist charges.

Sixth, strict adherence to 'rules' established by Syria to govern state/Hezbollah relations during conflict periods were an important means of warding off Israeli and American pressures on the Lebanese authorities to halt the party's military activities.

This analysis leads to conclusions about the future of Lebanon, Israel, Syria, and Hezbollah and the role of Islam in the region. It also covers the nature of terrorism and US involvement in the Middle East, and the likely impact of Hezbollah's jihad on the Palestinian *intifada*.

*Hezbollah: The Changing Face of Terrorism* differs from other works on Hezbollah by dealing in depth with its strategic and foreign policy thrust and focusing on the interrelationship, dynamics and manifestations of the terrorist/resistance controversy. In contrast, most recent books on Hezbollah have focused on the interplay of Shiite religious doctrine on the Party of God's political positions, Hezbollah's origins and development during the first decade of its existence and the party's alleged involvement in the terrorist activities that followed the 1982 Israeli invasion.[2]

The interesting development of Hezbollah into a mainstream party is also covered here. In 1990, Hezbollah faced a dilemma common to all radical parties that decide that a moderate political approach is more useful: this dilemma centres on how that transformation can be accomplished without losing the allegiance of core constituents, who are likely to view any relaxation in doctrine and goals as tantamount to treason.[3] At the same time, transforming radical parties must allay the suspicions of other groups in society that this change is not merely opportunistic.[4] The discussion of how Hezbollah handled this process and how well it was received in Muslim and Christian circles in the Lebanese population is as relevant to radical Irish splinter groups and the Basque ETA as it is to Palestinian fundamentalist organizations such as Hamas and Islamic Jihad.

Finally, this book fills an information gap on the politics of Israeli withdrawal from Lebanon in 2001 and on the military tactics and media campaigns designed by the Party of God to speed up this withdrawal. Similarly, an analysis of the political and strategic repercussions of Hezbollah's actions has been neglected and is found herein. The analysis provides information about Hezbollah's present status and the solidity of Syrian/Lebanese and Iranian support for its continuing struggle with Israel.

The book also provides insights into America's anti-terrorist goals in Lebanon and the various means used by the Bush administration to cripple Hezbollah's jihad activities along the Lebanese/Israeli frontier. Why American policy failed and why and how it might succeed in the future are also part of the book's important conclusions, with implications for regional stability that have not been previously addressed.

For these reasons this book should be useful to scholars, practitioners and those simply interested in acquiring a better idea of Israel's problems with Hezbollah and how they relate to the broader Arab/Israeli conflict. Above all, I hope to provide a greater understanding of why Hezbollah is lionized in the Arab and Muslim worlds and condemned as a terrorist organization in Israel and the West.

# Chapter One

# Hezbollah's Version
# of Political Islam

Islam', 'Muslim', 'fundamentalist', 'jihad' – these words resonated in the USA, Europe and around the world and were associated with mindless terrorism after the catastrophes of 11 September 2001. When America's most wanted terrorist list was published on 10 October, men identified by US intelligence units as Hezbollah members were given top billing with al-Qaeda operatives and other master criminals. When looking at the photos published of the 22 Middle Eastern men in the 'terrorist rogues' gallery', a western friend confided that he had seen in their faces 'the very incarnation of evil'.

This is not, however, how many of these men are viewed in the Middle East, where I live. Hezbollah, for instance, is considered a legitimate resistance force all over the Arab and Muslim worlds. This contradiction raises an important question: does a common and fervently believed faith – in this case, Islam – lead to the adoption of a single ideology and a common goal and practice? In other words, is Hezbollah motivated by the same issues that inspire al-Qaeda, the Palestinian organization Hamas and other radical fundamentalist groups, and are the practices it has adopted to achieve its goals similarly terrorist in nature?

Before this question can be adequately addressed some information about the Muslim faith and the several issues that spurred its resurgence in the Middle East during the 1970s will be helpful.

## ISLAM IN PERSPECTIVE

Mohammed Ibn Abdullah, born in Mecca of a noble family in 570 AD, was a tradesman until he reached the age of 40. At that time, the angel Gabriel appeared to him with revelations that he was to pass on to his family. Later, however, God commanded him to deliver his message to all mankind and Mohammed thus became known as God's Messenger – the Prophet. The Muslim holy book, the Koran, is a compilation of the truths revealed by God to Mohammed. Since these truths cover all aspects of human existence, the Koran functions as a spiritual guide. Faithful Muslims also try to emulate the *sunnah*, the exemplary behaviour of the Prophet, consisting of statements, deeds and judgements. Orthodox Muslims consider neglect or deviation from these norms and principles as a return to *al-jahiliyyah* – the time of chaos and idol-worship that preceded Islamic society.

For a pious Muslim, there is no thought of any separation between religion and other aspects of life or between church and state. Politics are deeply and explicitly embedded in Islam because they are believed to be a critical part of social existence and community well-being. In fact, the religious community (*umma*) formed by the Prophet between 622 and 632 AD serves as an everlasting model of virtuous governance and human society since God's rules and principles were put into everyday practice there. One of the energizers of the religious revival that swept the Middle East in the 1970s was precisely the fact that governments were compared to the Islamic model that was believed to be the only answer to the many ills afflicting Middle Eastern life.

After Mohammed's death, a controversy broke out over leadership of the community of the faithful, since the Prophet had not designated a successor (*khalifah*, or Caliph). Choosing successors based on a consensus among the leaders of Mohammed's tribe, the Quraysh, solved this problem. Nevertheless, conquest and materialism soon entered the picture. When the third Caliph, Uthman, was killed during a mutiny in 656 AD, Mohammed's cousin and son-in-law, Ali, succeeded him. This resulted in some companions of the Prophet and his wife, whose relatives belonged to another tribe and opposed Ali's succession, eventually leaving the community. These defectors preached that anyone who closely followed God's laws might become Caliph and that it was not necessary to keep the line of succession within the Quraysh. Ali's supporters, on the other hand, insisted on the sanctity of the Prophet's line through Mohammed and his daughter, Fatimah. When one of these opponents, Muawiyah, assassinated Ali in 661, a split occurred between his partisans and the rest of the community, who constituted the majority and are known as the followers of Mohammed's *sunnah*, or Sunnites. Those who comprised Ali's faction were known as Shiites (*shiat Ali* – the faction of Ali). Since members of the two sects regarded each other as heretics, the Sunnite/Shiite division within the Muslim faith caused serious problems for some Muslims. For instance, in light of the persecution often visited upon them by Sunnite authorities, Shiites adopted dissimulation and political passivity as safeguards.

Another important doctrinal difference between Shiites and Sunnites is the Shiites' belief that the twelfth Imam in the line of Ali has gone into hiding. The result of this belief is that the *maraji*, the high religious authorities that are believed to bear the divine testimony and succession received from Mohammed and the early imams, assume the dominant politico-religious role in the community.[1] Preoccupation with who should rule and the special qualities of the rule constitutes the main distinction between Shiite and Sunnite political thought.

## THE ISLAMIC RESURGENCE OF THE 1970s

Like many other peoples, Arabs tend to turn to religion during crises.[2] The latest manifestation of this crisis-reaction phenomenon came to a head in the 1970s as a result of a number of interrelated crises that faced the Middle Eastern Muslim community at the same time.[3] In addition to the crisis of secularism, others were government misrule and corruption, economic mismanagement and the uneven manifestations of modern-ization. Another potent factor that increased the aggravation energizing this politico-religious backlash was the abject failure of Middle Eastern governments to eliminate Israel – the country considered the usurper of holy Muslim lands and the latest manifestation of western imperialism in the region. These issues produced great anxiety among the Arab peoples, making them question their identity and place in rapidly changing societies.[4]

Islam's appeal was that it offered solid community attachments, a network of religious and charitable institutions to answer members' spiritual and material needs and an alternative model of governance. In its political sense, it thus held out a ray of hope that it might be possible to improve things.

The Islamic revival in various countries was led by religious leaders with different interpretations of the causes of and solutions to these crises. Those who believe in a literal interpretation of the Koran and espouse a return to the ideal model of society that Mohammed created are widely labelled fundamentalists. One expert on Islam defines fundamentalism as 'politicized traditional religion' and emphasizes that fundamentalist leaders of all religions use religion to construct ideology and organize movements aimed at purifying social existence.[5] It should be emphasized, however, that Middle Eastern fundamentalist groups that exhibited extreme reactions to the problems mentioned above and urged radical Islamic solutions were in a minority. Moderate Islamists who interpreted the scriptures in a way that justifies working within non-Islamist governments to promote reform rather than undertaking jihad to overthrow them were far more prominent.

A classic example of the different interpretations of Islam and the solutions offered by reformist and fundamentalist leaders at different times and in the same society is found in Egypt. During the economic and political crises that arose between the two world wars, an Islamic movement emerged that had a lasting impact on that society, as well as on others in the Arab World. Hassan al-Banna founded that movement – the Muslim Brotherhood (*al-iqwan al-muslimin*) in 1929. Banna emphasized that his organization was 'a new soul in the heart of this nation to give it life by means of the Koran...'[6] Seeking reform of Egyptian society rather than the violent overthrow of the government, the Muslim Brotherhood contested elections whenever the government did not proscribe it. It campaigned as an Islamic and therefore universal party rather than as a purely Egyptian one.

Banna's condemnation of Egyptian political parties was based on their wide-scale corruption and cooperation with the British colonial authority rather than on their neglect of religion. By the 1940s, the government found itself facing a well-developed opposition and took steps to deal with that threat. In 1949, Banna was assassinated and the movement was dissolved.[7]

The views on how to solve the problems of Egyptian society expressed by another member of the Brethren, Sayyed Qutb, contrasted radically with those of Banna. Reacting to the failures and corruption of the Abdul Nasser regime in the late 1950s and 1960s, Qutb advanced radical Islamic solutions. Considered the father of modern radical Islam, his views inspired militant Islamic groups everywhere by introducing the idea of militant jihad as a duty for all Muslims that was almost as important as the faith's four basic pillars – prayer, charity, fasting during Ramadan and accomplishing the pilgrimage (*hajj*) to Mecca. According to Qutb, non-Islamic governments fit the category of *jahiliyya*, or pre-Islamic conflict and ignorance, and were thus fair game for Muslim radicals. Practising what he preached, Qutb was hanged in 1966 for plotting the violent overthrow of the Egyptian state.

These two men, Banna and Qutb, the 'founding fathers' of modern reformist and radical fundamentalism respectively, demonstrate the distinctions between these ideologies in practical terms. Banna was willing to work towards ending the various manifestations of Egyptian government corruption while the very fact of its secularism was, in Qutb's view, enough reason to overthrow the regime. Crises of secularism and government corruption were common complaints suggesting that Islamic movements grow in the same socio-political hothouse regardless of the solutions they propose to solve crises and purify their societies. However, for an adequate understanding of the Islamic resurgence and its impact on today's politics, this example suggests that ideological and practical differences between one Islamic group and another cannot be ignored.

The following discussion demonstrates distinctions between one fundamentalist group and another based on varying reactions to the crises fuelling the Islamic revival in particular countries. As will be seen, these reactions are shaped by specific Islamist ideologies and the unique characteristics and experiences of the societies in which fundamentalist movements and organizations are embedded.

## THE CRISIS OF SECULARISM AND FUNDAMENTALIST REACTIONS

Although secular trends and values were well advanced in the Middle East, the effects of these trends were more pronounced in some countries than in others during the 1970s. In Syria, for instance, the secularization of the political system caused a particularly violent reaction from the local branch of the Muslim Brotherhood. This occurred after a considerable period of political upheaval in that country. A series of military *coups d'état* and an abortive effort to form a union with Egypt in 1962 had followed Syria's crushing defeat in the 1948 Arab-Israeli war. In the 1960s, Jamal Abdul Nasser, Egypt's president, was leading a pan-Arab movement aimed at unifying the countries of the region along cultural rather than religious lines. The main purpose of this movement was to stand up against Israel and the USA and to put an end to western domination of the region, economically, culturally or otherwise. During the same period the formation of a secular organization, the Baath (Renaissance) Party, took place in Syria. The Baath's motto is 'Arab unity from the Atlantic to the Gulf'. The secular trend gathering steam in Syria along with other factors discussed below, spurred the Society of Muslim Brothers to a revolt in the provincial city of Hamah in April 1964. The government permanently outlawed the fellowship after the Syrian army crushed the rebellion.

Airforce General Hafiz al-Assad, a Baathist, came to power a few years after that incident, after Syria had suffered a second defeat by Israel in the 1967 Arab-Israeli war.[8] Destabilization of his government became the Muslim Brotherhood's goal and a series of assassination attempts against Baath Party professionals, government figures and security agents soon took place. In 1976, a protest against the assistance provided by the Assad government to Christian militias struggling against a Muslim-leftist coalition in Lebanon was launched and three years later, in June 1979, in a direct challenge to Assad, the Brotherhood struck again, killing 83 mainly Alawite artillery cadets in Aleppo. The following year, demonstrations and boycotts in the cities of Hamah, Homs and Aleppo occurred and were followed by severe crackdowns by government forces.

In July 1980, Law 49 made membership in the Sunnite fundamentalist organization punishable by death.

The final straw for the Baathist regime, as far as this jihad was concerned, however, was the three-week-long Hamah revolt staged by the Brotherhood in 1982: the armed fundamentalists held off army regulars until Assad ordered heavy artillery to level whole sections of the city where the fighters were concentrated.[9] After this knockout blow, bulldozers razed the area and rapidly repaved it. Ever since this incident, the Syrian branch of the Muslim Brotherhood has kept a very low profile.

During the 1970s, the inroads made by secularism were also fanning discontent in Egypt, where Abdul Nasser's Arab socialism had failed to deliver economic development and social justice to the burgeoning Egyptian population. Anwar Sadat, another member of the Free Officer's circle that overthrew King Farouk's government in 1952 and who came to power after Nasser's death, was viewed through the same lens by fundamentalists. A series of kidnappings, murders, riots and fundamentalist-led attacks on Egyptian Christians began. The trip Sadat made to Jerusalem in 1977 and the subsequent peace treaty he signed with Israel furthered the decline of his popularity and created more unrest. In 1981, he ordered the arrest of thousands of people and placed all the country's mosques under his direct control. This action only poured more oil on the fire. Sadat was finally assassinated in 1981 by members of the Jihad Organization (*tanzim al-jihad*), a militant group based in Upper Egypt.

Hosni Moubarak, who succeeded Sadat as President of Egypt, ordered the fundamentalist perpetrators of the assassination hanged. Those that escaped either left the country or went into hiding like Ayman al-Zawahiri, subsequently Osama bin Laden's top lieutenant.

Prominent radical groups also operating in Egypt are the Islamic Liberation Party (*hizb al-tahrir al-islami*) and the Society of Muslims (*jam'at al-muslimin*). Both were born along with the Jihad Organization, in the crisis setting that followed the 1967 war with Israel. They are all direct descendents of the Society of Muslim Brothers, but they do not share the Banna wing of the Brotherhood's general objection to violence. Mohammed Atef, for instance, is widely considered to be al-Qaeda's second in command and head of its military operations. He is said to have planned the September 11 attacks with al-Zawahiri, who founded the Islamic Jihad Organization. These men appeared at bin Laden's side in the first video produced after the New York and Washington attacks. Five other individuals on America's most wanted terrorist list are also Egyptians, which gives that country the dubious honour of having produced more effective terrorists or, according to fundamentalist values, more valiant holy warriors, than any other country – eight out of 22.[10]

Manifestations and sporadic outbursts of fundamentalist violence against Christians who constitute a large minority in Egypt continue to plague the Egyptian government.[11] However, the Muslim Brotherhood tries to work around the government ban maintained on their organization's electoral participation by presenting their partisans as independents or negotiating alliances with other legal Egyptian parties. Signs of the Brotherhood's continuing influence are seen within the parallel economy and welfare system of a network of Islamic schools, medical centres and welfare organizations operating independently of the state sector. The growing influence of political Islam in Egypt is also measured by the proliferation of private mosques which grew between 1962 and 1982 from 14,000 to around 40,000 compared with an increase from 3,000 to 6,000 government-controlled mosques in the same period.[12]

Sudan's Islamists also reacted negatively to the inroads of secularism. As in Egypt, the appeal of secular movements such as Nasserism and Baathism had worn thin in Sudan by the 1970s. Experiments with liberal democracy had failed and military *coups d'état* began. Severe economic decline was another crisis affecting the country, as was the rebellion against the Arab government, which arose out of an African (Negroid) Christian and animist culture. These problems prepared the way for a religious revival similar to that occurring in other parts of the Arab world at the same time.

Interestingly, the midwife of the Sunnite Islamic Republic that emerged in the 1980s was the military establishment. However, the road was well prepared in advance by the Islamic National Front (INF), a coalition of Muslim groups led by Dr Hassan Turabi. Turabi had founded the Sudanese Muslim Brotherhood Society, a prominent part of the Front, in 1949. The popularity of the INF led Jafar Nimeiri, an army officer who had come to power in a coup, to try to co-opt it and use Islamic ideology and precepts to create his own power base. Nimeiri proclaimed an Islamic Republic soon afterward, but this experiment was short lived, since he was ousted by another coup in 1985. After that government also failed, General Omar Hassan al-Bashir, today's president, took the reins of power and, in June 1989, formally established the Sudanese Islamic Republic. Turabi was the de facto leader, the first Muslim Brother who had fully realized the Islamic ideal. Turabi accomplished this feat patiently, in the Banna tradition, through political groundwork and by his group's participation in elections.[13]

Unlike other fundamentalist movements, the Brotherhood's social base was drawn from the educated urban middle class, rather than Sudan's large amorphous underclass. Turabi himself was educated at the University of London and the Sorbonne and eschewed the robes and turbans worn by other fundamentalist leaders of the region for sharply tailored western suits. Erudite and articulate, he appealed to reason and used moral persuasion rather than force to achieve Islamic goals. Taking a moderate position in comparison to most of the other fundamentalist leaders already discussed, he stressed that Islamic groups should participate in non-Islamist Arab governments as his party had done, in order to Islamize them and ultimately achieve both Arab and Islamic unity. Good relations with Iran, whose leaders provided military and economic assistance to Sudan, caused considerable concern to neighbouring states, which feared an Islamic domino effect.

Turabi's own moderate brand of political activism, however, did not preclude his support of fundamentalists from other countries who advocated violent action to purify their societies. In fact, he opened the door to Islamist exiles and Arabs who were training for revolutionary action against non-Islamist regimes such as the one backed by the Soviets in Afghanistan. Turabi's agenda during this period meshed well with United States interests in the region and received its full support.

Bin Laden was apparently sheltered at one time by the Sudanese authorities and is alleged to have recruited operatives for his al-Qaeda organization in that country. Turabi, however, flatly denied this link as well as any connection between his government and the five Sudanese nationals arrested for their involvement in the plot to blow up the New York World Trade Center on 26 February 1993. He also denied having invited Omar Abd al-Rahman to visit him and having been his host for two weeks. Rahman is the Egyptian cleric who blessed the New York operation and who was convicted of conspiracy in a New York court in January 1996. 'Carlos' – Ilich Ramirez Sanchez – who had been wanted for terrorist acts for more than two decades was also welcome in Sudan for several years. Bashir finally handed him over to the French authorities that wanted to try him for murder when he decided to make a gesture that he hoped would remove Sudan from the list of countries sponsoring terrorism.

When terrorist bombs destroyed the American embassies in Tanzania and Kenya in 1998, the USA staged retaliatory air strikes against Sudan as well as against al-Qaeda training camps in Afghanistan. Bashir, echoed by Turabi, vigorously denied any implication in those attacks.[14]

The prominent role Turabi had played in Sudanese politics ended in 1999 when Bashir stripped him of his power. The rift between the two leaders had arisen over the issue of how to deal with the confrontation still raging in the South with the Sudan People's Liberation Army (SPLA) – Turabi apparently backed a more conciliatory approach to the rebels. He was placed under house arrest in 2001. Recently, however, the Sudanese president did a 180-degree turn and opened talks with the rebels. An understanding might be being hatched under which the SPLA will drop its demand for a self-determination referendum in the South, in exchange for Khartoum conceding over the issue of separating state and religion. As the Bashir government tries hard to end its reputation for terrorism to avoid US sanctions within the framework of the 'War on Terror', members of Turabi's Popular National Congress have been causing disturbances that have led the government to accuse the party of planning acts of sabotage to create a state of instability. On 29 August 2002, Turabi was moved from house arrest to the central prison, where he remains, 'for his own safety'. From these incidents it appears that Sudan's fundamentalists will not be taking their altered position lying down.

The problem of secularism also surfaced in Saudi Arabia, because of American forces stationed there during and after the Desert Storm military operation against Iraq of 1990–1991. Many pious Saudis believed that the continued presence of these troops – some of them women in what they considered inappropriate dress – polluted Islamic soil and would eventually introduce secular values and practices into the kingdom if the American presence there was not ended. While this issue is important, it is not the main problem facing 'establishment Islam' in that country as will be seen below.

Iran underwent a crisis of secularism akin to Syria's in terms of its importance and violent outcome, but in this case the fundamentalists triumphed. In 1979, the Shah's secular regime was replaced with an Islamic Republic. This successful revolution was partially the result of the close relationship of Iran's ruler with the USA (see Chapter 2). America viewed this oil-rich country, whose northern border fronted the Soviet Union, as an important ally during the Cold War and had thus attempted to beef up its armed forces and ensure its stability in different ways. The powerful Iranian Shiite clergy (*mullahs*) decried the country's growing dependency on the USA and viewed with concern the growing influence of America's secular culture on Iranian society. Moreover, to the mullahs, the Shah's efforts to modernize Iran along lines urged by the USA represented a serious threat to Islam and Islamic institutions. These men also realized that the rapid changes the Shah was promoting in the 1970s would undercut their own authority.

One of those mullahs, Ayatollah Ruhollah Khomeini, played the leading role in mobilizing resistance to developments in Iran. That resistance eventually took the form of a fully fledged popular revolution, which overturned the secular government and forced the Shah to seek refuge abroad. Khomeini then returned from his exile in France to huge popular acclaim. Within a short period of time, his Islamist partisans had eliminated the other groups in the revolutionary coalition that had brought down the Shah's government. Having fully consolidated his power with the help of the Revolutionary Guards – an officially recognized standing militia – Khomeini then took the steps necessary to establish an Islamic republic, in which he became the all-wise Supreme Jurist (*al-wali al-faqih*) – the stand-in for the missing twelfth Imam. Henceforth, Iran would be governed in accordance with religious law (*sharia*), as interpreted by the Supreme Jurist in consultation with the mullahs, who were members of the state's governing institutions.[15]

The lessons of the Islamic Revolution rippled throughout the region, especially in the Gulf States, the West Bank and Gaza, but it had its most direct and profound impact on the circle of young Lebanese mullahs who formed Hezbollah, who identify with the Revolution's ideology and embrace the principle of government by the Supreme Jurist. This means that these Lebanese clerics profess complete allegiance to Iran's spiritual leader – first Ayatollah Khomeini and, after his death, Ayatollah Ali Khamenei – and consider their organization to be under his guidance.

Hezbollah's version of fundamentalism thus embraces the principles of Iran's Islamic ideology including its belief in the importance of struggling against secularism, injustice and the oppression of Muslims by foreign imperialists spearheaded by the USA and its regional manifestation, Israel.[16] The Party's vision of the creation of a wider Islamic community beyond the boundaries of its own country follows Ayatollah Khomeini's goal of exporting the Islamic Revolution throughout the region. Removing the Israelis from Jerusalem and the Holy Land and restoring the rights of the Muslim community was a sacred imperative.[17]

The belief that armed struggle was not only justified but also a sacred imperative to erase oppression, usurpation of rights and restore Muslim lands opened Hezbollah to practices which had traditionally been rejected by Shiite leaders over the centuries in favour of passive political positions.[18] The forceful expulsion of western forces from Lebanon in the 1980s and the jihad against the Israeli military forces that had been in South Lebanon since 1978 and established a 'Security Zone' there in 1985 were therefore fully justified on religious grounds provided by the radical Shiite ideology emanating from Iran. Hezbollah's leaders, all students of the same seminary in Najaf, Iraq, where Khomeini had studied, connected this ideology with their desire to deal real blows to their country's invaders. Since this struggle would also serve other, more mundane interests of the Iranian and Lebanese clerics and their adherents, cooperation between the two groups where these interests coincided was natural.

The direct and unprecedented cooperation that resulted between this revolutionary Islamic regime and its fundamentalist adherents in another country was a new phenomenon in fundamentalist and Middle Eastern annals. The USA and Israel considered the development an attempt by Shiite fundamentalism to put an entirely new face on terrorism.

But here the question arises as to whether Hezbollah's establishment occurred as a directive of Ayatollah Khomeini, a simple meeting of minds between the clergy of two countries on a political course of action, or whether it had its roots in some of the same crises that had triggered fundamentalist activism in other countries in the region. For instance, had the inroads of secularism, which had so dramatically destabilized Iran and Syria, had any effect on Hezbollah's rise?

In Lebanon, unlike other countries in the region, the issue of political secularism was specifically championed by Muslims and some Christians and was very important in fuelling the civil war that began in 1975. A brief look at the country's political system and the breakdown that led to what many believed to be intractable communal strife is instructive.

The political system set up after the French Mandate ended and the country's independence was achieved in 1943 was widely perceived in Muslim and Christian circles at the time as the most useful way of representing the 16 formally recognized religious sects residing in Lebanon. The 1932 census that served as the basis for the distribution of power revealed that among these sects Maronite Christians were in the majority while Sunnites and Shiites comprised the next two largest sects respectively. A gentleman's agreement between two prominent Lebanese leaders, a Sunnite and a Maronite, which became known as the 'national pact', produced a political arrangement where the most important government positions were determined on the basis of sect size while seats in parliament were determined on a presumed 50-50 ratio between Muslims and Christians.[19]

Although the national pact was widely supported at the time, many Christians and Muslims still had strong reservations about it. At issue was what sort of state Lebanon should be: a unique entity culturally and politically tied to the West, as many Christians and some Muslims wished, or a state attuned to its Arabic heritage and well integrated in the region, as desired by Muslims and some Christians. Here it should be noted that Lebanon had been part of Syria until it came under the French Mandate established by the League of Nations after the First World War. Both Muslim extremists and nationalists, including some Christians, believed that Lebanon should not have been removed from its Syrian matrix, while Christian extremists hoped that Lebanon would become an exclusive homeland for their members. These positions were never entirely abandoned.

As time passed, dissatisfaction with the effects of Lebanon's political system increased, since a political establishment composed of Muslims and Christians had arisen whose common interest lay in maintaining the status quo rather than addressing the problems its critics raised.[20] Moreover, no census was ever again taken to indicate whether a different distribution of power among the sects should be undertaken. The secular arrangement of 1943 had thus ossified into a system that guaranteed Christian political domination regardless of that sect's size in comparison to that of the other confessional groups suspected of outstripping Maronite numbers over the years. Besides this grievance, the political elites of this system all derived their political authority from familial, confessional and location sources and maintained their influence by distributing to their constituents the resources available to them through government connections.[21] The result was the almost permanent incumbency of a handful of powerful men in each sect who did their best to rebuff challengers and to pass on their positions to nearest eligible male relatives upon their death or retirement.[22] Because of this situation, counter elites or regime opponents had little chance of ever replacing the 'establishment' through legal or normal political channels.

Besides political grievances with the sectarian system and its imbalances, rural citizens received a much smaller portion of the benefits of modernization. These benefits were clearly noticeable in the capital and its contiguous Christian areas. By all measurements, peripheral regions such as the Bekaa Valley and the South where Shiites are concentrated were severely deprived of even such basics as sewer networks and clean water distribution. Lamentably, that still remains the case. As a result of rising discontent in the 1950s and 1960s, the issue of social justice became another bone of contention between those who desired reform of the system and those whose interests lay in retaining it unchanged. The preference of most Muslims and some Christians for a pro-Arab position in regional and world affairs rather than the pro-western one desired by a majority of Christians only deepened the chasm dividing the two groupings.

A debate about Lebanon's identity – whether Arab or Lebanese – that had surfaced in the 1943 discussions and had been resolved by a compromise – neither too western nor too Arab – heated up soon after the establishment of Israel. Egyptian leader Jamal Abdul Nasser mobilized many Lebanese Muslims and leftists who sympathized with his views and regarded the Palestinian's plight with outrage. With the influx into Lebanon of thousands of Palestinian refugees, their mobilization and growing military strength acted as a catalyst for disgruntled Muslim-leftists who formed a coalition against the armed Christian forces that had sprung up in the 1970s.[23]

These two coalitions fought each other without mercy for 17 years using kidnappings, assassinations, car bombs and random shelling of each other's areas to try to gain the upper hand. The Lebanese army almost disappeared as, over the years, officers and soldiers abandoned their posts to join the militia of their confessional affiliation.[24] However, while this struggle was going on in and around the capital, the Palestinian Liberation Organization (PLO), an umbrella group that included a number of leftist and Muslim groups, had entrenched itself in the South and was attacking Israel by cross border raids. These attacks and Israeli retaliations spurred an exodus of Shiites from the area to an overcrowded suburb of Beirut – the *dahiyeh* – where they squatted with little if any government assistance. As far as many Shiites were concerned, the confessional political system prevailing had not offered much in terms of social benefits, political representation and security. These complaints were much like those that had been advanced by Muslims in secular states to justify system reform or radical change along Islamic lines. However, in this case, the Muslims thought their best chance for development and influence lay with taking the religious component out of the governing formula completely or at least reforming the system in their favour.

Hezbollah emerged in this tense and precarious atmosphere. Yet unlike other fundamentalist organizations, replacing the Lebanese government with an Islamic Republic was never the leadership's main preoccupation despite the emphasis placed on this issue by the leadership in the 1980s. However important it was for the mullahs that formed Hezbollah to resist the inroads of secularism by propagating Islam, Lebanon's structural restraints, the large Christian community, and the traditional antipathy between Shiite and Sunnite effectively precluded the achievement of this important goal.

Instead, Hezbollah leaders made their sacred obligation to conduct jihad against 'the usurpers of Muslim lands' – the Israelis – their top priority. Since that struggle would require broad national backing it was thought to be more important to soft-pedal the idea of a republic ruled by Muslim religious law for Lebanon and to accede to the kind of reforms the Muslim-leftist coalition was stressing. In this way, the campaign begun against Israel in southern Lebanon in 1985 would not be jeopardized by raising undue apprehensions about the party's radical ideology and ultimate goal for Lebanon.

Furthermore, and in contrast with other fundamentalist movements of the region, after Hezbollah's transformation into a mainstream political party, it actively sought accommodation with the Lebanese authorities and worked out a number of cooperative endeavours through which it could achieve thorough integration into Lebanon's socio-political life. This strategy is discussed in detail in later chapters.

Notwithstanding Hezbollah's limitations in achieving the power necessary to fulfil the Islamist dream in Lebanon, the expansion of fundamentalism in the Shiite community is well documented and a number of Sunnite fundamentalist movements also seem to be fairly well entrenched.[25]

## GOVERNMENT CORRUPTION AND THE PURIFICATION OF SOCIETY

As mentioned previously, secular governments generally failed to deliver on the promises of social justice and political modernization that they made. However, particular incidents or patterns of misrule and corruption in some countries stimulated Muslim discontent to a heightened degree. In reaction to these crises, fundamentalist leaders promoted the establishment of Islamic governance as the only way of purifying and healing their societies.

The Saudi group *al-salafiyyun* exemplifies this concern with political corruption but within a reformist framework. Osama bin Laden and other Saudis on America's Most Wanted list, as well as other 'neo-funda-mentalist' groups operating in the Kingdom and outside it, are part of this political current, which aims at purifying the present Saudi regime and bringing it back to the principles of Islamic governance on which it was founded in the eighteenth century. Mohammed Ibn Saud, the tribal chieftain who unified most of the Arabian Peninsula, had achieved that feat with the man who was to give his kingdom its Islamic ideology, Sheikh Mohammed Ibn Abd al-Wahhab, at his side. Sheikh al-Wahhab accepted only the Koran and sunnah as guides and rejected all other interpretations or innovations. Emphasizing the 'oneness' of God (*tawhid*), his followers were *al-muwahhidun*, commonly known as the Wahhabis, the followers of Sheikh al-Wahhab. In later years, however, a current developed *within* the Wahhabi religious establishment known as *al-salafiyyun* – the followers of pious ancestors (*salaf al-salih*). The movement was composed of preachers, prayer leaders, Islamic professors and other pious individuals, mainly from the Najd region. This group wanted to return Saudi society to Islamic basics and accused members of the clergy of quietism concerning the excesses of members of the ruling royal family. The salafiyyun charged these rulers, whose numbers ran into the thousands, of looting the treasury, gambling, womanizing and other forms of corruption. What they wanted was purification of the government that guards Prophet Mohammed's birthplace and Islam's holiest shrines and a return to Mohammed's sacred and ideal model of governance. Prince Abdullah, who heads the government today as a result of King Fahd's disability, is a pious individual who is presently seeking ways to deal with opposition currents in his country. For its part, the Bush administration is pushing the Saudi government to crack down on Saudi citizens and charitable organizations it suspects of links to al-Qaeda. The fact that bin Laden and 15 of the 19 individuals directly involved in the September 11 attacks are Saudi nationals has caused Riyadh severe embarrassment, while Bush administration accusations that not enough is being done by the Saudis to crack down on such terrorists is raising hackles in government quarters.

Across the Persian Gulf in Iran, the Shah was also widely criticized for corruption. Tyranny and profligate spending were some of the charges levelled against him. As opposition to his government grew in the 1970s, the Shah used his secret service – Savak – to savagely root it out. The mullahs and a large part of the Iranian population considered this behaviour as the absolute antithesis of all Islam stood for in terms of merciful and consensual governance.

The Shah's abuses of power were fully exploited by Ayatollah Khomeini in his campaign to mobilize and unite the opposition against his continued rule. According to Khomeini's plan, his ouster would usher in the epitome of clean and just rule since it would be based on interpretations of the Prophet Mohammed's own words and deeds as expressed in religious law. There is no sign that this system is wavering, although the mullahs face increasing public pressure for political reform.

In Syria, Hafiz al-Assad's illegal seizure of power, autocratic rule and repression of opposition forces were some of the other reasons that made his government a target of the Muslim Brotherhood. Another important factor that drew their ire was his membership in a sect considered heretical by Sunnites and his placement of co-religionists and family members in important positions within the state's security apparatus. Assad's attempt to create a political dynasty by arranging for his son Bashar to succeed him is also considered corruption in the eyes of the Brotherhood.

Government corruption also played an important role in the emergence of grassroots movements like Hezbollah and its secular Shiite rival, Amal. As explained previously, the political domination of a Christian sect that was thought to have lost its majority by the 1970s was a problem for many Lebanese and especially for the Shiites who believed their own community had become the largest group in the country.

Equally disturbing to the Shiites, an agricultural people concentrated in the South and the Bekaa Valley, was the collaboration of their elected representatives with a regime that short-changed the peripheral areas of the country.[26] The level of deprivation of these people as compared to those of other communities was one of the reasons many Shiites turned to secular leftist parties like the Communists, the Baathists and the Syrian Social National Party to try to improve their lot.[27]

The plight of the Shiites was worsened by Israeli retaliations against Palestinian fighters that had entrenched themselves along the Lebanese/Israeli frontier. No compensation was forthcoming from the state for lost income or destruction of property suffered by the inhabitants of the area. This situation led to general Shiite political mobilization, of which the fundamentalist circles were a part. However, the impotence of the

Lebanese government was not the main reason Hezbollah took form. The trigger of the party's emergence had more to do with the disappearance of the leader of the mass Shiite movement that had evolved by 1974 – Imam Musa al-Sadr – than anything else.

Imam Musa al-Sadr, a Lebanese of Iranian origins who was helped by various religious groups in Iran to found a number of charitable institutions in South Lebanon during the 1960s, had, by the end of that decade, succeeded in establishing the Higher Shiite Islamic Council, an institution that for the first time gave the community formal recognition at the state level and looked after its interests. Al-Sadr was its first president. Later, as Israeli raids in retaliation for cross-border attacks by the PLO damaged or destroyed southern properties, the Imam voiced demands for government compensation to the individuals who had suffered such losses. In his book *The Imam*, Fuad Ajami, a Lebanese-American Shiite scholar, describes the emotional impact of this activist clergyman on youths who had never experienced anyone like al-Sadr, as nothing short of a revelation.[28]

In 1974, al-Sadr established the Movement of the Disinherited (*harakat al-mahrumin*), a broad-based organization that stood for the reform of the present Lebanese system. The movement's goal was universally expressed as seeking social justice for all deprived Lebanese, although its Shiite social base was well known. In actuality, it was the first Shiite political organization.

The feverish arming of various Lebanese militias as the 1975 civil war approached encouraged the development of a fighting wing within al-Sadr's movement, the Battalions of the Lebanese Resistance (*afwaj al-muqawamat al-lubnaniyya* – Arabic acronym AMAL). Led by lawyer Nabih Berri, presently Speaker of the House, Amal acquired the resources necessary for collective action in the same way most of the other militias had – by assistance from an Arab state – in this case Libya, a client of the Soviet Union at that time.

Al-Sadr's abrupt disappearance on a trip to Libya in 1978, some say as a result of a dispute over funds with President Muammar Khadafi, and Berri's ensuing control of Amal wiped out the Islamic content of the mass movement. Hussein Musawi, a leading cleric in Amal, broke away from the movement to establish an Islamic counterpart of Amal in the northern Bekaa with the announced objectives of fighting injustice and the 'infidels' – the Israelis – in South Lebanon. Musawi's actions constituted the magnet that attracted a group of fundamentalist clerics, who had all studied under the Shiite religious scholar and theorist Baqir al-Sadr at a religious seminary in Najaf, Iraq – the same place where Ayatollah Khomeini and the Lebanese mullah Mohammed Hussein Fadlallah had also been educated. Other Shiite fundamentalist splinter groups were also drawn to this movement out of which Hezbollah eventually emerged.

Musawi and the other leaders' goal of purifying Lebanon's corrupt system by radically changing it remained a cherished ideal but jihad against an enemy of the faith – Israel – took precedence, especially after the experiences of the 1982 Israeli invasion which spawned the Sabra-Shatila massacres in the refugee camps of Beirut's southern suburb.

## COLONIALISM AND ITS DISCONTENTS

Another factor that added steam to the Islamic revival in the 1970s was a further defeat for Arab forces at the hands of the Israeli military in 1973.[29] The Israelis were thought to have muscled their way into the region through deceit and imperialist design and were blamed for forcibly displacing thousands of Palestinians – mostly Muslims – from their homes in 1948. In Arab eyes, Palestine was then illegally colonized by Zionists. That was not, of course, how the Israelis saw the bloody birth of their nation or the foundation on which their state was built.

Israel's foundations were laid in the latter part of the nineteenth century, when the founders of Zionism, the ideology whose aim is to establish a homeland for the Jewish Diaspora, decided on Palestine as its locale because of its ancient connection with the Israelite tribes. At the time – the late 1800s – the population of Palestine was Arab with a few minority groups including Jews living among them. Jewish agencies were established to raise funds to purchase land in Palestine and resettle Jews there from all parts of the world and immigration began. The hope of the organizers of the movement was that one day, as a result of the ingathering of millions of Jews, a Jewish state might arise in the Holy Land with Jerusalem as its capital.

During the Second World War, with the British Mandate over Palestine in place, conditions matured for this enterprise to take place and a state was declared in 1948 against the objections of the resident Palestinian Arab population, which, despite heavy Jewish immigration, remained in the majority. Arab citizens rejected a UN decision to partition Palestine into two states, one for each community, and they were supported by Arab and Muslim governments who went to war to stop what they considered was robbery backed by the West.

The story of the 1947–1948 war and its aftermath is well known and needs no elaboration here. The point is that, despite the fait accompli, Muslim fundamentalists continue to vehemently reject Israel's right to exist based on the deepest principles of the Muslim faith. They believe that no exceptions or trade-offs can be made where God's will is concerned and therefore insist that the millions of Palestinians whom they believe were violently driven from their homes by Zionist agencies and armies must be allowed to return to their homes. Moderate Muslim leaders in the region, however, generally agree that this would be impossible, as it would alter Israel's *raison d'être* as a Jewish state. They believe that some other solution must therefore be found. As Arab governments for various reasons began to recognize Israel's right to exist, fundamentalist anger against the regimes willing to turn their back on jihad to recapture the Holy Land intensified. While secular Arabs viewed accommodation with the Hebrew state as unforgivable and a calamity, fundamentalists called it heresy. President Sadat paid for that heresy with his life.

Middle Eastern governments were also harangued by fundamentalists for collaboration with the United States of America, which had become Israel's main supporter. The latter was the case in Iran, where Ayatollah Khomeini not only blamed the Shah for the relationship he entertained with Israel, but also took him to task for the behaviour of his closest ally, the USA, in condoning and abetting crimes against Muslims in Palestine. After the Shah's defeat, the Islamic Republic sought to expand its influence in the region by exporting its revolution and involving itself in the anti-Israel/anti-USA struggle going on in the region. It found a means of accomplishing both goals in Lebanon, as we shall see in a later chapter.

The Saudi royal family's close connections with the USA are also condemned by religious conservatives on the basis of America's support for Israel[30] and the suspected perpetrators of the World Trade Center and Pentagon attacks explained their operations as protests against American support of Israel.

Interestingly, while fundamentalist leaders of all colours and stripes have been protesting against the Israeli 'occupation' of Palestine for decades, Palestinian radical fundamentalists emerged somewhat later than those already mentioned. Palestinians had been active in the Society of Muslim Brothers and the Communist Party, but it was the organizations that formed outside the Occupied West Bank and Gaza, such as Yasser Arafat's Fatah and the Popular Front for the Liberation of Palestine formed by Christians George Habash and Wadih Haddad, that were the militants in the struggle against the Israelis using whatever locales and tactics were available. The stories of hijackings, murders and massacres are legion. In the end, however, it was the ineffectiveness of such organizations in addition to the inability of Arab states' to make any real change in the Palestinian situation that allowed radical Islam's entry onto the Palestinian political scene. Such Palestinian fundamentalist groups espousing jihad, established much needed networks of social support and proclaimed appealing activist ideologies. This fundamentalist trend was further energized by harsh Israeli policies and economic deterioration in the West Bank and Gaza in the 1980s.

Ironically, the Israelis themselves had nurtured fundamentalist groups like Islamic Jihad and Hamas by turning a blind eye to funds being sent from the Gulf area to the Islamists for the purpose of building mosques, sports clubs and community centres. Yet, while the Israelis succeeded in their plan to undercut the appeal of Fatah and other groups in this fashion, they also shortly found themselves confronting *mujahidin* (jihad warriors) ready to fight to the death.

Sheikh Abdul Aziz Awdah, for instance, left the more quiescent Muslim Brotherhood to become the spiritual guide of an activist organization – Islamic Jihad (Arabic title *jihad al-islamiyya*). In December 1987, his partisans surged onto the streets and began lobbing stones at the startled Israeli troops on duty. Fired by this unprecedented event, many other Palestinians joined the battle and a full-scale popular uprising (*intifada*) materialized. This demonstration of peoples' power directly led to the Oslo Accord that resulted in Yasser Arafat's return to Palestine, the establishment of a Palestinian Authority in the West Bank and Gaza and the commencement of what turned out to be a much-troubled peace process.

The other Palestinian fundamentalist group – The Islamic Resistance Movement (*harakat al-muqawamah al-islamiyyah* – Arabic acronym HAMAS, or Zeal) – was formed by Sheikh Ahmad Yassin, the son of an impoverished family who was brought up in a refugee camp in Gaza. Yassin's family had fled their home in Askalan, Palestine during the fighting that led to Israel's statehood in 1948.

The resurgence of Islam in Gaza owes a great deal to the frail and crippled Yassin, since it was he who founded the Islamic Congress (*al-mujamaa al-islami*), an offshoot of the Muslim Brotherhood. Yassin was arrested in October 1984 by the Israeli authorities for his activities but was nevertheless released a year later on condition that he gave up politics. That was wishful thinking on the part of the Israelis, however, since his popularity had grown precisely because of his imprisonment. Hamas was born soon after his release. According to its founder, Yassin, the organization's explicit mission is the reclamation of all of Palestine – 'a religious trust assigned by God to the Muslims until the end of time.'[31]

Hamas and Islamic Jihad regard the peace process that got underway in 1993 as anathema. They completely reject the partial recovery of Palestinian lands that Arafat is willing to accept and that would doom a full return of all Palestinians who have been in exile since 1948. Nothing short of the complete dismantling of the state of Israel will do as far as they are concerned. They also regard Arafat's secular authority, tight grasp on power and corrupt cohorts as unacceptable in the eyes of Islam.[32] The basic conflict dividing the two sides has nonetheless been held at bay by attempts to avoid open conflict with Arafat that could weaken the struggle against the Israelis and alienate potential supporters.[33]

In September 2000, frustration and bitterness resulting from the failure to halt new Israeli settlements in the West Bank – the area targeted to be the Palestinian state if and when final status agreements are reached – boiled over when the then Israeli Defence Minister, Ariel Sharon, a proponent of settlement expansion, visited the area of the al-Aqsa Mosque. All Palestinians, including Israeli Palestinian Arab citizens who took to streets in a protest that led to the deaths of 13 of them, considered this act provocative and deliberate. These events sparked another far more deadly intifada, in which stones aimed at Israeli soldiers by bands of Palestinian youths are supplemented by deadly attacks on soldiers and civilians alike, engineered and executed by Hamas and Islamic Jihad volunteers.

This tactic, in which explosives are strapped to the bodies of willing martyrs, dubbed 'suicide bombers' in the West, who then explode themselves in areas of civilian concentration, aims at causing political dissension and demoralization. They embarrass the Israeli military, security forces and government leaders by their frequency and randomness and the tolls they take in terms of numbers of dead and wounded. Furthermore, there is apparently no shortage of individuals willing to gain martyrdom by turning themselves into human grenades. This means that some attacks will always succeed despite the most rigorous precautions taken to prevent them. This permits Hamas and other organizations that have copied this tactic to send the message that no Israeli man, woman or child is safe while the occupation of Palestinian land continues. To be noted here is the fundamentalist rationale behind this tactic that stands at odds with the common belief that terrorists are raving lunatics who strike out blindly at those they hate.

As Hamas leaders have observed, martyrdom attacks are the means they have at hand to effectively confront the Israelis. They also add that if they had alternative weapons like the American-made Apache helicopter gun ships and F16 fighter planes used by the Israeli military establishment, they would use them instead.

The suicide/martyrdom attacks, carried out for the purpose of sowing widespread fear among the civilian population to reach political goals, are called terrorism. At the same time, Israel's efforts to stop the attacks, for example the use of collective punishment – dynamiting of Palestinian homes and widespread arrests – are violations of the Fourth Geneva Convention for the protection of civilians during wartime and make them 'state terrorists' in the eyes of their opponents. America's position is that the Israelis have the right to defend their population against these terrorist attacks and the Bush administration has been trying hard to get Arafat's Palestinian Authority to help the Israelis crack down on the perpetrators.

A Hamas partisan provided me with the ideological underpinning for the organization's jihad tactics. Quoting the Prophet's words, he said that 'if there are twenty among you, patient and persevering, they will vanquish two hundred: if a hundred they will vanquish a thousand of the Unbelievers...' He also said that faithful Muslims are promised, 'Whatever you shall spend in the cause of God, shall be repaid unto you, and you shall not be treated unjustly'. (S. VIII, 65 and 60) Because secular Muslims also generally support the struggle to liberate Palestine, Hamas and Islamic Jihad have acquired broad public support as well as various types of assistance from interested regional state actors including Syria and Iran. This will be discussed in later chapters.

Hezbollah completely agrees with Palestinian fundamentalist groups on the use of force against the Israeli state to destroy it and takes every opportunity to spur Hamas and Islamic Jihad on. Both groups also struggle to remove Israeli occupation from Arab lands. Hezbollah's operations are meant to indirectly dislodge Israelis who have settled Syria's Golan Heights, seized during the 1967 war, and directly remove Israel's military presence from lands claimed by Lebanon. Hamas' efforts presently aim to force the Israelis – settlers as well as military – out of the West Bank and Gaza. The tactics Hezbollah fighters use in the struggle in South Lebanon against the Israeli military occupation, however, reflect the unique politico-military situation there as well as demographic and topographical conditions that are unlike those existing in the West Bank and Gaza.

Operating at first as an irregular force with no connection to the Lebanese government which was fighting for its life in the capital, Hezbollah, backed by Syria and Iran, began regularly attacking the Israeli soldiers and a local Lebanese militia assisting them – the South Lebanese Army (SLA) – in the 'Security Zone' the Hebrew troops had withdrawn to after the political aims of their 1982 invasion had fizzled. The tactics chosen to accomplish the campaign against the Israelis took into consideration the strategy's goals, battlefield conditions, resources available and likely Israeli and American responses. One dangerous response was pinning the terrorist label on Hezbollah, whom the Americans and Israelis considered an irregular mercenary force sponsored by two foreign states. Steps therefore had to be taken to avoid the onerous designation and therefore tactics of a different nature to those used by Hamas and Islamic Jihad were developed.

On the other hand, the earlier terrorist attacks against American and western civilians in West Beirut during the 1980s that the United States charges the Islamic Republic of Iran with sponsoring and Hezbollah with carrying out, do resemble the methods used by al-Qaeda, Hamas and Islamic Jihad, in that buildings full of people were destroyed by suicide/martyrdom attacks using ordinary vehicles. No matter that the alleged Hezbollah attacks were aimed at pushing the foreign troops in West Beirut back onto their ships and getting them out of the battle – from America's perspective fine distinctions between the aims and methods of these operations are not important. Terrorists are terrorists and these organizations are like peas in a pod no matter how their tactics evolve over time.

From the above discussion, it can be concluded that all the discontents and problems that had generated the wider Islamic resurgence – secularism, corruption, conflict and resentment of Israel – were present in Lebanon during the 1970s and were shared by members of the Islamic current developing there. Yet the doctrines and lessons of Revolutionary Iran had an unprecedented impact on the Lebanese Shiite leaders who formed Hezbollah and on those who gravitated toward its military wing. Furthermore, the particular conditions prevailing in Lebanon and the events precipitated by the civil war and the Palestinian/Israeli conflict in the South shaped Hezbollah's ideology and practices in ways that also set it apart from other fundamentalist organizations. America's charge of terrorism against Hezbollah and the Lebanese government's resistance defence after 1990 rest on selective applications and interpretations of these commonalities and distinctions.

# Chapter Two

# Hezbollah and
# the Outside World

A sustained military campaign against a regional superpower like Israel requires considerable planning, funding and logistics. How did the handful of Lebanese Shiite mullahs managing Hezbollah wind up with the support they needed to face down the Israelis and the surrogate force they had developed to ward off terrorism? Where did this support come from and why was it offered? The answers to these questions require a look at the geopolitical factors that led radically different states – one governed by Islamic fundamentalists and the other secular to the core – to join forces and enlist the Party of God as a foreign policy proxy.

## ANTI-IMPERIALISM AND COMMON CAUSE

Political alliances are sometimes formed by states with little in common besides converging foreign policy goals. In some instances, however, a common denominator of mutual hostility toward the same adversary might prepare the ground for cooperation. Such behaviour illustrates the old adage expressed by the eminent Caliph Ali bin Abi Taleb: 'The enemy of my enemy is my friend.'

Where Syria and Iran are concerned, geopolitical factors led to negative experiences with western imperialist countries that had lasting repercussions. These repercussions prepared the ground for foreign policy cooperation.

## SYRIA'S PROBLEMS WITH THE WEST

In Syria's case, westerners had distributed its land like slices of cake after the First World War. As mandate powers authorized by the League of Nations, Britain and France decided that part of western Syria would become Lebanon, another part would be annexed to Turkey, while Palestine and Jordan would be carved out of southern Syria. This dismemberment of Syria's territory frustrated its nationalist aspirations and engendered great bitterness. Worse still, by sponsoring Jewish colonization in Palestine, Britain encouraged the eventual emergence of the state of Israel whose existence has led to more than 50 years of hostility and several wars between the two states.

As the United States of America offered unequivocal support for Israel after its foundation and became a key element in that country's economic and military development, America became the object of Syrian resentment. These feelings were exacerbated when Syria again lost part of its national territory – this time, 1,860 square kilometres of the water-rich Golan plateau – during the 1967 Arab-Israeli war. The Israelis justified their seizure of the Golan and its subsequent annexation as having been carried out 'so that Syria would be unable to threaten Israeli citizens from that location again'. However, Syria was actually threatening Israeli paramilitary settlements that had been encroaching on areas previously established as demilitarized zones. The loss of the Golan Heights and its subsequent colonization by Israeli settlers triggered a crisis from which the Syrian nation has never recovered.[1] Recuperation of this area is Syria's major foreign policy concern today.

During another war with Israel in 1973, it became clear to Egyptian and Syrian leaders that their armies would not be able to dislodge the Israelis from Sinai and the Golan Heights by force. The fighter planes and weapons provided by East European countries of the Soviet Bloc were inferior to armaments provided to Israel by the USA, and the Israelis were far better prepared and trained in combat than their Arab counterparts. Considering that the time was right to push for bilateral peace negotiations between Israel and its neighbours and to remove them from the Middle East conflict arena, the USA brokered a separate peace deal between Egypt and Israel, which returned the Sinai Peninsula that had been seized by Israel, for permanent peace between the two countries. A peace treaty with Jordan followed. In both instances the deal was sweetened by America's promise to provide massive economic aid to the two Arab states.

On the other hand, a 'land for peace' deal between Syrians and Israelis was much more difficult to broker. While Egypt's Sinai had been occupied and colonized by settlers it had not been permanently annexed, as had the Golan Heights. The Sinai's Jewish settlers were therefore removed with relatively little fuss. Furthermore, the Sinai Peninsula is a desert, whereas the Golan is the major water reservoir of the parched region.

Recovery of the Golan Heights was a matter of national honour that Syria's President Hafiz al-Assad felt compelled to redeem.[2] He therefore took a firm position that no peace would be possible with Israel while Syrian land remained under its control and stuck to it.

The United Nations force that was stationed along the demilitarized zone on the Golan Heights to monitor any military developments there had little to do because Assad well understood that his conventional forces were no match for Israel's modern military forces. This meant that negotiations were the only means by which Syrian land could be regained. The problem was that Israel had little incentive to undertake negotiations as things stood in the 1970s. At that time, Israel and Syria had become involved in the Lebanese civil war, although each did its best to avoid the other's military forces stationed in Lebanon. Each wanted to somehow undercut the other's influence in that country in order to protect its flanks from attack while avoiding another direct military confrontation. As mentioned previously, a system of war by proxy forces was developed with Maronite militias assisted by Tel Aviv and the Muslim-leftist alliance aided by Damascus and other Arab states. That assistance continued until the civil war ended in 1990.[3]

But then events occurred in Lebanon in the 1980s that resulted in opportunities Assad could exploit in his campaign to regain the Golan Heights. One was the ousting of PLO fighters from the Israeli-Lebanese frontier in 1982, which left a politico-military vacuum there; the other was the reinforcement of Lebanon's border area with Israeli troops and a surrogate force – the SLA in 1985 (see Chapter 3 for details). Assad needed two assets: his own surrogate force that could provide the necessary disturbances and frictions that might keep the Golan issue alive; and some help with the logistics of the strategy he had in mind. As we shall see, Hezbollah and Iran provided these assets.

## IMPERIALISM AND THE IRANIAN EXPERIENCE

Iran was never dismembered by western powers as Syria had been, but fears arose for its territorial integrity and independence because of its highly strategic location.[4] During the Second World War, it became a supply route for the delivery of war material to the Soviet Union, and was then occupied by allied forces to exclude any Nazi penetration. Its ruler was deposed because of his Nazi sympathies in 1941, and his son, Mohammed Reza Pahlavi, was then placed on the peacock throne. Britain guaranteed the newly established Shah's tenure and kept an eye on his country's vast oil reserves.

The enmity that arose between the USA and the USSR after the Second World War was also played out on Iranian soil as America tried to prevent its enemy's encroachment in Iran. The CIA overthrew a Prime

Minister of nationalist sentiments in 1953 – Muhammad Mossadegh – who was considered pro-Soviet by the USA. With US assistance, the Shah was able to create one of the strongest military forces in the region, directly across the Persian Gulf from the oil-rich countries of the Arabian Peninsula.

A negative result of the Shah's close ties with the USA, however, was widespread public opinion that he had severely compromised the country's independence and that Iran had still not thrown off the shackles of imperialism that had begun years earlier when the British were calling the shots. As mentioned previously, another reason why Iranians began to withdraw their support from the Shah's regime in the 1970s was the failure of a modernization program that had been pushed by the USA. This angered the rural majority by raising expectations of considerable benefits but then failing to fulfil them. A faltering economy raised anger among bazaar merchants, who often took refuge in the mosques when their protests drew a reaction from the Shah's security forces. As those protests increased in number and the Shah became more and more isolated, he reacted by expanding an already formidable secret police organization – savak – to maintain order.

The dynamic and eloquent Ayatollah Ruhallah Khomeini – the Shah's arch-enemy – followed these events closely from Paris, where he lived in exile and encouraged the opposition forces in every way he could. By the time the regime fell to a united front of communists, fundamentalists and other groups in 1979, every sector of Iranian society had turned against the Shah.[5]

When the fundamentalist clergy led by Khomeini cleared away the opposition and established an Islamic Republic, Syria and the Soviet Union – the enemies of Khomeini's enemies – were the first two states to grant recognition to the new government.[6]

In November of the same year, in a gesture of defiance toward the USA, labelled 'the Great Satan' by Khomeini – the Revolutionary Guards surrounded the American Embassy in Tehran and held its occupants hostage for 444 days. During that period, President Jimmy Carter launched an ill-fated helicopter raid to try to rescue the hostages that, much to the glee of the Iranian authorities, never got close to the capital. The USA then applied economic sanctions against its enemy and froze the huge assets that had been deposited in American banks during the Shah's regime. Some of the frozen funds are now being awarded to individuals who were kidnapped in Beirut in the 1980s since the USA claims it has proof that Iran was behind these incidents.

In September 1980, Iraqi forces invaded Iran and bombed Tehran and other cities, in what was the beginning of an eight-year battle for supremacy in the Persian Gulf region.[7] Syria immediately broke relations with Iraq, accusing its leader, Saddam Hussein, of doing the CIA's dirty work. Was there any truth in that remark?

As it happens, recent information on the Iran/Iraq war indicates that CIA officials supported a covert programme to defeat Iran but were not directly involved in it. The details of that programme were revealed recently by a reporter who interviewed military officers with direct knowledge of America's secret effort to assist Iraq during the Iran-Iraq war. According to these officers, the USA had decided that it was vital for Iran to lose the war so that it could not overrun the oil-producing states in the Gulf. The USA thus provided intelligence assistance to Iraq in the form of satellite photography to help the Iraqis understand how Iranian forces were deployed against them. Senior US military officers also reported that this covert US programme assisted Iraq, although American intelligence agencies knew that Iraqi commanders would employ chemical weapons in waging the decisive battles of the Iran-Iraq war. Although Iraq's use of mustard gas, sarin and other poisonous agents was publicly condemned by those agencies, President Ronald Reagan, Vice President George Bush and senior national security aides never withdrew their support for the highly classified programme, in which more than 60 officers of the US Defense Agency were secretly providing the Iraqi general staff with detailed information on Iranian deployments, tactical planning and bomb-damage assessments. The Iraqis shared their battle plans with the Americans without admitting use of chemical weapons, the military officers said. Fully aware of US-Iraqi cooperation, the above incident provides yet another reason for the Iranian leadership's abiding hostility toward the USA.

On the other hand, Colonel Walter Lang, the senior Defense Intelligence officer at the time, was also quoted in the article as having the following to say about the reasons American agencies turned a blind eye toward Iraq's use of chemical warfare against its neighbour: 'The use of gas on the battlefield by the Iraqis was not a matter of deep strategic concern. What Reagan's top aides were concerned about, was that the Iranians not break through to the Fao Peninsula and spread the Islamic revolution to Kuwait and Saudi Arabia to the south.'[8]

Sharing Iran's hostility toward the USA and Iraq, the Assad government did what it could to exploit the situation, while assisting the Islamic Republic's campaign against its neighbour. In May 1982, after signing a ten-year trade pact with Iran, Damascus closed its border to Iraq and the pipeline for Iraqi oil exports through the Mediterranean. That act deprived Iraq of about 40 per cent of its oil revenues. A month later, foreign policy reciprocity between Syria and Iran led to an immediate announcement of support for Syria and Lebanon by the Tehran authorities as the 1982 Israeli invasion of Lebanon got under way.

While the Iran-Iraq war was continuing, Iran was also searching for other ways in which it could expand its influence in the region. Lebanon seemed a fertile field. The mainly Muslim PLO operating against Israel from South Lebanon could be assisted with the recruitment of Shiites, while Shiites that had recently become politically active could be further mobilized along Islamic lines. Furthermore, Iran's only regional ally, Syria, was already deeply involved in Lebanese politics, trying to counter Israeli influence in that disintegrating state.[9] Having vowed to export its Islamic revolution, to destroy Israel and recapture Jerusalem, what better place for Iran to start than in Lebanon?[10]

## LEBANON: AN ARENA FOR FOREIGN BATTLES

As explained earlier, armed clashes between Lebanese militias in and around Beirut were not the only conflicts taking place on Lebanese soil that interested Syrian President Assad in the late 1970s and early 1980s. Palestinians from Lebanon's refugee camps were also engaging in cross-border attacks against Israeli villages near the Lebanese frontier that often drew military responses from the Israeli army.[11] How was it that these groups could operate so freely within Lebanon's borders that the whole southern part of the country had been sarcastically labelled 'Fatahland'?

In an Arab League meeting in Cairo on 3 November 1969, the newly founded PLO headed by Yasser Arafat had been given the green light to conduct these operations from Lebanese soil. The Lebanese government at that time found no way it could deny access to the fighters without alienating other Arab states and causing further expansion of the already widening Muslim-Christian rift in the country.

Although Assad was never friendly with Yasser Arafat, because of the latter's unwillingness to integrate his resistance activities with the policy directions of the Syrian regime, the Assad government did appreciate the pressure being placed on the Israelis in South Lebanon by the PLO, as it sought ways to defeat the pro-Israeli Christian factions involved in the civil war going on to the north.

The Israelis, however, sought a solution to their problem with the PLO by approaching Christian and Shiite inhabitants of the South who strongly resented the Palestinians' presence among them, or who simply remained there rather than fleeing north, to join an auxiliary force they were forming. This local militia would help repulse the PLO, thereby protecting Israel's northern frontier. Saad Haddad, a Christian who had been an officer in the Lebanese Army, commanded this force – the Southern Lebanese Army (SLA). Despite this precautionary measure, however, cross-border attacks continued against Israel's northern settlements, although they had drastically decreased by the late 1970s.

In fact, on the eve of the massive Israeli invasion of Lebanon in 1982, something like a ceasefire was prevailing along Lebanon's southern border. Nevertheless, the invasion was justified by Tel Aviv as a means of ending terrorism there. Israeli authors Schiff and Yaari dispute that rationale and claim that the real motive for the military incursion that year was the right-wing Israeli Likud Party's ambition to destroy remaining resistance from Syria and the PLO and impose a unilateral Pax Israeli on the region. This would include incorporation of the West Bank and Gaza into greater Israel.[12]

In that operation, entitled 'Peace for Galilee' and directed by Defense Minister Ariel Sharon, Israeli forces went all the way to Beirut in hopes that they could smash the Palestinians and their Muslim-leftist allies and work out an arrangement with Israel's Christian allies that would produce an Israeli-Lebanese peace treaty. If that could be done then Syria would be the odd man out.[13]

The goals of that strategy were not achieved due to strenuous opposition from pro-Syrian groups and the assassination of the militiaman Israel had counted on to swing the peace treaty – Bashir al-Gemayel. Gemayel's aim was to sweep every inch of Lebanon clean of Palestinians and to radically alter the political system in favour of the Christians. Even more unfortunately for the Israelis, the battle of West Beirut and its occupation by their forces radicalized some Shiites, led to their cooperation with Syria and Iran and finally resulted in the war of attrition that is still causing them grief today.

## IRAN ENTERS THE BATTLE FOR WEST BEIRUT

The Israeli bombing raids on Palestinian targets in West Beirut that went on during the summer closed down Beirut, crippled electricity and water networks and left the Lebanese citizens panicky and exhausted. Yet the most horrific events were still to come. Just after Bashir al-Gemayel was elected president of the republic, he was killed in an explosion on 14 September 1982, which buried him under his party's branch office in Ashrafieh. Hysterical with grief, his partisans refused to believe their leader was dead for more than a week. Bashir's death was immediately avenged by Christian partisans who entered Sabra and Shatila Palestinian refugee camps in Beirut's southern suburb and between 16 and 18 September machine-gunned at least 1,500 men, women and children and anything else that moved – dogs, horses, sheep – to death. Then, on 19 September, Ariel Sharon's troops who were presumed to be protecting the people in the camps from just such an eventuality, apparently did not see Bashir's Lebanese allies cleanse the camps of the '2,000 terrorists' Defense Minister Sharon insisted had remained on the sites. As a result of that action, hundreds of Lebanese and Palestinian civilians were subjected to three days of torture, rape and killing while many others were arrested and trucked away never to appear again. In all, an estimated 2,000 civilians were either killed or made to disappear in that operation.[14]

A four-nation international force, including 1,400 US marines, was dispatched to Beirut immediately after the massacres to take charge of the further deteriorating situation and to organize the evacuation of Palestinian fighters to Tunisia, whose government agreed to accept them. Order, however, did not prevail. In December of the same year, the American mission seemed to change course when the American battleship *Virginia,* anchored off the coast, fired projectiles at Muslim-leftist coalition forces whom it was claimed were threatening the Lebanese army positions. Since army units that had remained intact were cooperating with the Christian militias, this act was heralded by the local press as the end of America's neutrality in the Lebanese civil war. United States strategy had moved from evacuating Palestinian fighters from Lebanon to intervention in the civil war on the Christian side. Both these developments pleased their Israeli friends.

The car bombing of the American Embassy in Beirut took place four months later, on 18 April 1983, leaving 63 dead. The blast that left the front of the building in rubble occurred at a very opportune time, since Beirut CIA operatives were meeting there with other members of that organization. In October of the same year, 243 marines were killed when a truck loaded with explosives crashed into their barracks near the international airport. The blast left a crater more than 4 metres deep. Twenty-six minutes later, the building housing members of the French contingent of the multinational force went up the same way with more than a dozen killed.

While no individual or group had claimed responsibility for the attack on the American Embassy, this time phone calls to an international press agency revealed that these acts had been carried out by an unknown organization that called itself Islamic Jihad. The caller identified his group as 'soldiers of God yearning for martyrdom' and said that their goal was an Islamic Republic for Lebanon and the expulsion of Israelis and their supporters. A new force had been added to the struggle for Lebanon.

As a result of the recent revolution in Iran and the references made to martyrdom and an Islamic Republic for Lebanon, attention immediately focused on Iranian backing for these deeds although the local operatives could not be clearly identified at the time. From discussions with senior Lebanese officials at the time, I learned that it was thought that fundamentalist groups or even a few individuals recruited by Iran and/ or Syria had set up these operations and found martyrs willing to carry them out.

In November 1983, Israeli headquarters located in the southern port city of Tyre were car bombed as well, with considerable loss of life. Hezbollah claimed that attack, while categorically denying that the others were the handiwork of their operatives. However, they admit to fully understanding and sympathizing with the rationale behind the terrorist acts. In fact, Sayyed Mohammed Hussein Fadlallah, a top Shiite religious leader later said to be Hezbollah's Spiritual Guide, characterized the Beirut and Tyre bomb blasts as the response of the weak to oppression by the powerful. Shortly thereafter, a car bomb thought by many to have been planted by CIA operatives, went off near Fadlallah's home killing 83 Lebanese civilians but leaving him untouched. According to information pieced together by terror expert Magnus Ranstorp from local and international press accounts, the key figure in the anti-American and French bomb attacks was a man later indicted by a US court for hijacking TWA 847 and murdering an American citizen on board, Hezbollah member Imad Mugniyeh, who was none other than Sayyed Fadlallah's body guard at one time.[15]

The kidnappings of Americans and other westerners living in Lebanon – begun after the Israeli invasion in 1982 with the disappearance of the Acting President of the American University of Beirut, David Dodge – continued throughout the 1980s. All told, more than a dozen individuals, including Terry Waite, a representative of the British Archbishop of Canterbury, were kidnapped between 1982 and 1992 with no public announcement of who had done it or why. A major part of this campaign was meant to disrupt western intelligence networks by forcing them to look to their security as any remaining male western presence in Beirut was eliminated. However, Ranstorp claims that the kidnappings occurred in stages as a result of several different motivations on the part of the perpetrators and their Iranian backers and that five of the victims died or were executed by Hezbollah, including Army Lt Colonel William Higgins and William Buckley, the chief of the CIA's Lebanese operations.[16] It is worth mentioning here that friction arose between Syria and Iran over the kidnappings that occurred after mid 1980, since Damascus was controlling security in West Beirut at that time and was unable to find the sequestered victims or prevent more kidnappings.

In 1984, the US battleship *New Jersey* went into action to try to relieve a unit of the Lebanese army that had been surrounded by opposition militias in the mountains above the Beirut International Airport. More than 300 projectiles were fired causing considerable destruction to homes and businesses in the target area. The *New Jersey* was anchored less than a quarter of a mile from my home, and the first blast of its giant guns shattered all windows facing the sea and blew my front door right off its hinges.

TWA flight 847 was hijacked in 1985 and a US Navy diver aboard was murdered and brutally thrown out onto the tarmac. The USA was able to gather information on the three perpetrators and indicted them in absentia on charges of murder before a US court. The evidence in this case is said to indicate that all three men were members of Hezbollah, and their names are presently among the 23 most wanted terrorists on the list published by the US government in September 2001.

The above information about Israel's 1982 invasion and the events unleashed in its wake provides some insight into the climate of fear, anger and bitterness that fuelled the continuing civil war and the struggle against Israel simultaneously taking place in the South during the 1980s. At this time, many believed that the Lebanese crisis was simply intractable, since each side's view of the other side had dramatically hardened. For Ronald Reagan, president during the 1982 invasion, America's major enemy was the 'evil empire' (a reference to the Soviet Union). Soviet clients, some of the Arab regimes such as Libya and Syria, the Palestinians and the Lebanese locals fighting with them were naturally also on Reagan's blacklist. Iran was also high on that list, for reasons already discussed. American 'friends' were the Israelis, the Lebanese government and the Christian militias that were allied with it. Those who opposed this group, whom they called 'imperialists and lackeys', also saw the situation in terms of black and white, good and evil.

## DAMASCUS AND TEHRAN STRIKE A DEAL

While chaos was occurring in Beirut and its surrounding areas, Assad was considering how to deal with the politico-military vacuum left by the PLO in Lebanon's border area. Replacing the Palestinian fighters with a surrogate force that would be amenable to his command was highly important to his campaign to regain the Golan Heights because it would allow him to attack Israeli soldiers in Lebanon while protecting the Syrian army from a direct confrontation with Israel's far superior military establishment. These attacks would serve as 'reminders' to Israel that Syria had not given up its quest to have the Golan Heights returned.

The lush and remote Bekaa Valley, which had remained under Syrian control despite the Israeli presence in the capital and areas surrounding it,[17] was an ideal location for the training and arming of clandestine fighting units. This area had been off-limits to the Israelis, just as the border area had been to Syria, as a result of the tacit agreement made between the two states to avoid direct clashes.[18]

Assad thus took steps to energize his plan to introduce Lebanese fighters into the border area. These combatants could be recruited from the Bekaa area and trained right there near the ancient Greco-Roman temple complex of Baalbak. The irregular force would operate against the Israelis in coordination with Syrian headquarters in Lebanon.

Iran was ready to join forces with Syria in this enterprise because Damascus' territorial preoccupations provided a way for Teheran to realize its own foreign policy ambitions. Its main goal in this respect was 'to break out of the narrow geopolitical confines of the war with Iraq and reach a wider constituency within the Arab world'.[19] A clear arrangement with Syria that incorporated jihad against the Israelis by Lebanese Shiite fundamentalists provided the framework for Iran to actualize its strategy.

In the deal worked out between the two countries, Syrian strategists and politicians would handle the timing and targeting of the attacks against Israeli and SLA troops by the selected irregular surrogate force in ways that would convey the messages Syria wished to send to Israel and the USA. Syrian troops stationed in the Bekaa would provide the security necessary for the training camps set up and help with logistics. For its part of the arrangement, Iran would provide the fighters with training and monthly salaries and take care of benefits for their families. Weapons sent from Iran for the mujahidin would be forwarded over land in Syrian trucks to the Bekaa and other locations in Lebanon. The Lebanese government did not enter into this picture at all, since it was completely powerless to prevent the activities going on in the Bekaa. The national army had been so weakened by the defection of its troops to the various militias that it was pinned down and fighting for its life in a very small part of East Beirut and adjacent areas. For all intents and purposes the authorities had simply abandoned the peripheral areas during the civil conflict. Thus the only thing left to do was to decide on the human resources that would conduct the actual fighting against Israel.

## HEZBOLLAH: THE ONLY CHOICE

As we know, Lebanese Shiite fundamentalists were looking for a role in the struggle against Israel and some had split from the Shiite Amal movement to find one. These men, and others like them, suited Iran's foreign policy requirements in terms of their ideological commitments and willingness to act upon them, as some had already demonstrated in the terrorist operations allegedly sponsored by the Islamic Republic in West Beirut. These men and other committed Shiite fundamentalists who, after 1979, were swept up by the Iranian Revolution and shared its goals could be helped by Iran's Revolutionary Guards to form an organizational structure and to cohere around a local leadership that would be able to exploit the opportunity for militant jihad being offered. Potential mujahidin were plentiful in the Bekaa where Hussein Musawi, the leader of the breakaway group Islamic Amal, resided and other young Shiite men from the dahiyeh, Beirut's suburb, and the South could also be encouraged to commit themselves to the holy struggle against the 'usurpers of Palestine'.

Iran's support for this group, which would eventually become Hezbollah, could deliver two important foreign policy goals: the capacity to fight Israel through a proxy, which allowed it direct entrance into the Middle East war/peace equation and the expansion of Shiite Islam's influence in Lebanon through Hezbollah's developing role there.

How would Syria react to a fundamentalist militia as a foreign policy surrogate? Although Damascus' past experiences with fundamentalism had been extremely negative, Assad expected to have as tight a grip on Hezbollah as he had on all the other parties under the Syrian politico-military umbrella. This expectation was tested in 1987, when Hezbollah partisans refused to remove a checkpoint from the road before their West Beirut barracks on the orders of the Syrian troops that had arrived to control the area. The Syrian officer in charge simply arrested the two-dozen or so men involved, lined them up and shot each one through the head with his pistol. This kind of 'Hamah solution' was not quickly forgotten by any of the West Beirut parties, although it did eliminate other frictions between the Party of God and the Syrians during the late 1980s. The tensions at times between Hezbollah and Syria and between Tehran and Damascus illustrated the fact that the three-sided relationship was obviously a marriage of convenience and only later became a closer one.

With the decision that Hezbollah would spearhead the struggle against Israel in South Lebanon, Iranian Revolutionary Guards were sent to the Bekaa to help PLO instructors train Hezbollah fighters. According to Israeli information, by the mid 1980s Hezbollah was estimated to have mobilized some 7,000 partisans there. Many unemployed youths who were galvanized by faith to join Hezbollah also found a means of making a living in that depressed area by becoming a mujahid, since Iran footed the monthly salary of each enlistee and provided benefits for him and his family. It is somewhat ironic that the Islamic Republic of Iran should have thus become the largest employer in the Bekaa region.

When Israel announced in 1985 that it would not completely withdraw its troops from Lebanon, but would establish a 'Security Zone' some 10 kilometres deep and 79 long inside Lebanese territory to protect its northern villages from possible future infiltrations, Hezbollah was ready to challenge that decision with arms. The Israelis, however, needed their own surrogate force in the area to be occupied. Recognizing Amal as a moderate force that wished to prevent military operations in the border area that might draw Israeli retaliations, the Israelis first tried to negotiate some sort of security arrangement with Berri. However, although Amal had even disarmed some Hezbollah fighters and stopped armed shipments to the South, it could not permit itself to be linked with any activities that could be viewed by the Syrians as pro-Israeli. Thus the South Lebanese Army (SLA), which had been formed in 1978 under the direction of Major Saad Haddad to help the Israelis control the border area, continued to do so with a minimal number of Israeli troops stationed there.

With their mission cut out for them, Hezbollah field commanders coordinated most of their activities with Syrian officials but also had to be given some leeway in working out tactics and finding the opportunities to use them to best avail. Amal was later allowed more limited activities along some of the edges of the zone. As the operations conducted by Hezbollah began to take their toll on the occupation forces, the Israelis found that their plan of minimal exposure in the zone could not be sustained. More men were added to the Lebanese component of the defence force to beef it up. Casualties were attributed to terrorism by Iranian-backed irregular forces and Hezbollah's name began appearing more and more frequently in the regional and international mass media. The question that was still to be answered, however, was whether a policy designed and implemented by two foreign powers – Syria and Iran – would remain in force once the civil war wound down and a new Lebanese government was installed in office.

# Chapter Three

# The Mechanics of Hezbollah's Transformation from Radical Militia to Mainstream Party

The internal and external dynamics of Lebanon's civil war were important factors in Hezbollah's rise and its course of development. However, it was Syria's gradual political ascendancy in Lebanon and the post-war role it achieved in that country that enabled Hezbollah to continue its jihad activities against Israel under the auspices of the post-war Lebanese regime. This development legitimated the Party of God as an authentic Lebanese party and cast its struggle against the Israeli military and the SLA in the guise of national resistance. If Hezbollah's terrorist image were ever to be overridden, this tricky manoeuvre would have to be dealt with first. Was Syrian arm-twisting involved as the post-war government formed or had Hezbollah smoothed its transition to mainstream party status through its own efforts? Before these questions can be addressed a brief review of the events and political dynamics that produced Lebanon's post-war political order is required.

## SYRIA GAINS THE UPPER HAND IN LEBANON

In previous chapters we have seen the importance attached by the Assad government to the foreign policy strategy it had begun with Iran in the mid 1980s. As events transpired in the civil war, it was therefore essential that everything possible be done to ensure the continuity of Hezbollah's activities in the border area. The desired scenario was that Syrian allies would come out on top in the struggle against the Christian militias, or at least fight them to a standstill, so that Damascus could translate its power on the ground in Lebanon into some sort of internationally accepted role to resolve the impasse and ensure stability in the political order that would be emerging after hostilities ended. If that could be achieved somehow, the delicate operation of securing foreign policy coordination with the new Lebanese authorities in the face of undoubted Christian opposition would have to be managed. Finally, a deal between the government and Hezbollah would have to be brokered so that the change of face that would defeat accusations of terrorism would receive official endorsement. Since the Party of God had no history as a political party this situation would also require considerable handling by Damascus and by Hezbollah itself, as we shall see later.

As events proved, Syrian ascendancy in Lebanon was certainly not straightforward or rapid. The Christian Lebanese Forces militia tried to carry on the campaign begun by Bashir al-Gemayel before his assassination in 1982; however, after the Israeli troops were withdrawn from Beirut and surrounding areas, the new leadership failed to hold the positions evacuated by their allies and were handed a series of stinging defeats by Muslim-leftist fighters. However, there was enough strength left in the Christian forces and the Lebanese army to signal a strong rejection of the 1985 peace arrangement – the Tripartite Accord – that Syria tried to set up with the heads of leftist-Muslim militias and a Christian renegade.

Two years later, however, Syria scored a diplomatic and tactical breakthrough when Prime Minister Selim al-Hoss and his cabinet members requested the presence of Syrian troops in West Beirut to maintain order among the feuding militias in that sector. Syrian troops pitched tents here and there and requisitioned apartments for officers for a long stay. One of those bivouacs was on the top floor of my own building. A communications centre was set up in the lobby, the windows were sandbagged, and the soldiers hunkered down for a seven-year stay. Several conferences were then arranged in foreign capitals to bring the feuding parties to some sort of peace agreement to end the interminable struggle that seemed to have reached a stalemate. No results were forthcoming. Hoping third-party mediation might work, an Arab initiative supported by the international community to try to tie down Lebanon, the region's loose cannon, was launched in 1989. Representatives of King Fahd of Saudi Arabia, King Hassan of Morocco and Chadli Ben Jadid, Algeria's president, mediated the Lebanese conflict aided by the Assistant Secretary-General of the Arab League, Lakhdar Ibrahimi.[1] Lebanese MPs who had been elected before the civil war began and had assembled at Taif, Saudi Arabia in the autumn of 1989 formally accepted the arrangement worked out to end hostilities.

Although Christian parliamentarians signed the Document of National Reconciliation (known as the Taif Accord), agreeing to a change in the ratio of Muslim-Christian seats in parliament in the Muslims' favour and that Lebanon's face was Arab rather than Phoenician or particularly Lebanese, as Christians liked to think, they were very apprehensive about some parts of the text. Objections were raised over a clause acknowledging Syria's 'special interest' in Lebanon. The Accord also stated that Syria was to assist the Lebanese government to extend its authority over all Lebanese territory by disarming the militias and providing security while the national army was being reconstituted.[2] This point was a bow to Syria's undoubted power on the ground and acknowledged the fact that no other power besides Syria had the will or muscle to control the warring factions and deal with any hold-outs. It is worth noting in this respect that the USA went along with this arrangement so that the civil war in Lebanon could be shut down and full attention could be turned toward the establishment of a peace process that would finally resolve the Arab-Israeli conflict. Ironically, leaving Syria in charge of Lebanon established exactly the conditions Assad needed to guarantee the sustainability of Hezbollah's jihad in South Lebanon and the Party of God is presently doing its bit to end the floundering peace process.

The Accord stipulation that generated the strongest outcry, however, concerned the means by which Syrian troops would eventually be withdrawn from Lebanon. A two-year timetable for the gradual withdrawal of the approximately 40,000 Syrian troops in Lebanon to the Bekaa was set up; however, a decision on their final departure date was left to negotiations between the Syrian and Lebanese governments. Many Lebanese, and especially the Christian opposition, feared that the weaker party would actually have little to say in this decision and that the clause seriously jeopardized Lebanon's independence. Since Syria is still in Lebanon allegedly because security conditions are not yet assured, this sentiment has grown.

After the Taif Accord had been signed, Syrian troops aided their allies in the final battles against the decimated Lebanese Army led by Maronite General Michel Aoun. Aoun, who had been tapped to head a caretaker government in 1988, violently opposed the Taif Accord for giving Syria a free hand in Lebanon. He was finally sent off to house arrest in France in 1990, where he remains today. His adherents in Lebanon do their best to agitate for Syria's withdrawal, but have a hard time with security forces and police who break up manifestations none too gently and arrest political activists.

With the Christian opposition fragmented, its leaders either outside the country or keeping their heads down, or co-opted, the stage was set for the commencement of the post-war period and the election of a new government. What the Assad government needed now was an agreement with the new Lebanese governing elites on 100 per cent coordination of their country's foreign policy toward Israel with Syria's. A major feature of this coordination would be an agreement to keep the two conventional armies on the sidelines so that Hezbollah, with some assistance from Amal, would continue to be the sole military force facing the Israelis and the SLA in the effort to recoup national territories.

## GUARANTEEING JIHAD

The authority the Assad government had garnered through the Taif Accord and its military presence in Lebanon were important guarantors of foreign policy continuity, yet Damascus took no risks where government endorsement of Hezbollah's armed resistance activities was concerned. Thus, as the post-war period began, it was quickly understood by Lebanese politicians in search of top governmental positions, that no individual would secure any of the five most important governmental posts – president, speaker of the house, prime minister, minister of defence and of the interior – without total commitment to all aspects of the 'joint Lebanese-Syrian foreign policy' being orchestrated. Only those who would unswervingly support this strategy would receive the Syrian backing essential for election or appointment to those key posts.

Analysis of the political affiliations of the members of eight Lebanese governments between 1992 and 2000 reveals that the men who held the strategic positions mentioned above were indeed highly reliable Syrian allies.[3] However, this did not mean that they lacked popular support in their own right and were imposed on the public. On the contrary, Assad's strategy was to endorse popular Lebanese politicians for the vital positions that agreed with his interpretations of regional affairs and that had large followings. While the Christian opposition seethed over this situation and declared a boycott of the 1992 elections, it was powerless to counteract it. The boycott could not be sustained during the next elections as many Christians decided loyal opposition was better than 'staying out in the cold'.

At any rate, with Syria's interests widely understood, the men who would be the pillars of the post-war regime lined up and were duly elected in the parliamentary contest of 1992. 'Democratic process' legitimated the new political order Syria was stewarding.[4] Representatives of the two countries shortly thereafter signed a formal Treaty of Brotherhood and Cooperation that covered security and other arrangements between the two countries.[5]

## THE STATE/RESISTANCE DEAL

Smoothing the way for Hezbollah's insertion into the reconstituted political arena could not, however, be left entirely to Damascus' machinations. The main actors involved – Hezbollah and the Lebanese authorities – each had to come to terms with the novel situation gelling and actively promote it to make it work.

Situations like this are not uncommon and usually feature direct or implicit bargaining between radical parties wishing to transform themselves into moderate political actors and the governments holding the keys to the political arena. For a successful 'deal' to take place, the radical group must first foreswear its hostility to the state and promise to abide by the rules and regulations governing all other parties on the scene. For its part, the state guarantees the transforming party the protection and prerogatives that are due legitimate political organizations. Mutual interest underwrites this arrangement and demonstrations of good will and delivery on the promises made clinch it.[6]

In this case, for the deal to be swung between the radical Islamist party, Hezbollah, and the Lebanese authorities it had to be brokered by a third interested party – Syria. As we know, Syria's interest lay in bringing the two actors to an understanding that would safeguard the strategy it had developed years before with Iran. That strategy, it was hoped, would eventually prod the Israeli government into negotiating the return of the Golan Heights, the issue of vital importance to the Syrian government.

Whether the details of the agreement were actually articulated or not is not known to me, but here is what had to be agreed to make the Syrian-orchestrated strategy work under the new Lebanese political order. Hezbollah would have to shelve aspirations for an Islamic Republic ruled by Muslim religious law and forego the subversive activities that we have seen were applied against 'heretical governments' by other fundamentalist groups in the region. Instead, the Party of God would leave its radical ideology behind or soft-pedal it, so that it could enter the political arena, just as any of the other Muslim-leftist militia leaders and their followers and other opponents of the 'old regime' would have to do. Hezbollah could assume an opposition position to the new government as its interests dictated, but it would henceforth be a member of the *loyal opposition*.

In return, the Party of God's jihad activities against the Israelis would receive official authorization to continue by virtue of the government's recognition of the armed struggle as a national resistance. The Lebanese government would therefore declare Hezbollah's right to recover national territory in its name in no uncertain terms and stay out of the Party of God's way while it was undertaking that mission. (Chapter 8 presents information on the specific 'rules' that governed that arrangement and demonstrates how difficult it was at times for the government to comply with them.)

What this 'understanding' meant in general terms was that each actor would have to accept the other's legitimacy, as hard as that might be ideologically or practically. For instance, Hezbollah's leaders would have to cooperate with a secular government instead of heeding religious imperatives to overthrow it, a move certain to be resisted by hardline party ideologues. Moreover, at a time when the post-war government would be most anxious to extend its authority to all areas of the country as quickly as possible, how would leaders feel about the southern border area remaining off limits to the army? The hardest mouthful to swallow, however, would be Hezbollah's allegiance to Iran and close coordination with Syria rather than with the Lebanese authorities in that theatre of operations. To handle this potentially contentious situation, exasperated government leaders would have to keep their eyes firmly focused on the possibility of recovering a big water-rich chunk of their country's territory if the plan being hatched was successful.

## PUBLIC REACTION TO HEZBOLLAH'S NEW FACE

Was Hezbollah's entrance into the post-war political equation palatable to the Lebanese public, or were the 'terrorists', who had entered the House of Representatives in 1992, simply shoved down their throats by Syria and Iran, as Israel and the USA saw the situation?

By 1990, when Hezbollah began making plans to field candidates in the forthcoming elections to demonstrate the sincerity of its trans-formation, it had been operating a wide network of social and public services in the Bekaa and Beirut's dahiyeh for a number of years (see Chapter 6). As we know, mainstream parties and politicians generally undertake such activities to secure constituents' support. Still, Hezbollah was best known for fighting the Israelis and their surrogates in South Lebanon, where it was acting more like a militia than a party, to say the least. The question many people were pondering as the elections approached was whether this performance would earn Hezbollah the votes needed from citizens of different faiths that were necessary for seats in parliament and the legitimation of the armed struggle.

Regardless of their sentiments about the post-war power equation or their lingering suspicions about Hezbollah's Islamic plans for Lebanon, a consensus seemed to have formed among the Lebanese by the beginning of the 1990s that the Party of God was doing a good job on the battlefield against the Israelis and should continue its operations. Hezbollah had been carrying out resistance activities within the 'Security

Zone' since 1985 and knew the ropes. So well, in fact, that while the Israelis had originally counted on retaining a minimal number of troops in Lebanon to direct and work with the SLA, military strategists soon found that these soldiers needed far more support against Hezbollah than had first been planned. This was because the fundamentalist combatants had been taking a constant although never overwhelming toll of Israeli and SLA troops deployed in the area. In effect, over the five-year period between 1985 and 1990, Israel began to experience its own small-scale Vietnam.

The general antipathy felt toward the Israelis since the highly destructive 1978 and 1982 invasions, plus the fact that a local force was imposing costs on their occupation, had thus already gained the Party of God considerable public respect as the post-civil war regime was forming.

Another reason Hezbollah's military activities were generally approved was that there was apparently no other way to evict the Israelis. The Lebanese military was incoherent and undergoing reconstruction, and the Syrian army could not take on that job without risk of unacceptable losses by Israel's overwhelming conventional forces. Furthermore, the Syrians would draw widespread international condemnation for instigating a regional conflagration that, theoretically, they should have nothing to do with.

Suspicion of Israel's motives in South Lebanon also generated support for Hezbollah's jihad activities. Israel had been pumping the precious water sources that arose inside Lebanon from almost the moment it had occupied the Lebanese border area. (See Map 2) Despite Tel Aviv's repeated declarations that it had no ambitions in Lebanon other than to protect its own citizens from cross-border attacks, these actions seemed to belie their words.

There was also considerable public sympathy for the Lebanese who were caught against their will inside the 'Security Zone'. Economic, social and business links with the rest of Lebanon were difficult if not impossible, and harassment of young Shiite and Christian men to join the SLA was a well-known fact. Many parents sent their sons away to avoid this problem and, once they had left, visits were impossible, for obvious reasons. Those individuals and families who objected to the occupation and were suspected of cooperation with Hezbollah were expelled from the zone by the Israelis and often had to leave with only what they could carry. Such treatment of civilians is forbidden by international conventions and was roundly condemned.[8] For these reasons, many southerners harboured deep resentment against the occupation forces and found sympathy among the Lebanese public. The group punishing the Israelis and the SLA and attempting to liberate the area therefore won approval regardless of its backing by outside powers.

On the other hand, the Shiite and Christian inhabitants of the 'Security Zone' who found work and good educational possibilities for their children inside Israel and were cooperating with the SLA and its directors were considered collaborators by many Lebanese and reviled. Thus, for whatever reasons the occupation had been set up, it is fair to say that most Lebanese saw it as a blot on their national honour and an impediment to their independence that had to be removed. Since all resolutions of the United Nations Security Council since 1978, when Israel launched 'Operation Litani', that had branded the ensuing occupation of South Lebanon illegal and demanded Israel's immediate withdrawal had gone unheeded by Tel Aviv, many Lebanese agreed with Hezbollah and its sponsors that forceful resistance was the only option left to achieve Israel's retreat.

Finally, those who were very unhappy about the Syrian presence in their country came to believe that before Damascus would withdraw its troops from Lebanon the Israelis would have to evacuate the border strip. Under the circumstances, Hezbollah's actions to help matters along could be tolerated while objection might appear as a lack of patriotism. For these reasons, it looked as if Hezbollah might be well placed to win a few seats in the new parliament in the run-up to the 1992 elections.

The question of Hezbollah's chances in the upcoming elections was on everyone's mind in 1992 since its apparent about-face had drawn so much attention from the local, regional and international press. Thus a poll carried out by a local newspaper before the 1992 parliamentary elections took place sought the answer to that very question. The poll, whose results I analysed and published with an AUB colleague, confirmed the fact that many young Christian and Muslim adults from all areas of Lebanon would indeed be willing to elect a member of the resistance – a reference to Hezbollah. Of the 1,427 individuals polled, 62 per cent said that they would vote for a member of the resistance and 38 per cent said they would not. Although the respondents were not asked to explain their reasons, we believed it logical to interpret the results of the question as a public acknowledgement of the Party of God's contribution to the Lebanese 'cause' – reclamation of national territory.

Interestingly, only 19 per cent answered affirmatively when asked if they would prefer to see a militia leader elected. This response indicated to us that a clear difference had been made between the respondents' perception and regard of the wartime militias and Hezbollah, which was widely believed to be a resistance force. Although many individuals probably would have preferred a mixed group of fighters that would answer to Beirut first rather than the Islamist militants already in the field, still the results of the poll showed that Hezbollah had already earned considerable respect for its jihad by the beginning of the 1990s when the new Lebanese regime began. This fact certainly helped acceptance of the Party of God's transformation.

While Hezbollah's growth in popularity was undoubtedly furthered by its activities against the Israelis in South Lebanon, there was another, related but more mundane, reason why its members did well in the 1992 parliamentary elections. That reason was based on the failure of its main Shiite rival, Amal, to fulfill the expectations of many Shiites over the years. In simple terms, Hezbollah filled that vacuum.

Amal's grip on the Shiite population was wearing thin as early as 1983, as many Shiites in the movement began to doubt whether Berri's view that reform of the present political system and continued cooperation with the Maronite Christian establishment was still acceptable. Further- more, his stand on the Arab-Israeli cause was seen as wobbly, since he had opposed the PLO's presence in South Lebanon. This was because their attacks on Israel often provoked responses that were extremely detrimental to his Shiite brethren there. This position countered that taken by the Muslim-leftist organizations of the National Front – later the National Salvation Front – who were receiving assistance from Palestinian forces and their supporters during the civil war and who were generally viewed as the spearhead of the struggle against Israel.

Holding back from active participation in the Front, Berri nevertheless appeared unable to deliver anything concrete to his community on his own. In contrast, Hezbollah's proposed agenda of sustained jihad against the Israelis after the departure of the PLO from Lebanon and the promise it offered of various types of assistance that Iran was funnelling into Lebanon and that were obtainable through a linkage with Hezbollah, pushed many Shiites to gravitate toward the fundamentalist organization and away from Amal.

The rivalry between the two Shiite organizations that began in the mid 1980s, when Amal tried to halt Hezbollah operatives from entering the border area,[9] intensified over the years. The two groups used heavy weapons against each other in fierce combats during 1988 and 1989 for political control of the capital's southern suburb. Several times, I was caught in these skirmishes as I commuted to AUB from my mountain residence in the Matn along the coastal road near the International Airport. Hezbollah's victory led to the virtual elimination of Amal's political presence in the crowded Shiite suburb, a situation that remains to this day.

The minor role Amal was awarded in the struggle against Israel as compared to Hezbollah's also engendered lasting bitterness and jealousy, as we shall see in later chapters. Hezbollah's political hegemony in the dahiyeh meant that it would try to hang on to this area with its estimated population of half a million in much the same way that other Lebanese bosses maintained their fiefdoms – through services of all kinds. As we shall see later, the financial contribution made to this effort by Iran was crucial.

From this discussion, it can be seen that Hezbollah's own efforts in several different fields helped to smooth the transformation it underwent in 1990 and that these efforts were confirmed at the polls. By entering the 1992 elections, Hezbollah had sent a clear signal that it had changed its radical course and was abiding by the time-honoured rules of Lebanon's electoral game. Moreover, the game, as it were, quickly enhanced the Party of God's legitimacy as a mainstream party with a resistance wing, since as a result of its victories at the polls it fielded the largest single party bloc in the new parliament – 12 of 128 members. This development appeared to deal a blow to Israeli and American efforts to charge the Party of God with the wanton and unprincipled behaviour generally associated with mercenaries in western minds.

Now Hezbollah had to heal the divisions its accommodation with the Lebanese government had caused and convince pious Muslims that the leadership was more committed to the values and principles of Islam than ever before, despite some appearances to the contrary.

# Chapter Four

# Managing the 'True Believers'

O ne of the greatest dangers faced by parties transforming themselves from radical to mainstream status is the potential animosity and loss of core adherents who place ideological purity and principle above the demands of practical politics.[1] Fundamentalists integrating into secular societies and joining 'apostate' governments must therefore somehow convince pious partisans that despite all appearances to the contrary – including the reworking of party ideology to suit new mobilization and legitimization goals – God's sacred command to promote His rule on Earth is not being abandoned.

To what extent was radical backlash a problem for Hezbollah when the issue of accommodation with a non-Islamic government arose in 1989? What were the positions adopted in the internal debate and how was consensus achieved to join mainstream political life? What factors made swallowing the decision a little easier for highly religious partisans and kept the 'true believers' on board?

## ISLAM OR THE SYSTEM: THE INTERNAL DEBATE

Hezbollah enjoyed a remarkable degree of internal cohesion from its earliest days, and the information in the preceding chapters tells us why. All but one of its top leaders – Hussein al-Musawi – were Shiite clerics who graduated from the Najaf religious seminary in Iraq, where they imbibed the ideology of renowned clerics, such as Sheikhs Mohammed Baqer al-Sadr and Ruhallah Khomeini and put it into practice in Lebanon. Furthermore, all these mullahs were totally loyal to Ayatollah Khomeini, whose envoy, Fazlallah Mahallati, had helped establish Hezbollah's organizational structure in 1982. Almost all of the men who constituted Hezbollah's first *majlis al-shura* (consultative council) were mainly robed and turbaned religious men – Ibrahim Amin al-Sayyed and Hassan Nasrallah, Sheikhs Subhi Tufeili, Naim al-Qassim, Abbas al-Musawi, Abu Salim Yaghi and some dozen others – and have retained their seats to this day.[2]

Those elected to the highest council, the *majlis al-shura*, choose the organization's operational leadership – the secretary-general, his deputy and five of the nine members of the Executive Committee. It should also be noted that the organization's Combat Bureau, responsible for the Islamic Resistance and the Islamic Holy War, is directly linked to the Consultative Council and to no other office or department.[3]

In 1989, the organization underwent restructuring, adding an executive consultative council (*majlis al-shura al-karar*) as the second highest leadership authority and a politburo (*maktab-al-siyassi*), which coordinates the work of various committees under Jihad al-Binaa (reconstruction campaign), about which more will be said in Chapter 6. Recently, as it grew more important, Hezbollah's Information Department, the agency that controls its radio, television and newspaper sections, came directly under the authority of Hezbollah's secretary-general. Its director is a member of the party's Consultative Council. According to Ranstorp, these changes indicated that the 'Lebanonization' of Hezbollah had taken place, 'where the control of the overall organization has been made more open and expanded'.[4] The move away from secrecy to a more open organization in 1989 was consistent with the new, mainstream party face Hezbollah was preparing to present to the Lebanese and to the world. The later development of the Media Department was an important part of the campaign to deepen the party's integration by familiarizing the public with its various social programmes and military exploits.

From hints in the local press and interviews with 'high-ranking Israeli officials in the Ministry of Defense and Foreign affairs' in 1991, Ranstorp was able to gather some information on the organization of Hezbollah's 'Special Security Apparatus'. There are allegedly three subgroups: a central unit, a preventative one and an 'overseas security' group responsible for contacts with locals living abroad or foreign nationals or, as Israel and the USA claim, terrorist operations in foreign countries. According to Ranstorp, who heads research on terrorism at St Andrews University in Scotland, Hezbollah was able to maintain operational secrecy because it employed loyal family and clan members in these departments, some of whom had had experience with the PLO's intelligence and security organizations. One of the directors of the Hezbollah security units, according to Ranstorp's information, was alleged terrorist Imad Mugniyeh.[5]

The men who held the highest positions in the Party of God were popular clerics with considerable followings from various regions of Shiite concentration. Their particular functions, for that matter, may have been determined by their places of origin or residence and this could also have reduced competition among them. For instance, in Hezbollah's start-up period, Sayyed Hassan Nasrallah's residence in the dahiyeh influenced his position as liaison officer with Iran through the latter's Beirut Embassy. Financial transfers and expenditures became his concern. A southerner, Sheikh Raghib Harb, was the top official in that area until his death in 1984 at the hands of the Israelis. The Bekaa/Hermel area was Sheikh Subhi al-Tufeili's domain, along with Sheikh Abbas al-Musawi and Hussein al-Musawi, who lived there and who could therefore more easily mobilize young Shiites into Hezbollah's ranks. Since it was in this region that Hezbollah was busy forming military units with Iran's help and under the watchful eyes of Syrian officials, good relations with these men were highly important. Moreover, careful liaison work with the contingent of Iranian Revolutionary Guards that were domiciled in the Baalbek area was especially important to the Party of God's development during the 1980s.

Sheikh Tufeili's appointment as Hezbollah's first secretary-general rested on his close relationship with the Syrian and Iranian clerics. It was greatly aided by his ability to frame Hezbollah's goals at the time in radical ways that inspired young Shiite men to join the militia in droves. Personally very close to Ali Akbar Mohtashemi, the leader of Iran's ultra-orthodox faction, Tufeili performed this task brilliantly by quoting Ayatollah Khomeini's exhortations and referring to Iran's Islamic Republic as a model that, if adopted, could replace Lebanon's corrupt and worn out regime. The opportunity to belong to a universal movement, one that transcended the narrow limitations of Lebanon and their poor existence, probably fired the imaginations of young recruits and produced the zeal that has become so characteristic of Hezbollah's fighters.[6]

Despite the fact that Hezbollah's whole top echelon shared Tufeili's opinions, it was he, as leader, who drew the focus of the mass media. The Lebanese public therefore tended to identify Tufeili as the hardcore fundamentalist most deeply involved with efforts to Islamicize Lebanon despite its large Christian component and the presence of many Muslim groups that rejected this idea.

The cohesion of the men seated in the *Majlis al-Shura* appears to have been an established fact up to the time that Hezbollah's transformation to mainstream political party status began to be debated in 1989. Until that time, Hezbollah's singleness of purpose in terms of its pursuit of Islamic goals was apparently rock solid. Foremost among those goals, of course, was *jihad* against the Israelis.

Hezbollah's internal cohesion ended, however, after Ayatollah Khomeini's death in 1989. At that time, Ali Akbar Hashemi Rafsanjani, a more pragmatic mullah, became President of Iran and the country's foreign policy began to change. At the same time, the Taif Accord, which ended hostilities in Lebanon and recognized Syria's 'special relationship' with its neighbour, had just been signed. Rafsanjani and his circle were well aware of the heightened foreign policy opportunities now being made available to their country as a result of Syria's hegemonic position in Lebanon. They also knew, however, that a foreign policy pay-off could only be realized by their Lebanese connection if Hezbollah leaders could be induced to accommodate their organization with the post-war Lebanese government that would soon emerge – a government that would be stewarded by Damascus.

For the Hezbollah leaders, the Iranian turnabout presented a ticklish problem because of differences between pragmatic administrators in Tehran and the spiritual rulers who called the shots. Ayatollah Ali Khamenei was an Islamic purist like his predecessor and might not be happy to see the struggle for an Islamic Republic in Lebanon shoved to the backburner. Moreover, Hezbollah owed much of the massive support it had been receiving to the commitment and assistance of hardline Iranian religious groups and not the reformers represented by Rafsanjani. Hezbollah leaders would thus have to tread very carefully in deciding whether and how to proceed along the more moderate track that began to be discussed.

In fact, dissension within Hezbollah immediately broke out over what course to pursue. While all leaders found accommodation with a non-Islamic government objectionable, some found the advantages of accommodation less distasteful than others. Sheikh Tufeili, however, like his Iranian mentor Mohtashemi, was absolutely unbending in his rejection of any cooperation whatsoever with the emerging Lebanese regime. His position was reported in the media when a dispute between he and Sayyed Fadlallah, the highly respected Shiite theologian, reached public attention.[7] While supportive of Ayatollah Khomeini's form of Shiite activism, Sayyed Fadlallah had nevertheless always stopped short of calling for the establishment of an Islamic Republic in Lebanon. His belief was that such a system could not be imposed on Lebanon's large Christian community and would also be rejected by secular Muslims. Sayyed Fadlallah had therefore spent time and energy over the years in working to promote Christian-Muslim understanding and cooperation as a means of peacefully enlarging Islamic space in Lebanon rather than capturing it.

Sheikh Tufeili, on the other hand, was inflexible in his position that Islamists should neither forge peaceful linkages with non-Islamic authorities nor prostrate themselves before such a pluralist, secular system. Tufeili vigorously argued that if political accommodation with the state occurred, Hezbollah's religious obligation to wage jihad against the Israelis – the cause that lay at the very heart of the organization – would inevitably fall prey to political considerations and manoeuvring. Tufeili wanted a forthright and open declaration of Hezbollah's Islamic position and goals and totally rejected any hedging about them.[8]

Sayyed Hassan Nasrallah and Sheikh Ibrahim Amin al-Sayyed, on the other hand, understood exactly what positions and attitudes had to be adopted to guarantee their organization's struggle against Israel under Lebanon's changing circumstances. They saw that under the prevailing conditions ideological rigidity would deny their armed struggle the national legitimacy necessary to win it strong and continuous Lebanese support. The 'moderates' were therefore willing to look for ways around the ideological impasse that would allow pursuit of jihad without totally compromising other Islamic imperatives. Various conceptions of the concept of jihad itself, and interpretations as to when coexistence with a non-Muslim state might have to occur, offered a theological rationale for accommodation.

## RATIONALIZING COMPROMISE FROM AN ISLAMIC PERSPECTIVE

The concept of jihad is central to Islamic 'cosmology' because the Islamic injunction to fight injustice and eliminate usurpers obviously includes impious rulers whose governments do not apply Islamic law. But is there any dispensation from this obligation that would be understood by the *ulama* (Islamic scholars) as a justifiable excuse for Hezbollah to waive the obligation of jihad against a heretical government like Lebanon's? Could accommodation, for instance, be justified by reference to the Koran?

'Commanding the good and forbidding the evil' is the Koranic imperative that sanctions jihad against tyrants. In Islamic law, the word means armed struggle against the unbeliever, and this is also a common meaning in the Koran. According to Islamic scholar Rudolph Peters:

> The most important function of the doctrine of *jihad* is that it mobilizes and motivates Muslims to take part in wars against unbelievers, as it is considered to be the fulfillment of a religious duty. This motivation is strongly fed by the idea that those who are killed on the battlefield, called martyrs (shahid, pl shuhada) will go directly to paradise.[9]

As might be imagined, however, this injunction caused much deliberation over the centuries regarding the duty of obedience to an unjust ruler who caused disobedience to God. It also provoked theological debates over the justifiable courses of action that could be taken by the community if the abuse of authority made the state evil. Abdelazziz Sachedena, an expert on Islam, notes that 'in early Shiite history it had become firmly established that every pious Muslim was to oppose any nominally Muslim authority regarded as corrupt and degenerate', but with an important proviso: *'as long as such opposition did not endanger the believers' lives'* (my emphasis).[10] For instance, the Koran states: 'Cast not yourself by your own hands into destruction.' (2:195) This injunction was used by some Muslims to rationalize Arab paralysis in waging jihad against the superior forces of the western powers occupying Arab lands after the Second World War.[11]

These constraints and past experiences would be an acceptable justification for the conciliatory approach taken by Hezbollah in its relationship with the Lebanese authorities. This is because Shiite Islamists in Lebanon, who have yet to prove their political preponderance within even their own community, have little chance of seizing power or even eventually working their way up to a dominant power position in the country's heterogeneous society. If Islamists tried force, their efforts would most certainly place the umma in great physical danger; the more so since Damascus is so intent on preserving the status quo among Lebanese communities in its own interests.

Up against this omnipresent force, like all other Lebanese politicians and parties, Hezbollah leaders could count on widespread understanding of their decision to practise self-restraint and to cooperate with the Syrian and Lebanese authorities – especially since this cooperation was critical to the party's military agenda in the South.

On the other hand, other interpretations of the concept of jihad can also be used to justify Hezbollah's acquiescence to Lebanon's political order. Jihad need not be limited to the idea of 'holy war' in the militant sense. Its meaning can, in fact, be interpreted to cover a broad range of activities undertaken by pious Muslims who desire to follow God's injunctions. The word 'jihad' (verbal noun of the verb *jahad*) means to strive, to exert oneself, to struggle. The word has a basic connotation of an endeavour towards a praiseworthy aim. In a religious context, it may express a struggle against one's own evil inclinations – *jihad al-nefs* (the struggle for self-control) – or an exertion for the sake of Islam and the umma, such as trying to convert unbelievers or working for the moral or political betterment of Islamic society. For instance, writing against injustice, joining public demonstrations to achieve the rights of Muslims and articulating their demands in public forums are all activities that ultimately advance the Islamic cause.

In this respect, Hezbollah could easily justify membership in the Lebanese Parliament. Islamist MPs would be able to use that forum as a means of drawing attention to the sub-standard conditions in Shiite areas or to the administrative oversight or corruption that prevented improvement. Social justice might be broadened through this action.

As well as this flexibility in the concept of jihad, the Hezbollah leadership's deliberate vagueness about their goals when interviewed on this subject helped to defuse or shelve the contention that surrounded their change in direction. Time after time, when asked if accommodation with the government meant that Hezbollah had given up on establishing an Islamic republic in Lebanon, the response was neither a firm yes or no but an acknowledgement that 'objective conditions are not present for the creation of an Islamist state'. This response deliberately avoided the issue of whether or not the leadership had stopped working toward this goal while insinuating that all that could be done in this realm was being done. In this respect, the leaders assumed that their muted Islamic goals would be understood by partisans when the pursuit of militant jihad depended on that ploy. The practice of *taqiyya*, or strategic fibbing where one's religion is concerned, is very well understood by the Lebanese. In light of the ideological flexibility being practised by Hezbollah leaders in the early 1990s, 'true believers' would simply have to judge for themselves whether 'politics' had had negative effects on militant jihad as Tufeili had bitterly predicted.

As might have been expected, Tufeili was replaced as secretary-general of Hezbollah by the more flexible Sheikh Abbas al-Musawi, former head of the Islamic Resistance. The westerners who had been kidnapped in Lebanon began to be released in 1989. Closing one chapter of Shiite Islam in Lebanon was a necessary prelude to the new turn Hezbollah was about to make.

Hassan Nasrallah, a round and rather jovial individual in his forties who wears a black turban and dresses in long robes, became secretary-general after Israel used helicopter gun ships to assassinate al-Musawi in February 1992. I later learned that Nasrallah had actually won the most votes in the 1991 election but had stepped aside as a gesture to the Tufeili faction. Musawi, the man who had headed the resistance, was not very likely to let politics go to his head and forget armed struggle as Tufeili had suggested might happen.

Although he had been overridden, Tufeili did not resign. For their part, the new leaders made every effort to paper over the cracks in the organization's façade made by the heated internal debate for the sake of resistance unity. However, several years later when Tufeili organized a massive demonstration in the Bekaa on his own – 'the Revolt of the Hungry' – he apparently went beyond what Hezbollah leaders felt their new, moderate image could tolerate. Ever-conscious of the importance of their organization's accommodation with the Lebanese authorities, a day before the Lebanese Army moved in to break up the demonstration and arrest its leaders, Hezbollah cut all ties with the radical Sheikh.

Tufeili escaped the round-up of many of his partisans and went into hiding, where he remains today. Every now and then members of his circle issue a press release broadsiding Sayyed Nasrallah for neglecting the umma in favour of his deals with an apostate government. However, as election results have shown, the hardliners cannot compete with the Party of God's enormous influence in the Bekaa-Hermel region and they have therefore been effectively marginalized.

## CONVINCING THE GRASS ROOTS

Hezbollah partisans who were doubtful about their organization's new direction would simply have to wait and see, weighing the strength of their leaders' Islamic commitments against their actions. Since major programmes and policies are covered in later chapters, I will mention only a few of the activities that enhanced Hezbollah leaders' Islamic credentials at the time of its accommodation with the government. Among the most obvious were the public and social services offered to the umma and the burgeoning network of mosques and *husseiniyyas* (places of religious congregation). Furthermore, as jihad is not only the act of fighting but also doing anything conducive to victory – for example, providing financial support (*al-jihad bi-l-mal*) – Hezbollah's campaign against the Israelis in South Lebanon provides a means of fulfilling sacred religious obligations. When I asked an elderly partisan about this, he quoted the Prophet Mohammed: 'Whoever supplies a warrior in the way of god with equipment is also a warrior and whoever takes the place of a warrior in his family by means of wealth, is also a warrior.' He then added that he and other members of his family have been donating a percentage of their monthly income to the resistance for years. On this subject, one of my students from South Lebanon related that his brother was sponsoring a child whose father had been 'martyred on the battlefield' by committing a monthly sum to Hezbollah for its upbringing. In exchange they received pictures, report cards and other information about the child.

## AN EMINENT CLERGYMAN LENDS HIS AUTHORITY

Hezbollah had an invaluable asset in Sayyed Mohammed Hussein Fadlallah at transformation time. Fadlallah, a *marjaa* (one of the few Shiite clerics in the world elevated to the rank of Jurist), had always believed that implementing an Islamic regime in Lebanon would be impossible because of its demography. Instead, he advocated religious coexistence, an understanding of Islam and putting the religion's ethical principles into practice in daily life. These views must have mollified secular Muslims who were uneasy about the sudden prominence of Shiite political Islam on the Lebanese scene. However, Fadlallah had also published a book in 1981, a year before the Israeli invasion of Beirut and the catastrophic events that happened there, that explained the revolutionary notion of the logic of power within Islam from the Shiite perspective.[12] This ideology coincided with that adopted by the Hezbollah leaders and reached an intellectual audience. On the mass level, as Fadlallah had been broadcasting this galvanizing ideology from the pulpit every Friday for years and had taped many of his sermons, he was widely associated with the notion of the rightness of armed struggle against the enemies of Islam. During the 1980s, and especially at the time of the Israeli invasion and the American military presence in Lebanon, these sermons were enormously popular and hundreds of thousands of cassettes had been distributed in Lebanon, West Africa and other areas with substantial Shiite communities. His large following indicated that many Shiites found his views sound and in no way contradictory to the teachings of Islam.

Although Fadlallah never formally associated himself with Hezbollah (wishing as he did to remain above any political movement), his commitment to active Shiism was, like Hezbollah's, concretized by a number of important charitable institutions he established in the Raas al-Nabah district of Beirut. Among these institutions are an Islamic orphanage and a religious school. Recently, aided by a Shiite businessman from Kuwait, he opened a large modern medical facility – Bahman Hospital in the dahiyeh. The only other hospital in the seriously overcrowded area is the al-Rasul al-Azam Hospital, which was financed by Iran and is run by Hezbollah.

Both Fadlallah and Nasrallah use the pulpit to criticize American and Israeli foreign policy. As their views generally converge, the Sayyed became known as the Party of God's 'spiritual guide' and on many occasions eloquently interpreted and justified Hezbollah's deeds. Scholar Martin Kramer put his finger on exactly how Fadlallah contributed to the resistance by observing, 'He was capable of transforming resentment into resistance.'[13]

A connection of this sort with a respected religious leader, one who had never preached the overthrow of the Lebanese system but had earned the respect of thousands by working within the system for years, was of the highest value to a start-up party like Hezbollah in the 1990s. Although the relationship between the Sayyed and the fundamentalist organization has subsequently been tested by Hezbollah's ties to Iranian clerics who sometimes view things differently from Fadlallah, they continue to agree on most points. Above all, the Sayyed's strong support for the Islamic resistance ensures that he and other Lebanese Shiite fundamentalist leaders remain fellow travellers, if not always completely friendly ones.

In a nutshell, what kept the 'true believers' on board were: a desire to be deeply associated with a holy war against Israel; respect for the clergymen leading the struggle whose Islamic credentials were unimpeachable; and a clear realization that the geopolitical factors that had come together to produce such an opportunity for Islam were simply too outstanding to reject.

Hezbollah has not achieved a monopoly on Shiite allegiance, but all available information indicates that it was able to solidify a niche in this community at an early stage at least partially because its cooperation with a 'heretical' government was simply less important than its capacity to give 'the big one' – Israel – a drubbing on the battlefield. Hezbollah was able to expand its Muslim constituency for the same reason.

Now all the Party of God had to do to clinch its new moderate course was convince the doubters among the general public that what it was up to was for the good of the nation and would not be detrimental to the broader Lebanese community.

# Chapter Five

# Squaring Jihad with the General Public

A religious party headed by clerics had never before contested a Lebanese election let alone a Muslim fundamentalist one with a shady past. Therefore, as Hezbollah prepared to ditch its radical image by contesting the parliamentary elections in 1992, there was more than a little interest in what this development could mean for the political system. In this respect the record of achievement of fundamentalist groups in other Arab countries, and in Iran particularly, was not comforting. Moreover, the appearance of growing numbers of Lebanese women in black *chadors* and bearded men on the streets of Beirut raised eyebrows since this look was associated with Gulf tourists and Iranian men rather than nationals. Many began to wonder how far the 'Islamization' process undertaken by the Party of God was going to go.

How could Hezbollah convince the general public that the destruction of Lebanon's version of democracy and its replacement with an Islamic republic was no longer high on their list of priorities, or even there at all, when it was actively encouraging its version of Islam? Strident denials might alienate core supporters, while weak ones might not be sufficient to allay mistrust about the Party of God's ulterior motives. Although Christians were perhaps most concerned about Hezbollah's political designs, Muslims, including more secular Shiites, also viewed the newcomer with considerable disquiet. If Hezbollah leaders were unable to lay these negative attitudes to rest or at least considerably modify them, full integration into mainstream political life and legitimization of jihad as the expression of the national will would be extremely difficult. Thus Hezbollah would have to create some sort of a plan to get itself in contact with the Christian community and other groups and then win them over to full support of the resistance. How could the Party of God's leaders overcome their organization's rough beginnings and get this difficult task accomplished as time passed?

To address this topic, I must first return to the 1980s, when impressions of fundamentalists in Lebanon were first being formed. Were the terrorist acts attributed to Hezbollah as universally condemned as might be expected, and if not, why not?

## THE POLITICAL EFFECTS OF HEZBOLLAH'S VIOLENT EMERGENCE

The violence perpetrated against American and French installations in Lebanon during the 1980s and claimed by shadowy Shiite fundamentalist groups was deeply unsettling to most Christians and Muslims on ethical grounds. But apart from the repugnance these spectacular acts engendered, they were shocking because they vividly illustrated the fact that religious fervour could richly compensate for small numbers and relative weakness. After all, some friends pointed out, two fundament- alist drivers seeking martyrdom had killed and wounded a large number of Americans all by themselves. Moreover, as a result of their sacrifices, those two individuals had been highly instrumental in America's decision to get its troops off Lebanese soil and back onto the ships that had brought them.

While it was true that some Lebanese worried mainly about whether such capabilities might lead the perpetrators to force an Islamic political agenda onto their multi-confessional society, I found that others reeling from the battering given to mountainous Muslim areas by the battleship USS *New Jersey* in direct support of the Lebanese regime had a different reaction. They looked at the terrorist acts as a last resort, as having been used when no other means of removing the American presence, which might have turned the tide of the civil war, was available. Their reaction was therefore more like satisfaction that someone had punished those who had neither prevented Israel's invasion and its destruction of West Beirut, nor sufficiently laid blame on those who stood by and allowed Christian militiamen to perpetrate the massacres at the Sabra and Shatila refugee camps. There was a widespread feeling that the USA was perfectly capable of controlling its ally if it had wanted to.

On the occasion of the Sabra and Shatila camp massacres, the American University Hospital bulged with dazed men, women and children suffering bullet wounds. I saw them sprawled all along the hallways of the emergency section waiting for assistance when I went to see why my daughter, a hospital volunteer, had not come home for lunch. I could not call the hospital, as the phone lines were jammed. Admissions continued for days. Two students of mine, who had gone to the camps to help, later related nightmarish scenes of old women howling in grief as they waved the bullet-riddled bodies of dead babies over their heads. The acts that had brought about this ghastly scene were generally felt to be the very epitome of terrorism, defined as criminal acts perpetrated against innocent civilians for political purposes. Like all such dreadful acts, they can never be either forgiven or forgotten. For their part, Hezbollah leaders would later point to these massacres, undertaken while the camps were supposedly under the protection of General Ariel Sharon's soldiers, as a major factor in their decision to fight the Israelis.

The point to be made here, however, is that at the time the massacres occurred the groups that opposed them so bitterly had no means of avenging them, and this in itself constituted for many – both inside and outside Lebanon – another haunting Arab humiliation in need of assuagement. Thus, when US forces became openly involved in the civil war and took the side of the Christians who were fully supported by Israeli troops, many Lebanese on the other side of the battle line quite simply believed they got what they deserved for interfering when the suicide operations occurred.

Hezbollah has never admitted any involvement in these attacks and no concrete evidence has been presented by the United States government linking the fundamentalist group to them. However, although Hezbollah leaders later condemned the loss of innocent lives, they also flatly stated their belief, as did Sayyed Fadlallah, that the attacks had been 'the answer of the weak and oppressed to the powerful aggressors'.

These attacks naturally drew public attention to the very fact that the actual perpetrators were indeed unknown, although the hand of Tehran was suspected of having been behind them. At the time it was felt that a new stage in the struggle against Israel had begun, whose end results were unknown and especially frightening because of the total breakdown of the Lebanese government. Islamic injunctions to 'fight unbelievers until there is no persecution and the religion is God's entirely' (Koran 2:193 and 8:39)[1] came to mind and some people began to wonder whether the anti-US/anti-Israel campaign would stop there or whether it was just the first part of a general movement to establish a universal Islamic order.[2]

In the preceding chapter, I indicated how important Islamic ideology was in terms of mobilizing mujahidin for Hezbollah's struggle against Israel. I observed that Sheikh Tufeili and the other Lebanese fundamentalist leaders were all totally committed to the activist Islam envisioned by Ayatollah Khomeini and that they evidenced considerable doctrinal sophistication in interpreting its likely effects on the achievement of their own goals. Moreover, the skilful manner in which they made the Iranian revolutionary ideals accessible to young Shiite men was hardly the crazed rabble-rousing of medieval mullahs as Hezbollah's enemies tried to suggest. For instance, as a means of emphasizing the sacred nature of the commitment they were making, new recruits were asked to walk under a copy of the Koran held high and to kiss it as a token of reverence and steadfastness to its principles. One individual who participated in that ritual told me that he underwent a complete change at that moment and felt he had finally found something worthwhile to make of himself. 'I became God's soldier at that moment,' he said.

While all of this was critical to the formation of the fighting wing, Hezbollah leaders were canny enough to reason that an image of aggressive religious fanaticism would not do them much good in the Lebanese political arena, regardless of how chaotic it was then. Eventually things would get back on track and the Party of God would then have to deal with the fact that the bulk of the population would not much appreciate the fundamentalist way of thinking or behaving as it stood. A forthright declaration of the Party of God's identity would lift the veil of secrecy that had covered it since its inception, while a statement of its goals and strategies would relieve tension, especially among Christians, about who, exactly, Hezbollah's enemies were.

Hezbollah therefore sent an open letter to a Beirut daily newspaper in February 1985, in an attempt to set the record straight. The message presented major policy positions regarding military and political jihad and placed them in perspective from Hezbollah's point of view. A close reading of this missive illustrates that Hezbollah expressed *moderate political goals at the very same time as maximum efforts were being made to mobilize Shiites around a radical Islamic agenda!* The open letter therefore exemplifies early use of the tactic of ideological ambiguity – a technique that would later be applied whenever the public or its political representatives were the intended recipients of messages conveyed by the Party of God. Islam remained the backbone and essence of discourse when addressing the faithful. A less confessional and more conciliatory approach was considered more effective in the pluralist public domain, than the hard line used to rally 'true believers' and those young men being formed as fighting cadres. Before proceeding to the open letter, I should note, however, that this technique of ideological ambiguity is widely used by Lebanese politicians who need to retain the allegiance of their religious brethren without coming across as biased toward other communities with whom they must cooperate. Such are the demands of the Lebanese political system, as I explained in the last chapter.

## THE PARTY OF GOD TRIES TO CALM THE WATERS

The letter itself was divided into four parts: identity, struggle, objectives and 'a word to the Christians'.[3] In the letter, Hezbollah identifies itself with the vanguard that was victorious in Iran and claims it obeys Ayatollah Khomeini's commands. In view of this, it is added that Hezbollah is not 'a closed organization or party in Lebanon, nor a narrow political cadre. Rather, it is a society linked to the Muslims of the whole world'. The message emphasizes the fact that this connection gives Hezbollah's military apparatus 'inestimable importance' since it is not separate from the social fabric of the community. In other words, blows struck would be for all Muslims. Thus, 'each of us is a *mujahid* and when jihad is necessary, each carries out his assignment within the framework of the mission and under the tutelage of the commanding Jurist' (i.e. Khomeini).

It should be remembered here that this doctrine has not been formally rejected, but that, since 1990 and its accommodation with the authorities, more emphasis was placed on Hezbollah's Lebanese roots and authenticity as a national actor when groups other than Hezbollah's core sympathizers are addressed.

As far as Hezbollah's struggle is concerned, the letter identifies the USA as the major 'abomination', along with its allies and the 'Zionist entity' usurping 'the holy land of Palestine'. Israel must be wiped out of existence, the writer says, and the Islamic resistance must grow. However, there are Lebanese enemies as well, and the insufficiently protested massacres in Beirut's Palestinian camps in 1982, which were committed by Maronite Christian militiamen, are cited. Also mentioned is the destruction of homes and mosques in Beirut's southern suburbs, where Shiites are concentrated, which was ordered by Lebanese President Amin Gemayel in 1984.

Hezbollah then defines the aims of its struggle as expelling Americans and their allies from Lebanon and submitting the Christian militias to just punishment for crimes perpetrated against both Muslims and Christians during the civil war. With this statement Hezbollah clearly placed itself within the ranks of the National Movement that comprised Druze, Sunni, Shiite and leftist, secular groups – who were resisting the authority of the current Christian/Muslim establishment at that time. It is important to remember, however, that Hezbollah was never involved in meting out 'just punishment' to the Christian militias and had never kidnapped, car bombed or sniped at Lebanese civilians as most other militias had at one time or another.

The 'objectives' section of the letter dealt with 'domestic policy'. It is here that Sayyed Fadlallah's influence is suspected, for he has always stressed the importance of sound relations between Christians and Muslims. For instance, the writer stresses the importance of 'permitting our children to *freely choose* the form of government they desire', although he exhorts 'all to choose Islamic government' [my emphasis]. He continues: 'We do not want to impose Islam upon anyone... we do not want Islam to reign in Lebanon by force, which is what the Maronite Christians are using today. We wish to realize our ambitions by legal means... to adopt a regime fully desired by the Lebanese people.'

The letter follows these conciliatory remarks with strong words, however: 'Changes in the foundation of the unjust Lebanese regime are vital and no reform of the present rotten system can be satisfactory.' Is this a contradiction? Is it, after all, a call for the establishment of an Islamic republic? Hardly, since the message goes on to explain that what is required is 'real *reform*' (my emphasis), not just a reshuffling of cabinet members. This sounds much more like Hassan al-Banna than the radicals Ayatollah Khomeini or Sayyed Qutb. The statement offers no details about the mechanics of 'real' reform, but makes it easy to infer that the reforms demanded by the opposition coalition of leftist and Muslim groups would be adequate. In other words, if the political hegemony enjoyed by the present Maronite Christian establishment and its allies were ended and Muslim influence was increased in accordance with suspected demographic changes, Hezbollah would find such a system tolerable.

One can therefore conclude from this missive that as far as the Lebanese political system is concerned, militant jihad is repudiated and political jihad – in the sense of pushing for improvements such as social and political justice – will be Hezbollah's chosen tactic. This, of course, was exactly what justified transformation after the new political order had been established in 1990, as I noted in the previous chapter.

The final section of the letter – 'to the Christians' – criticizes the main Christian militias for founding their policies on bigotry, sectarian privilege and alliances with imperialism, a reference to France, the USA and Israel. The letter goes on to say:

> we are confident that Christ, God's Prophet, peace be on Him, is innocent of the massacres perpetrated by the Phalange militia [the major Christian organization whose military wing was Bashir al-Gemayel's Lebanese Forces] in his name and yours, and innocent of the stupid policy adopted by your leaders to oppress you and oppress us... Mohammed, God's Prophet, peace and mercy be upon Him, is also innocent of those who are counted as Muslims and who do not observe God's law and who do not seek to apply God's rules to you and to us.

The writer calls on the Christians to share some government affairs, indicating the nature of the reforms mentioned previously and clearly trying to lay to rest the idea of an Islamic republic. He then offers these reassuring words: 'If somebody has misled you, exaggerated matters for you, and made you afraid of reactions on our part to the crimes the Phalange Party has committed against us, then this is completely unjustifiable because peaceful Christians are still living among us without being disturbed by anybody.' (This is a reference to all areas of Shiite concentration where no charges of misdeeds had been levelled at Hezbollah.) The section ends with the words: 'We wish you well and we call you to embrace Islam... if you refuse, then all we want of you is to uphold your covenants with the Muslims and not to participate in aggression against them.'

I have given considerable space to this message because it includes all the elements that continue to define Hezbollah's 'Christian policy' during a period in which the results of the civil conflict were far from certain. With the contents of this message in mind, it might even be fair to say that what has been widely called Hezbollah's 'transformation' in the 1990s may have been more the transformation of the political system which opened the door to the Islamists to participate on the national scene, since some of the reforms the Party of God called for had been enacted and greater Muslim representation had been achieved. At that time, not only Hezbollah, but all the former leftist-Muslim coalition members were transformed from radical opposition groups to government loyalists.[4] This fact made it much easier for the fundamentalist group to move into the new political arena right along with the other new faces.

## ISLAMIST DISCOURSE AND INTEGRATION: JIHAD IN A NATIONAL CONTEXT

Islamic scholar Scott Appleby has argued that fundamentalist leaders must be more than theologians to successfully direct organizations seeking to root in generally hostile soil. While the divine will may be unbending, he says that fundamentalist leaders and operatives must be flexible in their pursuit and wielding of power. They must be practical and innovative men who can adapt to changing circumstances.[5] I would add that, in particular, they must master the ideological flexibility necessary to reduce antagonism among those committed to the separation of church and state, without abandoning the major precepts of their faith. Framing important Islamist issues in terms acceptable to the identities, hopes and goals of important non-Muslim and secular groups is therefore extremely important in allaying fears of a future resurgence of radicalism.

In the previous chapter, we saw that Sayyed Fadlallah's interpretation of Islamic principles conforms to reformist beliefs regarding how and against whom jihad should be directed. We saw that he felt that Lebanon's objective conditions were not conducive to Islamic governance and that jihad would have to be waged on the personal, political and social levels. It was pointed out that this argument would have mollified some Islamic hardliners and been convincing for the many pious individuals who revered Fadlallah and who may have wished for more but were rational enough to understand Islam's limitations in pluralist Lebanon.

Fadlallah's conciliatory interpretations and explanations on the issue of internal or domestic jihad now also served to soothe those who feared Hezbollah's present positions were merely tactical. In years of preaching and writing, Fadlallah had never hidden the fact that he believed an Islamic republic would be difficult for Lebanon to achieve and that dialogue and reconciliation between Muslims and Christians, rather than the use of force, was the only way to improve understanding.[6] Fadlallah's apparent position as the Party of God's spiritual guide, and his open support of Hezbollah's new political direction, provided additional evidence for some who doubted the genuineness of the organization's compromise with the Lebanese system.

In my own opinion, however, this was not the Shiite cleric's major contribution as a facilitator of Hezbollah's acceptance by various secular and non-Muslim Lebanese groups. True, as a man of religious authority and intelligence, the Sayyed did have an audience that was wider than the faction of the Shiite community with which he became associated. However, what made him so important were the nature and skill of his discourse. These gifts allowed him to explain Hezbollah's positions and goals in ways that made sense not only to secular Muslims but to Christians as well. For instance, on the subject of the 1983 suicide attacks against the US and French contingents in Beirut, Fadlallah echoed Hezbollah's Hussein al-Musawi's justification of these acts as defensive missions that were religiously legal measures against foreign occupation. Many Lebanese agreed with this definition. Moreover, in many other instances, the clergyman framed his discourse in an Arab nationalist context that appealed to individuals of different sects and political persuasions. The Sayyed took the position that although Arab nationalism had failed to rescue Palestine, its premises regarding the enemy were basically correct. Thus although he believed that Islam was the natural recourse, he could also explain blows struck for Islam as strikes against western imperialism by the Arab peoples.

Nationalism has also been used as a mobilizing ideology by other Middle Eastern fundamentalist groups seeking integration into secular societies. The most important English language writer on Algeria today, Hugh Roberts, found an Algerian Islamist group, the Islamic Salvation Front (ISF), had expanded its popular support by appropriating themes of both Algerian and Arab nationalism. For instance, since the Algerians had fought a bloody revolution against the French to obtain their independence, the ISF often generated support by its anti-imperialist posture and by claiming that the ruling party had failed to achieve the revolution's promises. References to Arab nationalist themes such as the recuperation of Palestine and the elimination of Israel also gained the ISF points with the Muslim masses, Roberts explains. However, he also observed that:

it was unclear whether the ISF attached importance to the Algerian nation as such or whether – as Islamist doctrine unquestionably enjoined – it took second place to the supranational community of the faithful, the *umma*... (but) for much of the Algerian public, the ISF convincingly established its nationalist credentials, and its leaders took care to ensure this.[7]

Similarly, the discourse of Sheikh Ahmed Yassin, spiritual leader of the radical Palestinian group Hamas, is considered to often be evasive on Islamic issues. Early ideological ambiguity 'allowed Hamas an advantage over secular rivals such as the PLO, since as the situation warranted, it could claim [to its core adherents] that while the liberation of Muslim Palestine remains the ultimate goal and jihad the ultimate means, the circumstances confronting the *umma* at any given time might necessitate a temporary and tactical halt or retreat'.[8] In other words, objective conditions explain this group's accommodation with the Palestinian Authority in 1994. The Hamas leader thus portrays Islamic jihad as a national jihad in much the same manner as Hezbollah came to identify its actions in the South against the Israelis.

Looking more closely at this ideological ambiguity as an important strategy to broaden support, we see that Hassan Nasrallah, Hezbollah's present Secretary-General, actually uses four different contexts or 'frames'[9] in presenting his ideas about Hezbollah's struggle against the Israelis, choosing one or another to suit the particular audience he is addressing. For instance, when speaking at a rally in the dahiyeh where the gathering is mainly Shiites and most are likely to be partisans, jihad is presented in its purely religious context as already described. Jihad is spoken of as a sacred religious duty that transcends all other aims. In this context the Israelis are referred to as infidels and heretics to be driven off Muslim soil. The present conflict is presented as but the first part of a campaign aimed at liberating Jerusalem and the other Muslim holy places.

On the other hand, when addressing a wider Lebanese audience of mixed faiths, Nasrallah presents jihad in nationalistic terms – as a patriotic duty to liberate the homeland and drive the Israelis out of Lebanon. In this context, Hezbollah represents the Lebanese people who are 'all resisting the enemy'.[10]

A third frame of reference used in the Hezbollah leader's discourse is trotted out when the target group is more likely to respond to an Arab nationalist context than any other. Then the struggle against Israel is promoted with reference to the harmful inroads of the West in the region as an effort to stand up to and defeat America's imperialistic designs. In this frame, Israel is identified as an American lackey or agent that must be resisted by the spearhead of the Arab nation – Hezbollah.

Jihad is placed in yet another context when Nasrallah addresses an international or global audience, as he often does on broadcasts by his organization's international television channel, al-Manar (the beacon or lighthouse). Here he expresses the idea of his organization's jihad as an internationally recognized right enjoyed by all peoples whose countries are illegally occupied. In this frame of reference, the Israelis are said to be violators of international accords, such as the several United Nations Security Council resolutions that have demanded Israel's withdrawal from Lebanon since 1978.

One fact stands out very clearly from this discussion: Hassan Nasrallah is an adept politician and a confirmed pragmatist when it comes to promoting his cause – quite a contrast indeed from the irrational terrorist his enemies try to portray him as.

To determine the social impact of this manoeuvring, the effects of Hezbollah's discourse and slogans have to be measured against public reactions. Some of these are dealt with in later chapters. But here a single incident, related to the struggle in South Lebanon, can be recounted that illustrates public acknowledgement of the ethical-religious principles and personal commitments that guided Hassan Nasrallah's behaviour. The general public was unaware that Nasrallah's oldest son, Hadi, was a common guerrilla fighter operating against the Israelis in the 'Security Zone'. His death in September 1999 in one of the actions there thus galvanized Lebanese from all walks of life. Furthermore, the Secretary-General's refusal to make any special deal with the Israelis to recover Hadi's body and his words – 'let them bury him with his companions in Palestine' – elevated Nasrallah's reputation to that of a man of unquestionable principle and patriotism. Thousands of Lebanese of all faiths, including busloads of youths from Christian areas, paid their condolences to him and his wife in Haret Hareik, where they found them relaxed and dry-eyed – content that Hadi had achieved martyrdom. Friends who were there told me that this display of faith had jolted them.

A similar appreciation of Hamas may have aided that group's capacity to integrate Palestinian society. According to Jean-Francois Legrain, a scholar of Palestinian politics, Hamas undercut Fatah, precisely because of the *patriotism* (my emphasis) it demonstrated in its willingness to take up armed struggle against the Israelis in comparison with the quiescence of the other party.[11]

In the case in hand, this public outpouring of respect apparently convinced the Hezbollah leaders that some sort of incorporation of non-fundamentalists in the fighting ranks would be positive for their struggle's highly important national image. After all, one of the best ways to discard the terrorist image was to prove that Hezbollah's activities had the whole country behind them. Later that autumn, a National Brigade was therefore formed under Hezbollah's auspices in which anyone who passed security vetting could participate in certain resistance operations under the Party of God's strict supervision. Several operations were then duly undertaken by this group and reported.

## *INFITAH*: SECURING CHRISTIAN UNDERSTANDING AND SUPPORT

Hezbollah members and sympathizers began active efforts to encourage Christian support for its resistance role immediately after the leaders' decision to enter the 1992 elections. Referred to as *infitah* (opening), this policy included several different approaches that have been vigorously pursued over the past decade and remain in force today.

One of these activities essentially followed Sayyed Fadlallah's lead insofar as it attempted to convince non-Muslims of Islam's peaceful approach to coexistence. In an interview with Fadlallah aired on the Lebanese Broadcasting Company's television channel in July 1997, the clergyman explained the Islamists' general approach to dialogue as follows:

> We carry on a dialogue with Christians without imposing any belief and without any prior conditions on either side. The basis of discussion should be to propose ideas as one of several around which debate revolves. Christians aim to win the other side over to Christianity and this applies as well to Islamists... there is nothing wrong with trying to convince individuals by civilized means.[12]

Hezbollah attempted to engage Christians in socio-political discussions in several ways – through formal and informal dialogue with notables and ordinary citizens of other sects, through the establishment of organizational linkages with different social, economic and political organizations and through various activities in areas under its control that embraced all residing there regardless of their religious affiliations. I will discuss these activities one by one below.

Formal dialogues with religious and social leaders of all denominations were begun early and have picked up steam in the last few years as a result of two major factors – events in the South and electoral participation.

In 1993 and 1996, Israel launched severe retaliatory raids against Lebanon to try to get the Lebanese authorities to rein Hezbollah in (see Chapter 8). After these onslaughts, Hezbollah leaders increased meetings with the Maronite Christian patriarch, Cardinal Nasrallah Butros Sfeir, and other groups such as the Maronite Brothers, to explain their positions and ask for outspoken support of resistance activities. As one of Israel's goals in launching the attacks had been to provoke dissension within Lebanese ranks, these meetings tried to encourage a united front as far as the national resistance was concerned.

Apart from these emergency meetings, however, there were also 'protocol' visits during which a wide range of issues facing the country were discussed. These visits paved the way for further exchanges of views. During one of these sessions, Christian opposition leaders who expressed disillusionment with the new regime were reportedly advised by Hezbollah representatives to 'integrate themselves into the political system despite their disappointment, and to respond positively'.[13] This advice could not have been further from fundamentalist orthodoxy and was all the more amazing since it was addressed to Christians! Regarding Hezbollah's multiple contacts with various groups, Sayyed Nasrallah observed in 1997: 'We have surpassed the stage of explanation and contacts are taking place with everyone and in depth.'[14]

Another example of Hezbollah's formal outreach policy occurred on 25 August 2001, when party representatives Nawaf Musawi and Mohammed Kamati spent an afternoon at one of Lebanon's mountain resorts with members of the Committee on Islamic-Christian Dialogue and a new Christian political umbrella group known as the Qornet Shehwan Gathering discussing current issues.

Nasrallah once described this openness policy as one of the principal characteristics of his organization.[15] He noted that it invariably promoted resistance discussions that in his opinion had helped to create a sounder political, intellectual and psychological environment for many Lebanese than had been the case in earlier years.

Infitah was not only directed at community elites, however. Early in 1990, Hezbollah partisans began hosting a series of 'get to know us' meetings in their own homes. An Orthodox Christian friend of mine who attended several of these discussions in West Beirut informed me that six other men had been invited to chat with Hezbollah's Deputy Secretary-General, Sheikh Naim al-Qassim, and that the conversation had been frank and wide ranging with emphasis on political and economic situations. This initiative is typical of the voluntarism and active networking vigorously encouraged by the Party of God.

Hezbollah youths were also mobilized to do their part in establishing relations with their uncommitted peers and those of other faiths. A Hezbollah official, Ali Fayyad, explained that this work was important because 'the student arena is one of the broad ones in the *umma* where committed Muslims mix with others who don't know much about Islam. Many think negatively of committed Muslims since we are portrayed to them by a hostile media as nothing more than terrorists and extremists'.[16]

A student mobilization unit was soon created. Composed of partisan students and teachers, its task was 'to Islamicize programs, criticize Western thought and forge links with young people on a Koranic, moral basis as Imam Ali instructed', according to Fayyad, the director of Hezbollah's Islamic research and documentation centre. Fayyad revealed that Hezbollah was also considering holding forums and sponsoring clubs and cultural events in Christian areas, so that the ordinary person could learn about the party in 'non-threatening, pleasant and instructive ways'. 'Dialogue,' said Fayyad, 'is the prophet's *and the apostles*' line of conduct.' [my emphasis] He noted that 'Jesus was always eager to deal with others as was Prophet Mohammed who invited everyone to embrace his religion'.

## POLITICAL NETWORKING WITH CHRISTIANS AND OTHERS

Apart from providing a broader support base for the resistance, Hezbollah's efforts to establish good relations with all sectors of Lebanese society made perfect political sense. Lebanon's version of confessional democracy requires candidates of different faiths to work together to create winning electoral tickets. That means that in many mixed confessional districts Hezbollah candidates stand with Christians on the same electoral ticket and must attract Christian votes as well as Shiite ones to win seats. In a sense then, infitah killed two birds with one stone. It helped Hezbollah to win seats in parliament while garnering specific Christian support for the resistance – both vital parts of the push to undermine the terrorist image.

Here, I want to use the case of a particular election to illustrate the extent of the overture made to Christians in 1999.

Thousands of families were forcibly displaced to other areas during the civil war and their return to their homes was a critical problem for the Lebanese government throughout the 1990s. The case of the dahiyeh was a particularly knotty problem. Before 6 February 1984, when the Shiite militia Amal attacked the Lebanese Army's positions in the area, there had been some 780 Christian families in the Harat Hreik district. All but 40 to 50 Christian families fled to Christian areas at that time, leaving homes and businesses to later be occupied by Shiites fleeing hostilities in the South. On the other hand, fearing a Christian backlash in February 1984, Shiites had left the Christian areas of Nabaa and Sin al-Fil to join their brethren in the dahiyeh.

Harat Hreik has about 9,500 registered voters, of whom approximately 4,600 are Maronites, 3,670 are Shiite, 700 are Sunnis and another 500 are Christians of various denominations. The problem was that in 1998, when general municipal elections were to be held, the Shiites and Sunnis were there but the Christians were not.

Although Hezbollah had not been involved in the displacement of the Christian population, the latter were not sure what they could expect in an area controlled by Muslim fundamentalists. Thus, in 1998, when the rest of the municipal elections took place, it was thought that the ground in Harat Hreik had not been sufficiently prepared for the Christians' return. The following year, though, it was thought that since financial allocations from the government to the displaced would begin in January 2000, at which time their involvement in municipal affairs would be important, the local election could take place. However, a lot depended on Hezbollah's reaction to this plan and on the party's efforts to promote acceptance of the idea among Shiites that Christians who were not presently residents of Harat Hreik should be allowed to stand for council seats.

The Party of God had no hesitation about fully cooperating with the government on the electoral project and immediately undertook negotiations with Christian notables to see what could be worked out as far as a division of seats between the two groups was concerned. By election time, 42 candidates had registered to contest the 18 seats available: 16 Christians, mostly Maronites, and the rest Shiites. The Christians were in favour of splitting the seats evenly, with the position of mayor going to a Christian, as historically had been the case. However, it was pointed out by Hezbollah spokesmen that things had changed a lot in the area since the last municipal election in 1963, when nine Christians and three Shiites had governed the municipality. Hezbollah's position was that if the Christians insisted on the mayor's post, they should accept a ten to eight Muslim majority. If that was not acceptable, the candidates would run individually and vote tallies would determine the outcome. This procedure would clearly favour a Hezbollah sweep, since the party's organs had been providing the municipality extensive public and social services since 1988 (see Chapter 6). In effect, its members and partisans, many from the important Shiite families in that district, had already proven themselves effective administrators.

The efforts of former Hezbollah MP Ali Ammar, current legislator Haj Mohammed Kamati and Christian MP Pierre Daccache finally led to a compromise only a few hours before the polls opened. It was decided that the council leadership would go to a Christian as a 'reassuring gesture' but that the Shiites would receive ten seats and the Maronites eight. In addition, to calm apprehensions and ensure a good turnout, the Christians would have one of their polling places set up on the outskirts of the densely populated Shiite municipality, along the airport road, and the other at a secondary school in the Bir al-Abed sector. When I visited these polling stations on election day, I found that all the Hezbollah posters, banners, and portraits of candidates and of Iran's spiritual leader, Ali Khamenei, usually plastered all over the district, had been removed from areas surrounding the Christian polling stations. I asked a young man wearing a Hezbollah t-shirt what had happened to the signs. 'We thought it was the right thing to do,' he said. 'They are not used to us.'

Other activities in which the kind of pragmatism illustrated by the infitah policy clearly stands Hezbollah in good stead involve its partisans' participation in the various professional syndicates in Lebanon, where they also rub shoulders with members of all faiths and political persuasions. An interview with Emile Saliba, the director of the Engineering Syndicate in 2000, revealed that the Party of God has approximately 350 active partisans out of a total syndicate membership of 23,000.[17] At present, Hezbollah partisans hold two of 16 seats on the governing council, one won in 1999 through the formation of a coalition with the Communist Party and various leftist currents, and the most recent by a complete ideological turnabout where the Party of God collaborated with the Christian *Phalange Party* [my emphasis] and the National Liberal Party, both of which were staunch allies of Israel during the civil war. Saliba found nothing unusual in Hezbollah's pragmatism and called it the 'typical Lebanese "get-the-seat" mentality with ideology out the window'.

A year earlier, in an interview on Future TV, Hezbollah MP Mohammed Fneish was asked why Hezbollah was willing to let its candidates appear on the same list with sympathizers of another wartime Christian militia, the proscribed Lebanese Forces, whose leader, Samir Geagea, is serving several life sentences in prison. Fneish said: 'We put political disputes aside.' Would his party ally with them again? 'In principle,' he said, 'Hezbollah has no problem dealing with any Lebanese group or current whatever their convictions might be. We have only one sensitivity and that is their relationship with Israel.'[18] The red line apparently is a group's very recent or present relations with Israel. The only group in that category is the South Lebanese Army, Israel's recent surrogates. Indeed, a joint statement by Amal and Hezbollah representatives, who were forming a list for municipal elections in the former occupied zone in September 2001, announced that SLA partisans would be the only individuals strictly excluded from that coalition.[19]

The above discussion indicates that infitah is not only desirable as a means of familiarizing other groups with Hezbollah's aims and creating solidarity for the resistance, but also an absolutely essential part of successfully playing the Lebanese political game. In all phases of professional and political life, sect numbers and proper representation require interaction by *moderate* members of the various communities – individuals who have no difficulty in allying with ideological opposites.

In this situation, Hezbollah members feel no constraints at all in joining the Communists and even cooperate with those implicated in the Sabra/Shatila massacres. Acting like everyone else certainly convinces many Lebanese today that Hezbollah is not likely to try to supersede the limits of the system it has worked so hard to join, while at the same time broad interaction with Christians appears to me to have greatly reduced the threatening image with which Hezbollah began.

Does this mean that Islamic principles have gone by the wayside? Not at all. However mundane the infitah's practical purpose, it is indeed always justified in terms of benevolent Islamic imperatives toward those of other faiths as first illustrated in the 1985 Open Letter.

Hassan Nasrallah explained to me once that

> a pillar of our movement is the need to respect others, whether Muslim or non-Muslim, and to forge relations with them on a Koranic, moral basis. As Imam Ali said, 'There are two kinds of people; either a brother in religion or a peer in morality – either a brother in Islam or an equal in humanity'.[20]

For his part, Deputy Fneish elaborated on his organization's stand on interfaith dialogue as follows:

> Dealing with the other person paves the way for getting acquainted with him and contributes to the development and progress of the society. This is our aim and hope as we hold sessions of Islamic-Christian dialogue – *in addition of course, to the promotion of a united position on the Israeli occupation and its resistance.* [my emphasis][21]

This blend of the pious and the practical has played an important role in assisting Hezbollah to remove doubts about its Lebanese character that its close affiliation with Iran raised. Here was an organization that was functioning within society and in the national political arena in completely traditional ways. Lebanese norms often require politicians to lie down with strange bedfellows to achieve their goals and in this case a rigid ideology and radical goals are entirely dysfunctional. These 'rules of behaviour' were very well understood by Hezbollah's pragmatic clerics and were deftly applied, as I have tried to show here. In short, these men were as opportunistic as anyone else when it came to the measures required to legitimize and sustain their struggle against Israel. These actions convinced many Lebanese that Hezbollah's radical militancy was reserved for the Israelis rather than the destruction of the freewheeling Lebanese way of life.

As later chapters will show, the infitah policy, in operation for more than ten years, helped to defeat repeated Israeli efforts to split support for the resistance along confessional lines. It also bolstered the authorities' refusal to send the Lebanese army to the South to protect the Christian population there, after Israel's withdrawal in 2000, a move that would have ended Hezbollah's capacity to undertake further operations there. And while many outsiders regard Lebanon's Christians as embattled and recall the massacres that took place in Christian villages during the civil war, the fact that Hezbollah achieved the support (tactical or not) of Christian spokesmen, made it far more difficult for its enemies to float the fundamentalist stereotype of a raging gang of religious fanatics whose main aim was to put enemies of the faith to the sword.

# Chapter Six

# Serving the *Umma*
# – Hezbollah as Employer
# and Welfare Organization

Feed those who need it, but do so especially when or where the
sources of sustenance, physical, moral or spiritual are cut off.
(Koran, v.6141)

Hezbollah's reputation in the West has centred on its guerrilla activities, but the dynamics of its growth and its achievement of mainstream status owe more than a little to its performance in the social arena, as we see later in this chapter. Hezbollah owes much of its appeal to the fact that it has been able to outstrip all other parties in the delivery of social and other public services in Muslim areas. Yet, unlike any of the other Islamic movements in the Middle East, the Party of God uses its good works as a means of underlining and enhancing its legitimacy as a bona fide Lebanese political party rather than as a means of challenging Lebanon's pluralist system. This is because Hezbollah's capacity to fight the Israelis depends on a positive relationship with the state and firm public support, and that sacred mission takes precedence over any other consideration.

Interestingly for Lebanon, what makes Hezbollah unique is the scope and range of the social and public services that it provides compared to other parties in Lebanon and fundamentalist organizations in the region. Although this is made possible by the large-scale assistance provided to the Party of God by the Islamic Republic of Iran, I emphasize the fact that these services are constantly evolving and that they are offered in a professional atmosphere that would not have been possible without careful planning and special attention to social and public service delivery systems, which form the specific contribution of sophisticated Hezbollah planners and modern administrators.

While commitment to the principles and values of Islam is obviously the wellspring of Hezbollah's behaviour – 'The man who feels no responsibility and thinks that he can do what he likes in life forgets his responsibility to God' (Koran, v.6135) – one should also consider the situational factors that facilitated the organization of the social and public services provided by the Party of God and enabled it to make itself indispensable to so many people.

## THE EFFECT OF LEBANON'S CIVIL WAR ON PUBLIC AND SOCIAL SERVICES

As a result of administrative and service gaps created by fierce fighting during the civil war, militia leaders had to create mini-public administrations in areas under their control. These handled essential tasks such as electricity, road repairs and the provision of educational and health services, to mention but a few. The factors that determined the shape and extent of these local governments were the strategic location of areas to be defended and administered, the material resources already in place, the size and cohesiveness of the population in question and the quality and extent of human resources which could be mobilized for defence and to direct and staff the service institutions.

While Hezbollah arose in this general atmosphere, its case differed from the Christian, Druze and the other Shiite militia Amal fighting in and around the capital, in that social services were first begun to support the needs of the mujahidin fighting the Israelis in the South and their families.[1] Gradually those services were expanded and extended to all needy civilians in areas under the Party of God's influence.

As mentioned previously, Hezbollah also differed from the other militias in the manner in which it was able to fund these services. Whereas the other groups had to exploit government resources such as port facilities and refineries to support their local administrations, Hezbollah's services were heavily underwritten by Iranian institutions called *bunyads*. These are foundations run by the clergy, whose large funds can be used to finance Iran's charitable and political agendas abroad. The direct political effect of the help from Tehran was that Hezbollah could never be viewed as having preyed on the disintegrating Lebanese state, a charge levelled against its major Shiite rival, Amal, and other political parties in Lebanon. In essence, Hezbollah's 'free money' and the disciplined behaviour of its partisans in comparison with that of Amal members encouraged the organization's 'Mr Clean' image.

While the phenomenon described above explains some of the tolerance afforded Islamists, the scope and variety of Hezbollah's social and public services also sets it apart from those offered by other Lebanese parties. Several factors explain this. In addition to the external assistance that has permitted expansion and development of service programmes over the years, the level of the Shiite community's needs exceeded that of other Lebanese communities. It has already been mentioned that areas of Shiite heavy concentration – the Bekaa and the South – were historically neglected in terms of infrastructure and social institutions such as schools, hospitals and clinics. Deterioration of already minimal and ageing infrastructure, population growth and damage caused by Israeli reprisal raids worsened the situation and hastened migration towards Beirut. There, the severe punishment the dahiyeh took from the Amal-Lebanese Army clashes in 1984 left whole neighbourhoods destroyed and further disrupted electricity and water networks that were already severely stressed due to the heavy increase of displaced persons in the area.

After defeating Amal in a skirmish for control of the dahiyeh in 1989, Hezbollah leaders found themselves responsible for the half million or so inhabitants and facing a fast-approaching social services crisis as thousands of families displaced by the fighting in the South continued to flood the overburdened sector.

## SERVICE DELIVERY IN THE *DAHIYEH*

Hezbollah tackled the severe public health hazards threatening the dahiyeh first. Daily garbage collection to remove the mountains of refuse that had built up over the years began in 1988, replacing a basic governmental function in several municipalities. This service continued for five years until the Lebanese Sanitation Department started to get back on its feet; however, and this is an important point, *Hezbollah still trucks out some 300 tons of garbage a day* from the dahiyeh and treats it with insecticides to supplement the government's service.

Hezbollah had been providing health services to the community since 1983. In 1988, however, the crown in the burgeoning network of Islamic institutions – al-Rasul al-Azam Hospital/mosque complex – opened its doors in the dahiyeh. The Iranian Martyrs Foundation, which pays all of the medical expenses for Hezbollah's wounded fighters and 70 per cent of the cost of caring for civilians injured in fighting, built the super-modern facility in order to handle war-related cases. Its services, however, are also available to all the residents of the area. Health facilities are woefully inadequate considering the size of the population in the dahiyeh and its expansion. Since only two other private hospitals operate there, one built in association with Sayyid Fadallah – Bahman Hospital – and another for Hezbollah, and there are no public hospitals in the area – the importance of the Islamist institution cannot be overestimated. In interviews I conducted with patients and unaffiliated doctors in 2001, I learned that doctors' fees and hospitalization costs are reportedly kept to a minimum and health care is excellent. I was therefore surprised when one young Shiite woman I knew expressed displeasure with the hospital. When asked for details, she said that her father had received excellent care there, but that she and her sisters had resented the fact that they were not allowed to accompany him inside the facility. This was because they were not wearing the headscarves required by the Islamic dress code! This anecdote illustrates the sorts of things that alienate some of the more secular-oriented members of the Shiite community who find Hezbollah too strait-laced for their tastes and lifestyles. On the other hand, it also sheds some light on how the meeting of material needs might override such feelings and encourage political loyalty after all.

On that subject, it is well to remember that Al-Rasul al-Azam Hospital and the new Hezbollah hospitals recently built in the South and in Baalbek employ large staffs and maintain substantial pools of medical professionals whose livelihood depends on Hezbollah. It is safe to say that these individuals too are likely to be among the ranks of those that support the Party of God politically.

These hospitals provide large-scale health service delivery. An illustration of simpler but no less vital work in this field is that carried out by a Hezbollah association, Jihad al-Binaa (Reconstruction Campaign [RC]), a charitable body registered with the Lebanese government and modelled on one established in Iran after that country's Islamic Revolution. One of this organization's major contributions was the installation of drinking fountains and decent toilets at public schools in the dahiyeh. I visited one school that had undergone this renovation and which had also been provided with new lighting fixtures and desks for all classrooms, courtesy of Hezbollah. This is a good place to mention that Hezbollah also runs its own primary and secondary schools and that these teach the national curriculum, with the addition of several hours a day devoted to religious study. Other schools are *madrasas*, or places of religious training, where clergymen are formed.

Emergency water delivery, however, remains the public service for which the dahiyeh residents I spoke with in 1993 gave greatest credit to Hezbollah. During General Aoun's administration (1988–1990), water and electricity services in the dahiyeh were almost completely cut off due to fighting. Through years of neglect and extensive war-related damage, an estimated 40 per cent of the water from Ain al-Dilbih, the area's major source of drinking water, had been lost and its purity had been gravely compromised. Several wells dug by UNICEF in the area reportedly failed. With help from the Iranian government, RC resolved this emergency by building 4,000-litre water reservoirs in each district of the southern suburbs and filling each of them five times a day from continuously circulating tanker trucks. Generators mounted on trucks also made regular rounds from building to building to provide electricity to pump water from private cisterns.

In 1992, when I interviewed Hajj Hussein Shami, Hezbollah's director for social services, water distribution was still continuing in this manner.[2] A decade after the election of the first post-war government, the southern suburbs' water problem had not changed. One might logically assume that the area's water problem would have been taken in hand by state agencies and solved. I was astonished to learn from the very same official in August 2001, however, that Hezbollah *still provides the major source of drinking water for dahiyeh residents*.[3] He further noted that, between 1988 and 1996, 57 artesian wells were dug and fitted with pumps, 15,000 meters of water pipes were laid, four water reservoirs were built and an additional 400 tanks for potable water were set up in various neighbourhoods in the dahiyeh by his party. Five electrical power stations and networks were also installed which included four stabilizers of 100–160kW and 25 generators of 250–500kW capacity, along with 4,100 metres of high-voltage wires.[4]

The fact that this work was undertaken by a political party and financed by a foreign country, Iran, rather than by the government's Public Works Ministry certainly removes all doubt about the state's capacity or desire to undercut the Party of God's services in order to reduce its political appeal. In fact, in both of my interviews with Shami, he strongly emphasized the point that if it were not for Hezbollah's cooperation in providing these basic utilities for the crowded suburbs, the government would have faced great social disorder and disruption. In his view, that could easily have been given a sectarian cast that would have shaken the regime since those wishing to accuse the government of religious discrimination could have simply pointed to the conditions prevailing in non-Shiite areas of Beirut. In those areas, the government provided a regular flow of clean water to homes and businesses.

Hezbollah also administers other projects that were originally designed to help the families of resistance martyrs become self-sufficient. Vocational schools for girls were established in Beirut and the Bekaa to train the daughters of fallen Hezbollah militiamen and subsidized workshops were set up to employ these and other dependents of dead or disabled fighters. As time went by, other programmes – some very uncomplicated but surprisingly effective – were initiated to meet public needs as the economy worsened. For instance, every autumn, when schools are about to open, textbooks discounted by up to 30 per cent of their original cost are set out for sale on street corners under the

Hezbollah banner. This provides a means of alleviating the additional financial burdens that afflict families at that time of year.

While the service orientation is old hat for many western parties, it must be heavily underlined here that in Lebanon, unremitting efforts by parties or politicians to serve the public in these ways are almost unheard of. The most citizens can expect is a road paved or some streetlights installed a day or two before the parliamentary elections – and this by exploiting the resources of state agencies.

## RURAL SERVICES AND PROGRAMMES

The point has been made that the Lebanese government still cannot cope with the basic needs of citizens in one part of the war-damaged capital and that a fundamentalist organization has picked up the slack. Before reviewing Hezbollah's activities in other parts of Lebanon, some information on the plight of residents in the Bekaa-Hermel region – Hezbollah's heartland – is instructive.

As in many backward regions of the developing world, land tenure and political domination were traditionally closely linked in the South and the Baalbek regions. With this connection broken or badly frayed after the civil war, large injections of aid were required to support the efforts of small independent farmers if sustained agricultural development and a rising standard of living were to be achieved. A survey undertaken in 1999 by the Economic and Social Commission for Western Asia (ESCWA), a UN agency, reveals how much there is to do in this respect. The report, entitled *Poverty and Gender Profile in the Baalbek-Hermel Region*, attests to the presence of situational factors that continue to fuel the expansion of Hezbollah's social and public services in that area.

For instance, the poor residents in the region (those householders who earn between $332 and $652 per month for an average household of 5.26 members)[5] 'utilize the services of dispensaries and health centers operated by non-governmental organizations [like Hezbollah] to a larger extent than the non-poor. Strikingly, however, 66 per cent of the "non-poor" uses them too'.[6] This is because of the quality care provided in contrast to the other medical facilities available. In the survey I carried out in the Shiite community in 1993 to determine the sources of Hezbollah's popular support, contrary to my expectation I found that this organization was *not* the exclusive party of the poor. As we have already seen in Chapter 1, scholars found that an important engine of Islamic expansion in the region was the worsening economic plight of the lowest sectors of society who receive material aid and consolation from Islamic organizations. But here 44 per cent of the Shiites sampled of *high* socio-economic status (SES) indicated affiliation with Hezbollah, while 53 per cent of those in the medium and 47 per cent of the low category respondents were also Party of God enthusiasts.[7] The poor health facility situation in Shiite areas combined with Hezbollah's better-run, cleaner and more up-to-date hospitals and clinics, is yet another example of how Hezbollah has been able to cut across class lines in its appeal and out-perform its rivals.

According to the ESCWA survey, 14–19 per cent of houses in Baalbek-Hermel are neither connected to a water network nor have access to water through artesian wells. This is high when compared with the national average, where only 5.6 per cent of total households do not have access to water networks.[8] Moreover only 66 per cent of the houses in Baalbek, as compared to 51 per cent in Hermel, are connected to the public network and less than half of the households have access to filtered potable water. Only 27.8 per cent and 9.4 per cent of homes in Baalbek and Hermel respectively, are connected to sewer systems. The study also reports that the area's poor have little access to resources, whether in the form of capital (credit) or in the form of equipment.[9]

Another source of worsening poverty is the fact that working the area's prime agricultural land is increasingly unfeasible as a result of the influx of cheaper produce from Syria and other Arab countries.[10] This leaves increasing numbers of farm families destitute or secretly growing drug crops destined for the international market. What was a dismal picture in the 1990s has today become a full-blown crisis in rural Lebanon, and the government is apparently completely impotent to soften the blow. How does Hezbollah tackle this catastrophe?

It is impossible to acquire any solid information about the extent of the funds coming to Hezbollah from Iran, but it is well known that it is in the tens of millions annually and is carefully allocated to all sorts of projects through Reconstruction Campaign. RC's by-laws list a broad array of welfare and developmental duties that have continually been expanded over the decade. This has encouraged organizational complexity. Helped initially by a gift of 30 tractors from Iran, a well-planned agro-technical programme has been carried out by this association in the Bekaa-Hermel area since 1988. Agricultural cooperatives, begun at that time, have opened at the rate of one a year since then. Pamphlets in Arabic on the use of materials and new techniques are distributed and field demonstrations and consultations are offered free of charge by a qualified engineering staff. Wells are dug where needed. Veterinary clinics have been opened, and a modern agro-technical centre and school in Hawsh Barada were also constructed in the mid 1990s. A total of 10 schools were established by RC between 1988 and 1996.

RC has moved on from providing free low-cost housing to those whose homes were destroyed by Israeli bombardments (see Chapter 8 for details) to making such housing units available to the general public. This work assumes greater importance since failure to adequately address the issue of low-cost housing is considered by many Lebanese to be a major failing of post-war governments.

Poor farmers are greatly assisted by the heavy machinery made available to them, at no cost, for collective usage and by the selling of seeds and fertilizers at below market prices from five outlets in the Bekaa and three in the South, where Berri's influence has traditionally been strong. The establishment of a model dairy farm, the setting up of pathology and soil-testing labs, and the construction of a tomato processing and canning plant to stimulate agricultural development are other facilities overseen by Hezbollah. The plant was processing more than 100 tons of locally produced tomatoes per day during the start-up stage.

Space does not permit a full listing of RC activities here, but a discussion of Hezbollah's rural services would not be complete without mention of two very important initiatives. These are the provision of poor farmers with credit and social security facilities.

Since 1997, small farmers in 190 Bekaa villages have had access to a credit system and many also received technical assistance and loans that are followed up by Jihad al-Binaa engineers. As of 1999, two social security funds have been serving the needs of farmers who do not qualify for the government system. One operates in the South, servicing more than 4,000 family members in 115 villages in eight participating districts. The second fund covers some 800 families from the Bekaa district. The membership fee costs only 10,000 LL (about $US7) per month and defrays the balance of hospitalization costs not covered by the Health Ministry. Since most hospitals in Lebanon routinely turn away patients who cannot pay for necessary procedures or guarantee them immediately upon arrival, the plan has literally proven to be a lifesaver and is now being extended to fishermen.

To energize this programme, contracts were signed with hospitals in the South and reductions in patient bills of 30–50 per cent were obtained. In addition, a network of some 120 doctors in the South provides consultations at greatly reduced fees. My own ENT specialist at the American University of Beirut Hospital recently accepted a request to update these men on recent developments in his field. Dr Osama Hadi said he delivered his lecture in a modern facility, complete with an extensive medical library, in the heart of the dahiyeh, and that he was impressed by the knowledge revealed by the questions asked by members of the audience. However, what most amazed him was the number of doctors ready to abandon far more lucrative practices in the capital for exceedingly low-paying work at the grass roots. Because he admired the commitment of these men, he said, he and other colleagues have decided that they will lecture whenever they are called upon.

I have made it a habit to mention such programmes to Lebanese acquaintances from all walks of life in order to gauge their reactions. They invariably express amazement at the extensive work Hezbollah is doing and regret at the government's failure to display the same initiative and commitment. Said one Lebanese Christian: 'Everyone knows the work is politically motivated but it also shows what faith can do.'

## SPEAKING FOR THE 'ABANDONED'

Like most other Hezbollah initiatives in the field of social and public services, the process of advocacy based on extensive fact-finding and teamed with grass roots support began early and developed over the past decade. This initiative began no less than a year before Hezbollah partisans competed in the parliamentary elections for the first time. Hezbollah had often mobilized dahiyeh residents for strikes and protests of one kind or another, but in December 1991 the party took a new track by encouraging the formation of residential and professional groups in each quarter of the southern suburb. The purpose of these groups was to help press the government for action on the water problem.

On 30 December 1991, the Dahiyeh Activists and Residents Committee, Hezbollah's Hajj Shami and Hajj Abdallah Kassir, the party's regional director for Beirut, met to consider a paper presented by Hezbollah's Center for Developmental Studies on the water problems of the area. The study was a detailed report on the developmental and financial policies of the state and the extent of general services and condition of infrastructure in the dahiyeh. Statistics were presented which compared the water resources of the dahiyeh with those of other urban areas on the basis of population size and offered solutions, including cost estimates. Other inadequate facilities were treated similarly, and this formed the basis of the new association's 14 January 1992 press conference, where a press release was issued. Entitled 'The Southern Suburbs: An Area of Misery Awaiting Solution', the communiqué contained the names of 27 individuals representing development committees and various professional and religious associations located in the dahiyeh. With this action, Hezbollah leaders began a pattern of mobilization and organization at the grass roots to support advocacy in and outside Parliament that has continued over the years. (See the following chapter for the political impact of this programme and other Hezbollah service-oriented initiatives.) In 2000, for instance, Hezbollah turned its efforts toward persuading the Ministry of Health to upgrade government hospitals. Statistics in hand, Islamist leaders pointed out in meetings with health officials that lack of modern equipment and poor professional standards sapped public confidence in these institutions and made people afraid to use them. As a result, the private and more expensive hospitals were overburdened with patients.[11] (Note how Hezbollah's findings dovetail with ESCWA's.)

Hezbollah's studies mean that ministry officials are equipped with useful information that can be used to push reform in full cabinet meetings while the Party of God's MPs handle the offensive in the legislature. Other Lebanese political parties and pressure groups lack the resources and/or the organization to carry out such a well-planned political campaign.

The major resource in play here is RC, and thus a closer look at this powerful organization is now in order.

## JIHAD AL-BINAA (RC) AS A MODEL RURAL DEVELOPMENT AGENCY

It should be very obvious by now that RC is not only functioning as an important supplement to the Ministry of Agriculture, but is also leading it in some very important directions. I wanted to know what operational structure and procedures had been adopted to facilitate and expand the important work of this fundamentalist association since my 1993 investigation. To my knowledge there is only one detailed study on the inner workings of Islamic welfare institutions since that time; it was commissioned by ESCWA in 1999, and carried out by Lamia al-Moubayed, who holds a Master of Science degree in Agriculture from the American University of Beirut. The object of the study was to investigate output and assess the quality of administrative and operational procedures of two rural development associations functioning in Lebanon – RC and a group operating in one village called the Arsal Rural Development Association.

Al-Moubayed indicated that she was given broad access to all RC operations and spent a great deal of time visiting various agricultural projects in the company of the director and/or various engineers and technical personnel. Interviews increased her understanding of the structure and the processes of planning, project selection, follow-through and evaluation, all of which, according to the researcher, 'had been rationalized and were well established to a surprising degree'.

The report explains that RC's agricultural projects are not identified by the traditional participatory approaches. That is, target groups are not actively involved in the definition of needs and prioritization of projects. Instead the association has a pre-defined plan, and priorities are defined by the field engineers themselves on the basis of needs they perceive during their field visits and upon interaction with the population – especially farmers.

Whenever possible and appropriate, the association attempts to seek cost-sharing agreements with groups that it intends to help, Moubayed reports. This practice is encouraged because experience demonstrates that more participation by the local community is insured and success is more likely when the local population feels it has a stake in the project.

The researcher was particularly impressed by the following operational features of RC that are emphasized here as they so dramatically collide with stereotypes of fundamentalist organizations as backward and perceptions of their leaders as ignorant fanatics.

Looking at the leadership from technical, human and conceptual skills of the supervisors, the organization seems to be remarkably organized. Their knowledge and ability is based on experience and educational achievement and they are quite aware of management techniques and processes. Their ability to build teamwork is obvious. They are the moral and technical reference of the group.

Although the number of employees is large (about 100), chains of command are short and communications in both directions strong by virtue of regular meetings and strong group interaction; meetings are held on weekly, monthly, biannual and yearly bases to review progress and revise work plans, exchange information, co-ordinate and share decision-making.

Written communication is strong and is practised by all staff at all levels. Everyone fills in a weekly report sheet that is submitted to immediate supervisors and others. Departments report progress on a weekly basis to the director-general who uses them to set meeting agendas; a four-day retreat which all employees attend is held annually in December. There the year's activities and expenditures are reviewed and evaluated and the discussions in which all employees participate result in a work plan and budget for the year to come.

A well-known private consulting and engineering company, Team International, has been contracted to undertake on-the-job training for technical staff in engineering, AutoCad drawing, computer training and management. Linkages with bilateral donors have resulted in training programmes financed by them. All staff is additionally encouraged to attend and participate in all events, workshops, seminars, etc. organized in Lebanon by the various NGOs, syndicates, and universities.

Extensive networking with line ministries such as the Ministry of Agriculture, Hydraulics and Electrical Resources, Environment, Water Authorities, High Relief Committee, Social Affairs and Public Works, with local municipalities and with the farmers of the region is carried out. Hizbullah partisans, it must be noted, often head or sit on local municipal councils.[12]

This report shows how RC takes every opportunity to improve efficiency and cut costs in a variety of ways that closely emulate modern management techniques. According to the management and staff, the major internal challenges faced by RC were related to training and to the updating of technical expertise. This was problematical because salaries are not competitive and the labour pool is specific to one politico-religious affiliation. They also found that this image was a problem. Although this was not explained, it was probably a reference to the fact that some potential beneficiaries and employees would hesitate to accept help from or work for RC because of its conservative Islamic orientation. Following up on this point, the report does note that the selection of projects undertaken is also based on political considerations that serve the overall objectives of Hezbollah and that this raises the question of whether the association's effectiveness would be as strong if it were not driven by a politico-religious mission. 'This commitment', the report concludes, however, 'remains an important constituent of this human, organizational and operational success story...'[13]

The political impact of Hezbollah's social and public services has assuredly been profound. None of their rivals, right or left, religious or secular, can compete with them as large patrons. While House Speaker Berri does have an important state resource he can manipulate in the form of a state fund earmarked for Southern reconstruction, the loose organization of his Amal Movement has meant that the establishment of a modern service organization – such as Hezbollah's social services bureau, or RC with its statisticians and fieldworkers – is completely out of reach.

Interestingly, Hezbollah not only outstrips its Shiite rivals but also outstrips all other local non-governmental service organizations, which distribute funds to 'small institutions' for 'small projects'. In a report published in May 2001 by the Lebanese Ministry of Social Affairs in cooperation with UNIFEM – a UN agency that assists women – the United Nations Development Program and the European Union, small institutions were described as those of one to five employees and that are informal and not registered as companies: 'They use primitive technology, but play an important role in development.' Activities might include growing vegetables or flowers, raising livestock, running mini-markets, providing transportation or mechanical services, engaging in construction, printing, etc. Women are engaged in many such activities.

Hezbollah heads the list of NGOs with an average of 7,500 loans per year. The organization in second place is Caritas, an international Catholic charity established by the Pope; it offers 1,500 loans per year. According to the government publication, the money set aside by Hezbollah for loans in 2001 was some $US4.5 million.[14] This information assumes greater importance when it is noted that of all the loans extended by the 40 Lebanese NGOs listed, some 25 per cent of the total were made by Hezbollah. When asked about this report, Hajj Shami tossed it off rather lightly, indicating that it reflects the contribution of *only one of the eight different welfare and charity institutions* associated with the Party of God, each of which works in different ways on other problems. The Public Health Association and RC, both licensed Lebanese charities, are two examples. Other associations have to do with civil defence, aid to martyrs and support for the resistance. Why the resistance belongs on the list was explained in Chapter 4, when I pointed out that according to the Koran a donation of money to a holy war confers the same blessing as fighting the enemy with weapons. Significantly, the *ulama* (spiritual leader) eventually decides how donated monies can be most usefully allocated to serve the interests of the faithful. Here the donation, collection and distribution of funds must be understood in the Islamic context.

In my interviews with Hezbollah officials, I discovered that the financial sources for the eight associations they run include contributions from Lebanese individuals, Hezbollah members, Iran (including charitable associations) and donations that are part of Shiite religious obligations to provide a fifth of one's income to help those in need. The families of the mujahidin can be considered needy.

## HEZBOLLAH'S 'GOOD WORKS': THE PROGNOSIS FOR GROWTH

So long as the government remains incapable of fulfilling its basic responsibilities toward its citizens, Hezbollah will no doubt continue to expand its social and public assistance work and to reap the rewards that spin off from these endeavours. These rewards are more solid anchoring in the social fabric of the Shiite community and increased legitimacy with which to continue to spearhead the struggle against Israel from Lebanon.

In this regard, a look at some dismal information recently furnished by ESCWA indicates that the authorities will be strapped for cash for a considerable period to come. Although Beirut struggled to manage the public debt throughout the past decade, the public workforce ballooned and government expenditures increased. By summer 2001, the total public debt had increased to $17 billion from $4 billion in 1992 and now stands at the highest per capita level of any emerging market economy. Although the deficit narrowed, interest on the debt still absorbs more than 80 per cent of state revenue. ESCWA's annual economic reports have shown negligible economic growth rates for Lebanon for some time, but in 2000, Lebanon achieved the unenviable position of being the only state in the region with zero growth, while (official) unemployment soared to 16 per cent, second only to Yemen's

16.5 per cent. According to the International Monetary Fund, the absence of growth continued in 2001.

In summer 2001, Beirut's failure to turn this situation around led to warnings by the World Bank that assistance could not be provided if the government did not find a way to increase its revenues – a very difficult thing to achieve when most Lebanese are too destitute to pay much in the way of taxes and in any event feel that they are not getting much for the little they already pay. This situation means that Beirut will continue to accept help from almost any source available that can forestall the social crisis that appears to be looming.

If past performance is any measure, Hezbollah's programmes will therefore continue to expand and diversify while the state struggles to get its act together. Whatever either actor can produce, alone or in tandem, to moderate the misery in Shiite areas will still be a drop in the bucket compared to actual need. It is probably fair to say that even if Iran were to scale back the funding of some of Hezbollah's associations and projects, even the more modest services the Party of God could still provide would continue to further its religious and political goals.

# Chapter Seven

# The Grass Roots Speak – The 1998 Municipal Elections

Highly important to the mainstream image and status Hezbollah was trying to promote was the party's capacity to continue expanding its support and to present irrefutable evidence of that fact. Hezbollah's candidates won 12 of the 128 seats in parliament in 1992 and nine in 1996, making it the largest single party bloc in the legislative chamber both times. Nevertheless, these elections were not a true measure of the Party of God's clout in the Shiite arena, since competition was restricted in 'resistance areas'. That meant that in the Bekaa and the South, the Party of God and its main rival, Amal, had to form single consensual lists rather than competing against each other for seats. This step was taken to forestall partisan clashes that would damage resistance unity. Only in the districts of Baabda (later Baabda-Aley), Beirut and Jbeil, where a total of five Shiite seats are available, was competition open for Shiite contenders.

In these competitions, candidates backed by Prime Minister Hariri, House Speaker Berri and Hezbollah staged fierce campaigns to win and Hezbollah had held its own. However, not too much could be made out of the Party of God's successes as a real measure of the level of its integration and expanding popularity within the Shiite community. The 1998 municipal elections could provide that measure if parties got into the competition, since no 'resistance rules' were in effect in this case. This was because the dynamics of the local elections had usually been provided by the competing families of the town or village, rather than by political party skirmishing as was the case in the national elections. This would, of course, change if parties got into the local competitions and ran candidates to fill council seats. If that happened and the record of other fundamentalist groups in the Arab world in municipal elections was any indicator of success, Hezbollah would do very well. Those elections favoured Islamic groups specifically as a result of the social and public services, which they, in contrast with their rivals, offered the neglected sectors of society as part of their religious obligations.[1] Of interest in this case, therefore, was not so much whether Hezbollah would do well in certain districts, for that was expected, but whether the Party of God had been able to penetrate Berri's South Lebanon fief. That would be a real measure of the inroads Hezbollah had made over the past decade.

However, election results are only one part of the story I want to tell here. We have already seen that an assumption of fundamentalist backwardness and rigidity is misleading where Hezbollah professionals involved in administrative work and health care are concerned. Now we see how the politicians measure up when they finally have a chance to meet their rivals head on. For real insights about the men leading Hezbollah and how they shucked off their party's negative image as a foreign graft, a very close look at the electoral strategies and resources they exploited to best their rivals is essential.

Having closely observed all the campaigns, I found three factors, besides Hezbollah's shrewd exploitation of its resistance record and public services, to be enormously important in the Party of God's electoral strategy. First, rather astonishingly, the fundamentalist party relied on democratic precepts to counter challenges from its rivals. Second, it adapted strategies and tactics that are traditionally associated with this type of election in Lebanon. And third, it used the election machine that had been finely tuned and polished after the preceding parliamentary elections and developed modern campaign tactics in ways that could not be matched by any single competitor or coalition of rivals. If there is interest in how political Islam advances or holds its own in secular societies, Hezbollah's electoral performance offers a fine example.

## THE STRUGGLE OVER ELECTION 'RULES'

Since it was expected that the Party of God would try to capitalize on its social and public services by nominating for election the very party members and close associates who had directed or been involved in that work, its rivals began to try to tilt the playing field in the direction of their own candidates or those of their cronies, months ahead of time. For instance, hoping to assist Bassam al-Sabbah, his Shiite ally and former minister of information, to blunt the Party of God's clout in the dahiyeh, Prime Minister Hariri announced that any party participation in the elections would be improper and should not be allowed. The sole criteria for municipal council membership, he said, should be a candidate's technical credentials and administrative skills. His or her political connections should not come into play at all. Politicians and parties, he argued, should reserve their manoeuvrings for the national arena and leave the local folks alone, as had traditionally been the case in Lebanon's municipal elections.[2]

As might have been expected of a rival of Hezbollah, Speaker Berri immediately took up this position by announcing that he and other senior leaders had asked close associates and members of their parties who had already announced their candidacies to withdraw them immediately. The effect was one of government solidarity to stop Hezbollah and again illustrates the incipient hostility against the fundamentalists that lies just under the surface of Lebanese politics.

The government's line, however, was not very convincing since although municipal elections in Lebanon were indeed 'family affairs', they had never been 'apolitical'. For instance, competing family factions were often divided along political lines and received support from the political bosses and parties with whom they were affiliated. Moreover, when the schism was more personal than ideological, the attractiveness of a list backed by a strong political figure or party sometimes determined a potential candidate's choice of one ticket over another. In like manner, politicians and parties often vied to recruit the family or clan member who could muster the largest number of votes for a ticket that could produce a 'friendly' council. This required an assessment of the divisions within and between families in each village and efforts to 'help' members of the faction that seemed the most likely to win votes. The coalition building that ensued therefore took into consideration the political colouration(s) of the villages, their confessional mixes, and the 'family politics' or rivalries that prevailed.

This kind of manoeuvring in past municipal elections made it quite clear that the authorities' effort to exclude parties was aimed at excluding popular Hezbollah candidates, and that in reality they too would be engaged in the competition by approving the candidacies of technically 'unaffiliated' individuals on lists they were either personally putting together behind the scenes or were known to favour. Such 'independents' would probably not remain independent for long, given the norms of reciprocity and obligation that are part of the Lebanese political game. When national elections rolled around, for instance, a municipal council member 'assisted' in this way would certainly be expected to help deliver local votes to his benefactor.

The authorities had successfully tilted the electoral playing field in favour of their own or their cohorts' candidacies in a previous election. A few days before the 1996 parliamentary elections were to take place

in Mount Lebanon, where the Maronite Christian opposition pre-
dominates, the government promulgated a patently illegal electoral law
that guaranteed the victories of 'favorite government sons'. The law
made it impossible for their rivals to compete with the well-oiled political
machines of certain ministers. At the same time, these men made
extravagant use of their state positions to garner votes and lock out
opponents.[3] The 'principled' stand these very same individuals had taken
against political parties' interference in the local elections thus rang
especially hollow to many Lebanese.

## HEZBOLLAH PLAYS THE DEMOCRACY CARD

Friction between Hezbollah and the government was palpable when
Party of God leaders made no bones about the fact that they would ignore
Hariri's injunction for parties to drop out of the local contests. On
television broadcasts and in newspaper interviews, Hassan Nasrallah
insisted that the candidacies of Hezbollah's members and adherents were
important precisely because *they had personally* demonstrated their
expertise and commitment to improving local conditions and governance
over an extended period of time. If members of other parties had not
been so engaged and had not won respect and popularity by similar
behaviour, that was too bad but not Hezbollah's fault. Why, he asked,
should individuals of proven capacity and dedication step aside for
alternative candidates who may have less or even no record of civic
achievement at all? And if merit was the aim, why should the government
assume that an independent would have more merit than a party
affiliate? Wasn't the aim to place the most qualified candidates in office
regardless of their ideologies or personal political persuasions? Why
might a party member hold a cabinet post in the national government
but not a seat on a town's board of directors? Nasrallah indicated that
in his opinion a party member in a local post would always outshine an
independent, simply by virtue of the fact that the former would have
the national aspirations of his party in mind, work harder and be held
accountable by his organization as well as the local population.[4] Sayyed
Nasrallah's clever references to democratic principles and processes were
not lost on anyone in this exchange and many people I spoke with
thought he was absolutely right. I personally found it very ironical that
a fundamentalist preacher favouring the rule of the Supreme Jurist
should be instructing the prime minister of a secular state on the benefits
of grass roots democracy... and making sense.

Nasrallah also emphasized in his reply to Hariri that his organization
well understood that other trends and individuals were important in
some locales, and that Hezbollah's aim was not to try to exclude
genuinely popular personalities or representatives of various political

currents from positions of influence. Rather, the Islamists sought to put together hard-working teams of locals who could get things done at the grass roots. In other words, the Islamists were not going to go their own way in the elections but would be open to bargaining and discussion to fill electoral tickets. While all this sounded good, whether it would happen or not on Election Day remained to be seen.

The controversy between Hezbollah and state officials over the participation of parties in the local elections became a full-blown campaign issue. Party of God members accused the government of trying 'to stifle what little of democratic political life still remains in Lebanon' and took every opportunity to criticize the Speaker of the House for his support of the government line. For example, in one speech Nasrallah denounced Berri for hypocrisy in demanding that parties abstain from influencing the elections, while at the same time allowing giant portraits of himself and Musa al-Sadr the founder of his party, as well as Amal flags and banners to be hung among the posters of candidates vying for council seats.

At a meeting in the Bekaa a day before the elections, the Hezbollah leader claimed that Berri was trying to eliminate legitimate democratic processes while he himself was practicing 'the old kind of feudal politics dressed up in modern clothes'.[5] This was an allusion to the high-handed and thorough manner in which traditional Shiite families like the Hamadehs and the Assads, who had held high government positions in pre-war governments, had dominated political life in Shiite areas before the civil war.

Interestingly, both the invocation of the rightness of the democratic process and the performance of party activities that supported that argument put the government on the defensive in much the same way as had occurred in other Middle Eastern societies where Islamist groups were building power at the grass roots.[6] The debate gave citizens a rare opportunity to ponder the contrasting versions of democracy being bandied about in the media and turned a spotlight on the electoral practices of the contenders.

## BEIRUT CAMPAIGNS AND ELECTIONS

While Hezbollah and its rivals were each seeking the moral high ground on this issue, the Prime Minister himself undertook the opening move in the Beirut municipal elections. On 6 May, the day officially consecrated to honouring the martyrs who gave their lives for Lebanese independence, Hariri organized a giant rally in the city centre whose reconstruction his company, Solidere, had been undertaking since the civil war ended. The political nature of the gathering was immediately obvious, since other speakers included al-Sabbah, who would be contesting one of the elections in Beirut's southern suburb, Press Association president Mohammed Baalbaki, and Nasri Maalouf – all solid members of the Hariri political machine.

Electoral outcomes in Beirut are always very important to Lebanon's prime ministers because their Sunnite constituency is concentrated there. Local elections therefore provide a means of demonstrating power between parliamentary elections and reinvigorating influence on the local level. In this case, however, the composition of Beirut's municipal council was far more important than ever before since renovation of war damage and the downtown project were the keystones of Hariri's programme. As the moving force behind Beirut's rebirth, the top official would therefore be loath to see influence over local affairs go to any individuals whose loyalty he could not count on completely. It is worth mentioning in this respect that the Council for Development and Reconstruction, in charge of the overall reconstruction plan, is headed by personnel and staffed by engineers plucked from Hariri's own contracting company, Oger Liban, and seconded to the state.

At the rally, Hariri did not miss the chance to air his views on democratic and open municipal elections and the need for apolitical technocrats on local councils again. Here, it should be pointed out that since Hariri does not officially head a party, those who are politically allied with him are thus technically all 'independents'.

In the weeks that followed, the Prime Minister went to work with other political leaders and parties, putting together a Beirut municipal council 'rainbow list' that could outdo any opposition's efforts.[7] In a 20 May television interview, he indicated that he had not endorsed any candidates in Beirut, and that he had agreed with other political leaders to support persons who were unaffiliated with a political current because 'if a party gets its candidates on the municipal council one can be sure that services will be guaranteed to one group and not another'. On the other hand, when the interviewer asked what would happen if the opposing list won half the seats on the municipal council, he answered: 'I'm very confident of *my own power on the ground*.'[8] [My emphasis]

In light of the verbal sparring going on between the Prime Minister and Hezbollah officials, there was intense interest as to whether Hezbollah would join Amal on the powerful Hariri-sponsored list in the capital, where three of the 24 council seats were reserved for Shiites. In conversations I held with Party of God members, I learned that there was considerable objection as a matter of principle to that option. However, in a perfect illustration of the non-ideological nature of the Lebanese political game, pragmatism prevailed, and Hezbollah leaders decided to place their candidates on the list of their major rival. Since many voters endorsed a whole list, the best chance to work for the city's benefit (and to win) lay with Hariri's coalition rather than with the list put together by his critics. Furthermore, it was also pointed out that membership on a popular, multi-confessional list further demonstrated Hezbollah's authentic search for interfaith cooperation rather than confrontation. Meetings had been undertaken with members of the Christian Phalange Party at their headquarters in Saifi to discuss election tactics. While the Phalangists were major Israeli allies during the civil war,[9] the party was one of the Christian factions that had agreed to cooperate with the post-war government rather than boycott elections and otherwise oppose it. At a joint press conference with Phalange leaders on 4 June, a Hezbollah official explained that the meeting was to ensure maximum cooperation between the two party machines.[10] I later learned that Hezbollah was urging its partisans to vote for the whole list being assembled and not to cross out the name of some Christian candidates who were being 'sponsored' by parties with whom the Party of God had formerly had hostile relations as a result of their behaviour during the civil war.

Lastly, since an Amal 'candidate' would also be on the Hariri list, it was a chance to see how well he would do compared to Hezbollah's man, the very popular director of the Party of God's *football team*, Amin al-Sharri. When I heard about this candidate I wondered if any other Middle Eastern fundamentalist party had a football team and played in a national league! I suspected, however, that this could only happen in Lebanon. The results of the election proved positive for Hezbollah, since al-Sharri made an excellent showing with 42,884 votes, approximately 2,000 more than independent Shiite MP Mohammed Youssef Beydoun's nephew, and far ahead of Amal's candidate, who was not elected. Commenting on the overall results of the elections, *Nida al-Watan*, a right-wing daily, noted that 'contrary to the government's claims, national politics played a prominent part in the Beirut elections, and Hariri, who imposed an initial veto on political parties' backing candidates, had to back down from this indefensible position and allow party participation in his own hand-picked electoral ticket.'[11]

## THE DAHIYEH DECIDES

At the same time that voting was taking place in Beirut, intense electioneering was taking place between Amal and Hezbollah in the large municipalities of Ghobeiri and Bourj al-Barajneh in the capital's southern suburb. After Beirut and the port city of Tripoli, Ghobeiri is considered the most important municipality in Lebanon because of its size and wealth. It contains 21,000 voters, of whom 2,000 are Sunnites and the rest Shiites. Since some of the worst slums in the area coexist with luxurious coastal tourist resorts, some believed it very inopportune for fundamentalists to control this area since their presence might scare the tourists. I spoke with the manager of one of resorts about this when I was lunching there one day right before the elections, and he said, with a grin, 'Not a problem – tourists who come to Lebanon are hardy.'

As the area was undergoing important government-sponsored reconstruction and development projects, it was natural for Hariri and other state officials to want to place people they could work with in positions of municipal authority there – this meant they had to work with Hezbollah's opposition in a district that had strongly felt the impact of the Party of God's public services. Hezbollah's strategy was therefore very clear – it must energize the political resources it had built up in the area over the years by placing on its list members of the organization who had been personally involved in its public and social programmes while also attracting popular figures regardless of their political and religious affiliations.

To fully understand the mechanics of creating a winning list, it is important to comprehend the importance of 'family politics' in Lebanon and the consequent electoral impact of family size. Most families accede to the political direction or preferences of the clan's key member – usually an older, respected male. Such an individual's endorsement is therefore the object of intense competition by list-builders, because the size of his family might be considerable. For instance, of Ghobeiri's 13 large families, the al-Khansas have 1,100 family members who are eligible to vote, the Khalils 750, the Kanjes 585 and the Farhats 497. The savvy list-maker must therefore attract or be open to the approaches made by members of these families, bearing in mind the popularity they enjoy within the family, as well as in the community as a whole, before deciding whether a place on the ballot is warranted.

In a nutshell, for Amal to regain political ground in the Ghobeiri area, and for Hezbollah to retain its influence there, the opposing list-makers had to work within the dynamics of inter- and intra-family forces, emphasizing or de-emphasizing ideological affinities as was necessary to woo the most popular individuals to their tickets.

Amal's job would not be easy since its wartime reputation in the area was not a positive one. Many of its gun-toting young militiamen had arrived in the southern suburbs with the waves of refugees fleeing the fighting in the South and had unfortunately used their party positions to intimidate the inhabitants of the district. Thus, although many individuals find Berri's personal dynamism and wit very attractive, the same affection is not felt for many of those associated with the Amal movement. The Shiite allies of Prime Minister Hariri would also have rough going since the government did not have the record of social and public services in the district that Hezbollah enjoyed. How did Hezbollah utilize its assets, and how did its rivals seek to undermine the Party of God's efforts in the southern suburbs?

Hezbollah chose Mohammed al-Khansa, a member of their politburo and former head of social services for the area, to head its list. Al-Khansa is not only a deeply pious, wealthy and charitable individual, but also heads the municipality's largest and most influential family. He would therefore be virtually impossible to defeat and gave the whole list an enormous edge. The other 21 members of Hezbollah's Ghobeiri list and the 18 candidates on the Bourj al-Barajneh ticket were also members of important families who were either fundamentalists themselves or were closely associated with the Party of God in one way or another.

Berri, on the other hand, tried to bar the way for Hezbollah by joining forces with a very influential resident of Ghobeiri, Riyadh Raad. He also tried to counteract Hezbollah's strategy by launching a press campaign ten days before the elections to try to turn the large families of both municipalities against the rival list. The slogan of the Berri campaign was '*let the people* (not a party) be given a chance to manage their daily affairs'. One Ghobeiri resident I interviewed to determine the impact of this slogan asked me the following question: 'Why should we leave the management of daily affairs to people Berri has collected? Hezbollah's people have been doing it for years and should continue doing it if they want to.' Another resident indicated that he thought Berri's list would fail because he simply was not the major list-maker (for which, read patron) in the area. For this reason he was unable to attract first-rank candidates to his tickets as Hezbollah had.

However, Berri sought the help of Prime Minister Hariri, whose close Shiite ally, Bassem al-Sabbah, could energize Amal's Ghobeiri list. Not only was al-Sabbah influential in the area because of the ministerial position he had held, but his alliance with the Sunni prime minister might also earn the ticket the votes of the 2,000 or more Sunnis living in the district. In addition, an estimated 1,800 individuals had recently been naturalized by the state and could be expected to show their appreciation by voting for the list heavily endorsed by the Prime Minister and the Speaker of the House rather than the one formed by the government's chief opposition bloc. With the Hariri-backed al-Sabbah on Amal's list, Hezbollah began calling for votes to 'fight big money and the hegemony of dwarfs'.

The campaigns for seats on the municipal council of Bourj al-Barajneh followed the pattern described above except for the fact that Amal was not able to count on Hariri's assistance in that contest. On the other hand, Hezbollah needed only to refer to the modern Rasul al-Azam Hospital and Mosque complex mentioned in the previous chapter, to point out its contribution to the welfare of Bourj al-Barajneh inhabitants.

Despite what was thought to be a clear advantage over Amal in this district, Hezbollah's efforts to get out the vote were not relaxed. In fact, observers commented about the fact that they matched those taken in Ghobeiri, where the race was considered to be much closer. Thus ambulances circulated continuously in Bourj al-Barajneh, transporting patients from Rasul al-Azam Hospital (some of whom were borne on stretchers to the polls), while mini-vans and other vehicles bore the healthy there. At these stations, as in Ghobeiri, Hezbollah volunteers waited, computerized voter lists in hand, to check off those who had come to vote and to pinpoint those who had not. Others then busied themselves canvassing the districts block by block to turn out those who had not yet voted and help them to the polls if they needed assistance. No such concerted activity by a Lebanese party had ever been witnessed. The numbers of volunteers involved in this operation – 400 according to one estimate – and the smooth functioning of this increasingly effective electoral machine demonstrate the importance Hezbollah attached to these elections as strong indicators of its popularity.

At the end of the day, Hezbollah had dealt Berri and Hariri a humiliating defeat in Ghobeiri by winning all 22 council seats, a fact that led al-Sabbah to declare that he hoped 'Berri will re-evaluate the political situation in the southern suburbs in light of the new facts the elections have brought to light and the imperatives of the coming period'. For his part, Berri indicated that despite the Party of God's sweep of both municipal elections, the results weren't too bad considering the 'particular characteristics of the *dahiyeh* that had endured for a decade' – an oblique reference to Hezbollah's dominance since 1989, after it had expelled Amal members by force from that sector.[12] In Bourj al-Barajneh, election results revealed another landslide for Hezbollah.

The party's strong inclination to cooperate with the authorities that was mentioned in the chapter on social services was echoed by newly elected council head al-Khansa in a newspaper interview. He said that the most important activity he foresaw was attempting to coordinate with the government and attaining full cooperation between the municipal council of Ghobeiri and government agencies to provide services for the locale. In this respect, he foresaw the creation of a taskforce to intervene when any problem arose over the implementation of the district's priorities, which he stated as improvement of health and water issues, work on the roads and other infrastructure.[13]

A minor diplomatic victory occurred as a result of Hezbollah's success in the dahiyeh local elections, when French President Jacques Chirac, meeting with French-speaking mayors on a state visit to Lebanon, warmly greeted and congratulated Khansa on his recent victory. This meeting was the French leader's first public encounter with an official of Hezbollah.

Reviewing Hezbollah's performance in the dahiyeh and in several municipalities in Mount Lebanon with an overwhelming Shiite population, the Party of God gained 90 council seats, shutting out Amal completely.

## THE ELECTORAL STRUGGLE IN THE SOUTH

Following the Party of God's success in the dahiyeh, all eyes turned toward the battle that would take place a week later in the South's municipalities. Imam Musa al-Sadr had begun the socio-political work that eventually led him to great prominence in the South, from where Berri hails and where the Amal leader's influence is thought to be at its highest level. Here, the question was not whether Berri's list would triumph but by how much in comparison with the coalition Hezbollah was putting together. This contest and the one to follow later in the Bekaa would be the first unrestricted match between the rival organizations.

As in the dahiyeh, Amal and Hezbollah did their best to draw popular candidates from the leading families of the two major districts where Shiites are concentrated, and neither was averse to seeking help from other attractive political contenders in this neglected and dangerous region. However, while Amal pushed the notion of consensual agreements with Hezbollah as a means of avoiding the polarization of families and clans – an indication of the movement's uncertainty – Hezbollah rejected any 'back room' negotiations that did not directly involve the families and indicated that while it did not object to consensual agreements where warranted, it would energetically refuse list negotiations with any political groups or notables that had no actual presence or influence on the ground in the locales in question. In other words, there would be no deals with Amal to divide up the cake in villages and townships where Berri's influence was slight or non-existent.

In the large town of Tyre, an alliance with Ali al-Khalil, a scion of the area's ruling Shiite family, would be a coup for the successful list negotiator. The level of influence al-Khalil enjoys can be measured by the fact that he has received important ministerial posts in almost all the post-war governments, despite advances in his domain made by other political currents over the past 30 years. Furthermore, since Berri apparently has a say on how the funds of the state agency formed for southern reconstruction are used and often gives projects in Tyre priority, an alliance between the two powerful governmental figures would produce a strong electoral ticket and a campaign that might shut out the Party of God's list in this district.

The 21-member ticket formed by Berri and al-Khalil was duly named Liberation and Development – the name of Berri's parliamentary bloc (this from the man who insisted party politics should be excluded from the elections) – and included four Sunnis and four Christians among the Shiite candidates. The official inauguration of the new Tyre municipal sports stadium took place only a few days before the elections, with Berri and his retinue doing the honours as a little reminder of which candidates to vote into office. Hezbollah's list, composed of 14 of its members or close associates and one member of the Communist Party and lacking any Christians, could not compete despite a campaign emphasizing Tyre's contribution to the resistance in terms of martyrs and the mobile medical unit and tractors that had been contributed through the auspices of the Party of God.[14] Amal spokesmen later claimed their movement had been victorious in a large majority of the municipalities in the Tyre district.

The southern district of Nabatiyeh and part of Rashaya abut the Israeli 'Security Zone' and thus contain locales where Hezbollah was militarily engaged with the Israelis and the SLA and where Israeli retaliation often occurred. That being the case, would the inhabitants censure the Party of God for having endangered their lives and properties time and again or reward the organization's fight against the occupation with votes? This question had never before been answered.

Hezbollah runs a modern hospital in the city of Nabatiyeh and Reconstruction Campaign has undertaken several development projects in the area and quickly repaired and sometimes completely reconstructed homes and businesses damaged as a result of clashes with the Israelis and their surrogates. If patronage is important to the largely poor, rural population of the South, then as Tyre rewarded Berri, Nabatiyeh should thank Hezbollah.

In fact, the electoral campaigns in Nabatiyeh were a great deal like those in Tyre, with the strongest power on the ground attracting the principal traditional leader of the district to support its lists. In this case Hezbollah partisans allied with Kamal al-Assad, a man who, like his father, ran the district like a feudal lord until the incursion of the militias. Unlike the leftist Ali al-Khalil, however, Assad and his followers were marginalized in the post-war period because of their sympathies with the pre-war establishment. For pragmatic Hezbollah leaders, however, Assad's spotty past presented no problem. Equally ironic was the fact that Communist Party sympathizers were represented on both Hezbollah's Nabatiyeh list and Amal's Tyre ticket.

Amal's strategy for the main localities of Nabatiyeh district was to resort to alliances with governmental figures, as had been the case in Beirut's southern suburbs. These included the Shiite minister of economy, Yassin Jaber, who is very close to Berri; MP Abdul Latif Zein; and former MP Anwar Sabbah. Hezbollah, however, was victorious in the city of Nabatiyeh, where it won 18 of the 22 seats on the municipal council and triumphed in many other municipalities in the district. Most observers reported a dead heat between the Shiite rivals in the South which testified to Hezbollah's rapid expansion in this critical region over the past decade. It is also very important to note that the election results also indicated that the Party of God's resistance operations would gain votes, not lose them. This further emphasized its legitimacy among the population most affected by it.

However, neither party was happy with the other's claims of victory. A heated quarrel over electoral statistics immediately erupted indicating the importance given to these electoral results by both parties. For example, out of 11 municipal elections in Bint Jbeil, another southern district, two lists had been decided by consensus between Amal and Hezbollah, five had been won by Amal and four by the Islamists. Hezbollah's total, MP Mohammed Raad claimed, was 31 of 66 contested municipal elections, while '*Amal's allies*', he said, 'were winners in nine other uncontested contests'. Raad went on to note that to cover up the important inroads the Party of God had made in the South, Amal was claiming as its own those council seats won by any candidates who were *not* associated with Hezbollah. In his view, a newly elected council comprised of partisans of the Syrian Social National Party or the Baath Party, while a defeat for Hezbollah, did not necessarily attest to Amal's influence or popularity in that locale. Raad virulently attacked Amal for claiming fictitious victories in 20 municipalities where no contest had taken place, in three where neither party had participated and three where there was a consensus between the two parties to share seats.[15] Hezbollah spokesmen also wasted no opportunity to point up the contrast between the stand Berri had taken on 'apolitical' elections and the fuss he and Amal officials were now making over 'Amal's so-called victories'.

A study published in 2000 on the Municipal Elections sought, among other objectives, to set the record straight. It concluded that in Nabatiyeh, Hezbollah-backed lists won 11 municipalities, while Amal lists won 12. However, the number of seats for each party on those municipal councils is almost equal – 97 to 94 respectively. In the South, including Tyre and Bint Jbeil, Berri's lists won 27 municipalities with 231 seats compared with 11 municipalities with 122 seats taken by Hezbollah. The author concluded 'Hezbollah proved that it is now a potent threat to Amal in its traditional stronghold'.[16]

## HEZBOLLAH'S BEKAA COUP

Since the Bekaa Valley had been under Syrian control for more than two decades and Hezbollah had enjoyed free rein there for a good part of that time, the dynamics of these elections would be furnished by the Party of God trying to reap the rewards it had sown by its many services to the region and by Amal's efforts to do anything possible to sidetrack the Islamist bandwagon. While Amal's efforts proved largely in vain, Hezbollah nevertheless met its Waterloo in none other than the city that Sheikh Tufeili had once pronounced the capital of Islamic Lebanon – Baalbek. This happened as a result of Sunni and Christian 'fatigue' over Hezbollah's attempts to make their city an outpost of Islam. Moreover, Sunni residents who had ably exploited the international tourist trade, attracted by the city's extensive archaeological site before the civil war, feared the effect of fundamentalist control over the municipality on the development of its tourism. Since this community constitutes 30 per cent of Baalbek's population and Christians make up another ten per cent, their support of an opposing list fatally damaged Hezbollah's chances. From interviews he conducted with some of the inhabitants of Baalbek on Election Day, a local reporter indicated that he had learned that while the inhabitants expressed full support for Hezbollah's resistance activities, they felt that 'business and politics could not be mixed'.[17] Five Hezbollah-backed candidates, including 3 Sunnites, were elected to the 21-member council, while the only candidate who was actually close to Amal on the opposing list – Ahmad al-Awada – was defeated. Could Amal turn this into a victory? Berri thought so, claiming that 'Baalbek remained faithful to the vows sworn to Imam Musa Sadr'. His top political officer, Mahmoud Hamdan, added that although 'Amal had not run any of its own candidates, by working to achieve a consensus among the participants it had proven itself an important electoral force in the region'. A Hezbollah sympathizer I spoke with regarding Hamdan's comment simply said 'Amal has no political presence whatsoever in Baalbek City or this region'.

If the literature on the expansion of political Islam in the Middle East is to be believed, the region of Hermel, with 100,000 impoverished agricultural residents, made it an ideal area for fundamentalist incursions. Some discouraging statistics about the standard of living in that area were presented in the previous chapter. Hermel, in fact, has been a major recruiting ground for the Islamic Resistance and thus residents' allegiance to Hezbollah was expected despite the fact that the Lebanese Baath Party is active in the area and Sheikh Subhi Tufeili is also still popular there. Campaigning under the slogan 'Loyalty to the Blood of Martyrs', Hezbollah easily won all six municipal elections in the Hermel area except that of Brital, Tufeili's home town. There, Hezbollah decided to forego a campaign that might have exacerbated tensions with Islamist hardliners loyal to the former secretary-general.

These elections made a number of facts about Hezbollah very clear. First, Hezbollah stands on solid records of achievement in social and military domains that have generated a great deal of popular support. It has therefore become the dominant list-maker in many Shiite areas and is thus capable of attracting the most influential and therefore desirable candidates to its tickets.

The heterogeneity of the lists formed showed that Hezbollah's fundamentalist ideology is neither overwhelmingly important in creating these lists nor greatly off-putting to those espousing secular and leftist views who join the list for opportunistic reasons. This finding fully supports another conclusion I drew from the previously mentioned survey I conducted in the Shiite community – to whit, deep religiosity and strong support of Islamic goals *were not significant* as a determinant of popular support for Hezbollah.[18]

Furthermore, the Party of God has adapted well to the rules of the Lebanese political game and was simply better at managing the competing ideologies, clan affiliations and local bosses that all co-exist simultaneously and vitally in areas of Shiite concentration, than its rival.[19] This kind of political skill combined with the institutional back-up and religious commitment Hezbollah leaders bring to all their tasks, makes them very hard to beat in open elections like this one. One Amal member I spoke to after the elections said that he had to give Hezbollah credit for its victory, because: 'All the assistance they get from Iran wouldn't mean a thing, if they didn't know how to make it work for them.' He felt that Berri would have to learn from Hezbollah's lesson and begin to reckon with Amal's lack of structure, discipline and popular mid-rank officials. He noted that the prominence and popularity of leading Hezbollah members is clearly an enormously important asset for the Party of God, whereas in his opinion Berri had foolishly ousted former party officials because he apparently felt threatened by their appeal. Soon after our conversation, I found out that Berri had begun new restructuring and recruiting efforts that were apparently aimed at a better performance in the 2000 parliamentary elections. This kind of manoeuvring between two mass parties makes Shiite politics far more interesting than the shenanigans that go on in the other Lebanese communities at election time.

Another point to note is that Hezbollah's growth has not provoked the apprehension that would normally be found in other Middle Eastern societies had a fundamentalist organization made the same kind of political strides. In Lebanon's case, however, the system clearly restricts the capacity of any one religious community or political current to dominate national politics. So, while the Shiite competition is open and furious, there is no chance at all for a party like Hezbollah to sweep to a national victory that would then permit them to deconstruct the system that brought them there.

Moreover, under the 'divide and rule principle' manipulated by Syria, where no party is allowed to deal a knockout blow to another, there are also strong obstacles to hegemony within the Shiite community itself. Syria – no advocate of fundamentalism – has a strong ally in Berri, who is one of the pillars of the pro-Syrian government. His key position as Speaker of the House provides the resistance with part of the official support it needs to pursue a national agenda. There is more about this interesting strategy in the following chapter, but here let it simply be said that, in addition to the above limits on Hezbollah's capacity to overwhelm its opponents, there is one more – and perhaps the most important – restriction operating today. Since the Party of God's priority is clearly the armed struggle with Israel and its maintenance, political self-aggrandizement must be subordinated to that end.

# Chapter Eight

# The Mechanics of Military Jihad[1]

The policies, programmes and strategies adopted by Hezbollah and discussed in the foregoing chapters were all developed with a particular consideration in mind: how best to secure the necessary popular base for resistance. Now it is important to see how the military policy developed by Syria and played out by Hezbollah and the Lebanese government unfolded – and by handing Israel stinging political defeats, provided the bedrock support for the Party of God's jihad. In doing so, I will also show how popular support garnered over the years was tapped at critical moments to thwart Israel's battle strategy.

Although Hezbollah has continuously been in the news as a result of its military operations – or 'terrorist activities', as the Israelis see them – the political strategy behind them and the domestic support that energizes them have been almost totally ignored. Below I rectify this omission by pointing out the connections between Hezbollah's military and political policies and how they contributed to the grand strategy designed by Damascus to try to bring the Israelis to the negotiating table.

In an earlier chapter I suggested that a militia operating at the behest of foreign powers *before the establishment of the new Lebanese political order* might provoke tensions with a government that felt insufficiently in control of the situation. I would argue that the policy devised to counter Israel's retaliatory attacks since 1992 owes its success precisely to that tension and to Syria's capacity to manage rather than to resolve it as Israeli strategists would like to see happen. In fact, my analysis shows that the Lebanese actors' strict adherence to Syria's unwritten 'rules' governing their behaviour during Israeli military operations has rendered and will continue to render Israel's use of force in Lebanon self-defeating.

On the other hand, this policy could not be sustained without the Lebanese population's capacity to absorb Israel's retaliatory strikes without altering its support for the struggle being waged by Hezbollah. In previous chapters, I pointed out how Hezbollah left virtually no stone unturned in its effort to gain this support. We will now see how meticulous political work at the grass roots, in parliament and on local boards, through dialogue and fraternization of all kinds, paid off when the crunch came. We will also see how Hezbollah leaders promoted their victories against the Israelis so as to maximize the political effects of Syria's 'state/resistance' strategy.

The analysis that follows is mainly based on my observations of Hezbollah and the Lebanese government's behaviour during Israel's 'Grapes of Wrath' military campaign against Lebanon in April 1996. This action left 150 people dead, the vast majority of them civilians, and caused millions of dollars in damage. It was strikingly similar to 'Operation Accountability', launched by Israel against the same 'targets' in July 1993. Statements by Israeli government officials, in fact, revealed that the two campaigns pursued the same goals and the same strategies. Both operations unleashed massive destruction in South Lebanon in order to pressure the Syrian-backed Lebanese government to halt Hezbollah's attacks on northern Galilee. The broader objective of the two Israeli acts was to drive a wedge between Syria and Lebanon at a time when Damascus counted on foreign policy coordination with the Lebanese government to achieve national and regional objectives. Considering Beirut the weak point in Syrian policy, the Israelis tried to exploit its often-tense relations with Hezbollah, the active partner in the arrangement. The most recent large-scale Israeli attack, in January 2000, sought the same goals but was more restrained in duration and the level of damage caused. Like the other military adventures in Lebanon, it was unsuccessful. Each time Syria was able to demonstrate its prowess in regional affairs by manipulating resources at hand in Lebanon – that is Hezbollah and the Lebanese government – from the sidelines. It was this ability to hand the Israelis repeated setbacks in their self-declared 'Security Zone' that led to the Jewish state's decision to evacuate it in 2000. What are the tensions between Hezbollah and the government that Israel would like to exploit and that Syria successfully manages?

## BEIRUT'S PRIORITY: EXTENDING CONTROL OVER THE SOUTH

Israel well understands the frictions between, on the one hand, a government seeking to recoup state authority after years of impotence at the hands of powerful militias and, on the other, an armed force conducting independent military activities in the country. Besides Lebanon's close post-war relationship with Muslim Syria – a situation

that, as we know, is highly resented and feared by the Christian sector –
other factors, too, place the government in an unenviable position in
terms of exercising full sovereignty. The most obvious of these factors is
the small, recently reformed Lebanese Army that is no match for Israel's
superior war machine. Additionally, an Israeli confrontation with
Lebanon's conventional forces would drag Syria into open conflict, a
situation all parties wish to avoid.

Thus, if pressure is to be kept on the occupying force to withdraw
from Southern Lebanon so that Beirut can recoup occupied territory
there, the joint Syrian-Lebanese foreign policy would have to be firmly
upheld. In essence this means that the Lebanese government must
abandon normal state prerogatives and assume an openly supportive
position toward the group most capable of doing the job – Hezbollah.

## INCIPIENT TENSIONS BETWEEN THE LEBANESE GOVERNMENT
## AND HEZBOLLAH

As already mentioned, the post-war Lebanese regime inherited an
ongoing struggle in the south of the country that had eluded the control
of the central authorities since it had been established almost a decade
earlier. Dealing almost exclusively with Iran and Syria in tactical and
logistical matters and fiercely opposed to Lebanese governing circles
during the civil war years, for most of its existence Hezbollah had had
no reason to build a working relationship with Beirut.

Further complicating any government initiative to influence activities
being undertaken by the Party of God in the South was the fact that
Hezbollah's popular support had grown over the years as a result of its
operations there. This made it very difficult for the authorities to do
anything to hinder these operations, which in point of fact had become
a national priority.

The type of warfare being waged by Hezbollah in the South made
things particularly difficult for the government.[2] Opportunities for blows
against the Israelis are planned in advance but often put into operation
as a result of a conjuncture of factors that are not easily predicted. Secrecy
is paramount. Thus the Lebanese authorities are not given advance
warning or consulted on field operations. Therefore, when the
government is confronted with massive population dislocation and
destruction as a result of hostilities between Israel and Hezbollah that
it can neither predict nor forestall, it can only react. This it does by
activating the official prerogatives that remain and by pursuing the
interest of the state. This entails ending the violence in the South by
bringing diplomatic pressures on Israel to end its occupation.

It can therefore be said that by campaigning for implementation of
UN Security Council Resolution 425 – which stipulated withdrawal of

all Israeli forces from Lebanon, the Lebanese authorities also hope to end the freewheeling activities of the last of Lebanon's operating militias and to initiate talks with Damascus about removal of Syrian troops from Lebanese soil. In other words, while taking draconian measures to avoid a run-in between the Lebanese Army and Israeli forces in the South, and staying out of Hezbollah's way, the *government is nevertheless pursuing a goal diametrically opposed to that of the Party of God*. The state's basic aim is to recover national territory but also to end the violence in the South, whereas Hezbollah's *raison d'être* is to single-mindedly fight the occupiers and – while they were still cooperating with the Israelis – their surrogates: members of the SLA. This is why Israeli strategists believed that Lebanese officialdom's shaky solidarity with the militant Islamic organization could be exploited if the cost of allegiance was made unacceptable through massive retaliation. Furthermore, the Israelis were conscious of the fact that Hezbollah's military exploits have not mobilized unqualified support for the Islamists. Apart from raising fears among government officials that Hezbollah's fighters might provoke unbearable military responses from Israel, the Party of God has been criticized by government figures for capitalizing on the struggle against Israel for its own aggrandizement. Nabih Berri and Amal partisans have particularly resented the political mileage that Hezbollah has gained from its military achievements while their own organization has played a more limited role along the edges of the 'Security Zone'. (See Map 1)

The other factor that creates tension between the government and Hezbollah concerns the political ends toward which the party's ascent may be leading. While it is widely understood that the Syrians would veto any attempt to radically change the Lebanese system, I have mentioned that many are still uneasy with the Party of God's strait-laced approach to aspects of Lebanese life that are valued by Muslims and Christians alike and really don't like Hezbollah much. Thus, although most Lebanese respect the party for its unshakable pursuit of the Israelis and its successes in inflicting damage over the years, Israel's strategists estimated that the reservoir of public support that the Party of God enjoys could dissipate if its tactics in the South continually drew Israeli responses that jeopardize citizens' security and damage infrastructure.

The question now is how Syria has countered this strategy and prevented 'state/resistance' antagonisms from erupting and spilling over into the public arena during periods of crisis.

## THE IMPERATIVES AND RULES OF SYRIA'S TWO-TRACK RESISTANCE POLICY

A review of the actions of the Lebanese government and Hezbollah leaders during Israel's Operation Accountability in 1993 will identify patterns of behaviour that can help clarify this question. Operation Accountability was launched on 25 July 1993, several weeks after Hezbollah guerrillas had rocketed northern Israel. The Hezbollah action had been in retaliation for the Israeli military's rupture of a tacit agreement that established the 'rules of combat' in the 'Security Zone'. Those rules essentially specified the legitimacy of military targets *within the zone*, but vetoed operations outside it. In this case, Hezbollah charged Israel with responding 'unfairly' to a legitimate attack on its military forces within the zone, and that drew the Party of God's cross-border response. (What Israeli officialdom had to say about a similar incident that occurred one year earlier, in 1992, is discussed in Chapter 11.) Speaking on Israeli radio, Foreign Minister Shimon Peres described the objective of Israel's massive attack in 1993 as follows:

> The Lebanese government has to decide whether Hezbollah represents it or not. If it does, then the whole of Lebanon is at a state of war with Israel and this also means that Hezbollah seeks the destruction of all of Lebanon. The Lebanese government will then have to cooperate with us in silencing Hezbollah and ending its activities.[3]

Beirut, however, did not cooperate. Instead, the Lebanese government pursued diplomatic efforts to end the conflict and limited its actions on the ground to assisting displaced people fleeing the South. The local press reported carping among cabinet members as to how much resistance Lebanon could tolerate, given the damage that Israeli gunners, helicopters and airplanes were inflicting. But throughout the period of intensified conflict, the central authorities made no attempt to discourage Hezbollah's incessant shelling of the Galilee panhandle.

During the hostilities, the Lebanese public showed somewhat mixed reactions to Hezbollah's performance, and there were no spontaneous or government-organized demonstrations of solidarity. In fact, when Hezbollah tried to mobilize a rally in Beirut, the government refused its application for a permit. Furthermore, the USA persuaded Lebanon not to bring the issue to the Security Council, arguing that a bitter debate might prejudice Secretary of State Warren Christopher's forthcoming visit to the Middle East to try to restart the stalled peace negotiations. Religious leaders met at the seat of the Maronite Christian Patriarchate to express support for the resistance *only after* a ceasefire had been achieved. However, although the media reported an 'undisclosed government position calling for restrictions on Hezbollah's activities along the border with Israel in order to synchronize its actions with government policy',[4] neither the public nor members of the government openly demanded these limitations during the hostilities. Operation Accountability therefore not only failed to exploit tensions between the

Lebanese authorities and Hezbollah, but also gave Damascus a key role in the situation as Syria mediated the ceasefire between Hezbollah and the Israelis, with the USA.

The actions of the Lebanese government and Hezbollah leaders during Operation Accountability indicate that each pursued its own goals efficiently using appropriate and distinctive resources: diplomacy and weapons, respectively. The evidence therefore suggests that Syria was able to defeat Israel's strategy of exploiting tensions between the Lebanese state and Hezbollah, not by smoothing them over or resolving them, but simply by channelling them to achieve its policy goals. The Lebanese actors were both fully backed by Damascus, yet their behaviour towards one another was apparently so closely regulated that any impingement on the other's sphere of influence was prevented. Implicit in this scenario are the following 'rules' established for Hezbollah and the Lebanese authorities:

1) Hezbollah is to pursue armed resistance in the 'Security Zone' while the Lebanese government resists by taking responsibility for civilians outside the combat areas where the state enjoys full sovereignty.

2) Furthermore, each party is given all rights by Damascus to exploit any political, military, or social means necessary to arrive at its own goals vis-à-vis the Israeli presence or Israeli actions in Lebanon. Each receives total Syrian support.

3) Neither party is required to coordinate its activities concerning the Israelis with the other because two separate tracks of resistance are vital to Syria's plan.

4) The latent conflict between Hezbollah and the Lebanese government is probably kept within bounds by a strict understanding that neither party can use force at the expense of the other's goals.

5) Additionally, Damascus' 'rules' seem to preclude the use of other Lebanese groups or external actors to promote their cause or derogate the other's with the Syrians. For instance, knowledgeable sources indicate that Hezbollah cannot use Iran to provide more effective influence with Syria at the expense of the state's goals; nor can the Lebanese government use an external actor – France, a traditional ally, for instance – to plead its case against Hezbollah.

6) Finally, only if the two parties reach total impasse in any dispute will Syria – and Syria alone – step in to arbitrate.

These hypothetical guidelines will now be applied to an analysis of 'state/resistance' dynamics triggered by Israel's 1996 and 2000 military operations in Lebanon.

## 'GRAPES OF WRATH' AND THE DYNAMICS OF SYRIAN FOREIGN POLICY

### Hezbollah's sphere of influence and actions

After the 1993 episode, Hezbollah stood by its commitment to limit attacks to the 'Security Zone'. However, in April 1996, in retaliation for an Israeli roadside blast that killed a teenager and wounded three *outside the agreed combat area,* Islamic guerrillas began firing rockets into northern Israel. As before, they claimed that Israel had broken its word. These attacks took no toll on life and did little material damage. Nevertheless, several days later, in a replay of Operation Accountability, the Israelis launched their Grapes of Wrath campaign. Using airpower to pulverize Lebanese infrastructure – highways, bridges, electric stations, etc., and blasting away at locations suspected of harbouring Hezbollah fighters, Israel warned the Lebanese government of even wider destruction if Hezbollah fighters were not brought to heel. Speaking on the second day of the raids, Uri Lubrani, coordinator of Israeli activities in Lebanon, warned that the Lebanese government's 'adoption of Hezbollah' would lead to the destruction of the country's economic and security accomplishments and that the damage that Hezbollah's shelling caused in Israel would be answered in kind anywhere in Lebanon.[5]

It was obvious, however, that a far wider game had been set in motion by the Israeli attack, one that had been anticipated in Lebanon since that February day when 64 Israeli civilians had died in two Hamas attacks. Following the twin blasts, a joint Israeli-American anti-terrorism campaign was launched to boost an image of Prime Minister Peres as a man who could handle security in Israel. Since a victory for Peres in upcoming Israeli elections was considered essential for continuation of the peace process, President Bill Clinton used that method to reassure the Israeli public of a strong US commitment to Israel's security. It was therefore widely believed in Lebanon that sometime before the June Israeli elections, Peres would demonstrate his resolve to fight terrorism by going on the offensive in Lebanon.

Hafiz al-Assad, on the other hand, was reportedly angered by Israel's abrupt and unilateral suspension of the land for peace negotiations with Syria after the Hamas attacks.[6] The Syrian leader was also alert to possible Israeli moves in Southern Lebanon and to opportunities to further embarrass Peres at this critical juncture in his career. The circumstances were ripe for the type of indirect confrontation between Syria and Israel that had been going on for years in Southern Lebanon. This time, however, the Labor government's overarching objective was to prove to the Israeli public that its candidate would not sit with arms crossed as Hezbollah attacked innocent civilians, while Syria's intent was again to deliver the message, in Assad's words, that 'there can be no security for Israel while Arab land is occupied'.

From the day of the Braachit blast that killed the teenager until the conclusion of a ceasefire agreement on 26 April, and despite all the havoc being caused by the Israeli Air Force, Hezbollah fighters relentlessly fired Katyusha rockets into northern Israel. The Israeli military was completely powerless to silence the highly mobile guerrilla units. This remains the case, by the way.

The machine-like quality of Hezbollah's operations and the hard line its leaders took in press releases and interviews gave the impression that the Party of God's embrace of the principle of jihad would make it impossible to stop it – *no matter what the consequences for Lebanon*. This is a good example of the conflicting goals of the Lebanese government and Hezbollah in operation. Comments by Prime Minister Hariri and by Syria's deputy foreign minister, Farouk al-Sharaa, about the *Party of God's* determination to take the battle inside Israel reinforced the impression of Hezbollah's unflinching and unmanageable pursuit of its goal. When Hariri was asked by a member of the foreign press why the Lebanese government could not stop Hezbollah attacks, he responded: 'If the Israelis with their war machine can't do it, how can you expect us to?'[7] Similarly, in response to an appeal from US Secretary of State Warren Christopher for Syria's intercession to persuade Hezbollah to consider a truce, Sharaa reportedly told the American secretary of state that *Hezbollah* (my emphasis) flatly rejected a ceasefire and that at that point Syria was simply unable to persuade them to accept one. The implication was that the Lebanese resistance was a force unto itself beyond the control of either Beirut or Damascus.

Hezbollah officials bolstered this impression by issuing strong policy statements on the ceasefire terms that *they* would or would not accept. It was reported that the Party of God was not willing to respond to mediation on any basis other than the understanding that had resumed after July 1993 about where it was proper to conduct combat. Nor would Hezbollah sign any written agreement with the 'Zionist enemy'. A US-French proposal was flatly rejected by the Islamists because, they claimed, the USA was not qualified to mediate because of its unambiguous support for the Israeli military operation.[8] When asked in an interview about the government's position vis-à-vis such uncompromising statements by an organization that lacked any authority to speak for the state, Prime Minister Hariri avoided the question, merely commenting: 'We will do our best to arrange a ceasefire.'[9]

Hariri also made it clear that strong public support for the resistance made it difficult to curb its actions. When asked how he explained his government's hands-off policy toward Hezbollah's activities when their continuous rocketing was causing massive destruction in his country, Hariri wryly remarked that any Lebanese official who tried to stop the resistance would be risking political suicide.[10] These statements clearly reaffirmed the position maintained by Beirut for years, that Hezbollah had the approval of the nation behind it and was completely within its rights to resist occupation.

Despite this public position, however, there is evidence that the government seriously discussed curbing Hezbollah's militants during the fighting. The Beirut daily newspaper *An-Nahar* reported on 22 April that this question was raised at a cabinet meeting chaired by President Elias Hirawi in the Prime Minister's absence. Another indication of the government's exasperation over its lack of control occurred when the Prime Minister and the Minister of Foreign Affairs cold-shouldered Iran's deputy foreign minister, Mohammed Kazem al-Khonsari, when he attempted to meet with them. This gesture was intended to show Beirut's annoyance with Iran's policy of dealing directly with Hezbollah and treating the Lebanese government as if it did not exist.

Presenting the Hezbollah fighters as an intrepid, autonomous force with a mission so important that it would compromise those who interfered with its operations, elevated *Syria*'s value as the player that could eventually persuade the Party of God to accept a truce. At the same time, it demonstrated how Damascus could inflict damage on Israel without direct confrontation.

### The Lebanese government's field of operations and tasks

The crux of Syria's policy was the Lebanese government's capacity to deal with Israeli punishment without cracking under pressure to rein in Hezbollah. Much of the Hariri administration's ability to carry out this task rested on the extent to which it could inspire strong public allegiance to its non-combative, supportive form of resistance. It could then credibly portray Hezbollah's actions as only one part of a national resistance that it, the state, was directing. This meant that members of the administration would have to work as a team, utilizing all of the state's resources to cope with the emergency.

During the Israeli assault, the state acted in a way similar to the way it had during the previous massive attack in 1993, except that its efforts had apparently improved with practice. Government activities were also covered more extensively by the local media, which had been induced to hold off all criticism during the crisis. The widest possible coverage was given to government, diplomatic and social assistance activities, as well as to the plight of the displaced and to demonstrations of public and private support for the *national* resistance. The media was apparently galvanized into taking this line by a proposal from Parliament's Defense and National Security Committee that a state of emergency be declared – which would have included control of the media.

This publicity had an important effect on Lebanese public opinion, however, because it drew the ordinary citizen into the heart of the state's efforts to repulse the Israeli attack, thus helping the government to shape a supportive national consensus. Detailed press and television coverage of all of Prime Minister Hariri's almost non-stop shuttles to regional and European capitals to present Lebanon's case during Grapes of Wrath repeatedly exposed the Lebanese audience to their government's version of the events.

During these visits, Hariri strictly adhered to the state's line while treading cautiously with regard to Hezbollah. When questioned about the Party of God's domination of the struggle against Israeli occupation, the Prime Minister retorted that the Islamists were not the only ones resisting – *all Lebanon was resisting*. The only way to end the violence in the South and terminate resistance activities along Lebanon's southern border, he observed, was for Israel to adhere to Security Council Resolution 425 and withdraw from the 'Security Zone'. Hariri assured press interlocutors that when Israeli forces did completely withdraw, the Lebanese Army, not the Syrians, would be responsible for security there.[11]

The Prime Minister also scrupulously avoided questions intended to draw him out about Hezbollah's policies or ultimate intentions. When asked at a press conference in Paris whether or not Hezbollah sought to destroy Israel, Hariri simply closed that line of questioning by tersely remarking: 'I don't want to discuss Hezbollah's political agenda.' After watching the replay of this interview, an acquaintance of mine who had often criticized the government in the past remarked that it was the first time the Lebanese had seen their government beat the Israelis at the propaganda game.

President Elias Hirawi's decision to personally deliver a complaint to the Security Council about Grapes of Wrath was another example of the way state prerogatives were maximized to turn the diplomatic tables on Israel. Successful efforts to secure international reconstruction assistance also improved the government's rating in the eyes of a national constituency accustomed to Israeli gains and Arab – especially Lebanese – losses.

The chaotic situation in 1993, with refugees frantically seeking places to squat in Beirut's mainly Shiite southern suburbs, was avoided in 1996 thanks to the coordinated activities of several ministries and state agencies. Government officials helped to install thousands of displaced families in public schools and centres throughout Mount Lebanon. Medical care, bedding and regular food deliveries were organized by ad hoc citizen committees. At the same time, the state's Council for the

South (*Majlis al-Janub*), which had been set up earlier to assist the South's recovery after other massive Israeli destruction, used Lebanese soldiers to distribute donated goods to the displaced. The Lebanese Army operated as a corps of engineers, constructing temporary bypass routes and erecting a bridge when main roads linking the South with the rest of the country were cut off because of Israeli bombardments. Army and civil defence units visited southern villages under fire to help evacuate the sick and wounded to regional clinics. Extensive day-long television coverage of these activities showed the government effectively managing a social crisis that would have daunted the most functional western government. This positive message generated a strong sense of solidarity among the populace and indeed crystallized a 'national resistance'. People throughout the country began to pitch in to help the war effort without regard to the confessional lines that generally divide Lebanese society. I saw students from the American Community School out on the streets collecting money to help the displaced. T-shirts painted with the letters FIT – Fight Israeli Terrorism – were hawked all over West Beirut by local students. Hezbollah volunteers were offering candies for donations at many intersections. During this period there was no carping about Hezbollah's activities.

The Israelis further contributed to Lebanon's mobilization when their warplanes dropped bombs that struck two electricity transformers in the heart of the Christian suburb of the capital on 14 and 15 April. This was a deliberate attempt to stir up opposition to the government's line from its main opponents. The effect of the raids, however, was the reverse of what Israeli strategists had wanted. Instead of using the attacks to criticize the government's tolerance of Hezbollah's behaviour and pushing for suppression of the Party of God's operations in the South, Christian leaders opposed to the post-war regime expressed outrage at Israeli aggression and rallied to the national effort. An unprecedented and heavily attended meeting of 'national solidarity with the South' was called in Achrafieh, the centre of Beirut's Christian sector.

On 18 April, an Israeli shell, claimed by Israel to have been fired at Hezbollah guerrillas nearby but to have missed its mark, landed on the UN base at Qana, killing 98 and wounding 101 Lebanese villagers who had sought refuge there. This tragedy brought national and regional outrage to a peak and was the turning point of Operation Grapes of Wrath. The situation was taken in hand by the Lebanese government with the massive participation of the media and used to drive home the brutal results of the Israeli campaign, as well as the sacrifice of 'national martyrs' – the murdered villagers who had resisted by refusing to leave their area. A national day of mourning was declared on 22 April and, after hostilities had ceased, an emotional state funeral was held at Qana where the dead were buried in rows of simple white cement tombs. This sombre place draws constant visitors.

On 25 April, Israel was condemned by the UN General Assembly and asked to cease its operations in Lebanon immediately. A day later a ceasefire agreement between Israel and Hezbollah was announced simultaneously in Jerusalem by US Secretary of State Christopher and Foreign Minister Shimon Peres, and in Beirut by Hariri and French Foreign Minister Herve de Charette. The final toll for 'Grapes of Wrath' was 165 Lebanese civilians killed, 401 wounded, 23,500 shells fired and 600 air raids in 16 days. Reading these figures in a local newspaper one of my university colleagues remarked: 'If that isn't terrorism what is?'

No Israeli casualties were reported.

None of this struggle, however, had any negative effect on Hezbollah's military operations, and out of it came major political victories for Lebanon and the resistance forces it claimed as its own.

## POLICY PAY-OFFS

The fact that Israel's use of force in Lebanon missed its political mark by a wide margin was a source of humiliation for the Peres government and gave the USA the embarrassing task of seeking Syrian assistance to arrange a ceasefire that would let its ally off the hook. The centrality of Syrian involvement in international efforts to manage the Israel-Hezbollah conflict was evident in the mechanics of the ceasefire negotiations. No fewer than seven foreign ministers were present in the Syrian capital toward the end of April as Assad conducted bilateral and trilateral consultations with them at his own pace and convenience. Although representatives of both the Lebanese government and Hezbollah were present in the Syrian capital, as was Iranian Foreign Minister Ali Akbar Velayati, they were not brought into the cycle of high-level meetings but were kept abreast of developments and consulted by Syrian Foreign Minister Farouk al-Sharaa. It was thus made clear once again that Syria was in command of the situation in Lebanon and that Assad's plans could be discounted only at the expense of those concerned.

The ceasefire negotiations reaped important rewards for both Hezbollah and the Lebanese authorities. The latter acquired equal membership status on a committee to monitor the ceasefire that also included representatives of France, the USA, Syria and Israel. This was headlined by the Beirut press as a breakthrough for Lebanon that won it international credibility.[12] Hezbollah, on the other hand, achieved reaffirmation of the tacit agreement with Israel that had been in place, *in writing*. This document, often referred to as the 'April Understanding,' made explicit the Party of God's right to continue resistance activities against Israeli and SLA combatants within the 'Security Zone'.

Affirmation of Hezbollah's right to resist Israeli occupation in an agreement signed by the USA, France and Israel seemed to deal quite a blow to the terrorist image the Party of God had been trying to shed. With international recognition of the role it was playing in the South, the Party of God seemed well placed to continue its armed struggle against Israel without further challenges based on alleged terrorist activities. Of course Damascus remained the only member on the new committee with enough influence over Hezbollah to 'reason' with the Islamists should their cooperation in calming Lebanon's southern front be needed in the future. Syria was also pleased that the monitoring committee idea initiated by France disturbed US hegemony in the region.

Among other Israeli notables disappointed with their government's Lebanon policy, Gideon Rafael, a founding member of the Israeli foreign ministry, also pointed out the negative results of Israel's use of force in Lebanon. On 14 May, shortly after the Grapes of Wrath campaign came to its disastrous conclusion, Rafael wrote a commentary that appeared on the Op-Ed page of the *International Herald Tribune*. In it he said: 'The complexity of the situation in Lebanon, and the way the recent conflict ended there, made it imperative to get direct negotiations between Israel and Syria over their "broader differences" back on track.' These negotiations, he added, should take into account Syria's special interest in Lebanon and also include the temporary situation (the Israeli occupation) in Southern Lebanon. As we know, this advice was not heeded by the Israeli authorities. Moreover, the strategy to pressure Beirut to curb Hezbollah by perpetrating massive destruction on the country's infrastructure was not abandoned but actually used three more times between 1999 and 2000 in various degrees. Each time this strategy proved as politically threadbare as previously and each time it again took unfortunate tolls in Lebanon far beyond the southern battlefield as will be described later.

## POST-'VICTORY' FRICTIONS

Strategic gains on the part of Syria and its allies, it should be remembered, were mainly the result of the containment of intense competition between the Lebanese actors. It is not surprising, therefore, that almost immediately after the ceasefire and the 'April understanding' between Israel and Lebanon came into effect, a much-publicized quarrel broke out between Prime Minister Hariri and Hezbollah officials. Hariri accused the Party of God of trying to monopolize and politicize the resistance, while Sayyed Nasrallah retorted that no one was barred from joining the resistance in its struggle to end Israeli occupation of the South. [13]

Government and Hezbollah leaders also squabbled over who had the right to assist those displaced in the conflict and who should allocate reconstruction funds. This friction arose because Hezbollah contested Damascus' 'rule' that the state has sole responsibility for citizens north of the 'Security Zone'. Acting for the state by channelling government assistance to southerners was the Party of God's rival, Nabih Berri. Although citizens were requested to reject indemnities from any agency other than the state's Council for the South (which answers to Berri), by the end of June Hezbollah's engineering and contracting group, Jihad al-Binaa (Reconstruction Campaign) heavily underwritten by Iran, announced that it had already rehabilitated more than 2,800 structures damaged by the Israelis in 106 locations in the South and would be undertaking reconstruction in the Bekaa and Beirut shortly.[14]

As charges and retorts flew back and forth between government officials and Hezbollah leaders, several impressive demonstrations took place in support of the latter. One of them featured an unprecedented parade of hundreds of cars carrying Hezbollah placards and flags that circled West Beirut one evening for several hours in a clear show of support. In the southern suburb, heavily armed Hezbollah fighters in black face masks and a group dressed in the white shrouds of martyrs made its way through a gigantic crowd assembled to hear an address by Sayyed Nasrallah. As might have been expected, Nasrallah adopted a mainly Islamist frame of reference for this speech and, in an oblique reference to the government's quibbling, swore that no power on earth could prevent his organization from accomplishing its sacred jihad duty.

I have devoted considerable space to the internal friction generated by Hezbollah's struggle with Israel, because it well illustrates a unique and serious problem with which Hezbollah leaders must still grapple from time to time. Fortunately for their jihad, Syria is there to remind government officials where their interests lie.

The controversy over how much and what kind of resistance had won the day, and who should assist the southerners soon settled down to normally stiff relations between Hezbollah and the government as attacks against the Israelis in the 'Security Zone' resumed. By the end of June 1996, only two months after the ceasefire had taken effect, the Islamic guerrillas had already killed nine Israeli soldiers and wounded 21. Dire consequences 'that would not spare Lebanese civilians' and 'that would surprise the terrorists' were threatened after each attack by spokesmen of the new Israeli government headed by Ehud Barak, the man who would finally preside over his country's troop withdrawal from Lebanon in spring 2000.

At that time the Lebanese actors' capacity to grapple with the various opportunities and emergencies that would arise as Israel prepared and executed its long-awaited departure would be tested.

# Chapter Nine

# The Collapse of the 'Security Zone'

As Hezbollah attacks inside the 'Security Zone' continued and Israeli casualties mounted, the Barak government began exploring the possibility of a unilateral withdrawal from southern Lebanon in exchange for security guarantees along the internationally demarcated Lebanon-Israel border. Hezbollah leaders immediately crowed that their fighters had 'brought the Israelis and their allies to their knees'. However, keeping the goal of their mission in view, they threatened dire results if withdrawal was attempted without concluding negotiations with the Syrian and Lebanese governments first.

That exchange in 1999 represented the opening thrusts of a new struggle that would be waged on several fronts to reap policy benefits for Syria and Lebanon out of the anticipated departure of Israeli troops and the expected defeat of the SLA. For this development to take place, several critical issues would have to be addressed. For instance, since Israel looked as if it might withdraw its troops without making a deal that would include negotiations with Syria over the Golan Heights, the question of how the resistance card could be retained in the aftermath of the withdrawal would require careful planning and tight coordination between the Lebanese and Syrian governments and Hezbollah. Another important concern was whether the coordinating parties could manage the controversy created by a few local Lebanese groups and encourage withdrawal without losing control over the areas that would be evacuated. Both internal and external pressure to send the Lebanese army into the vacuum created by Israel's departure was anticipated and this pressure would have to be countered if Hezbollah was to carry on its mission. These issues were extremely sensitive, since any mistakes would be extremely costly in terms of domestic and regional support.

Furthermore, in terms of the continuity of the struggle against Israel, Hezbollah's comportment during the delicate operation would be extremely critical in illustrating the difference between the image it had hoped for as a national resistance and the terrorist stereotype America and Israel were still insisting on. With the eyes of the world trained on South Lebanon in months to come, Hezbollah would have an opportunity to promote its resistance face through handling the withdrawal in a manner befitting a legitimate – and ultimately successful – resistance group. If past experience were any gauge, that politico-military struggle would be as complex and fine-tuned as any other one that had pitted this fundamentalist group against the Israelis over the past decade. Here, for the first time, is an in-depth analysis of exactly how it was handled.

## ISRAEL'S 'SECURITY ZONE' BEGINS TO SHRINK

Hezbollah leaders were very conscious of the opportunities offered by the plummeting morale among SLA fighters as their masters debated departure plans. The expectations of SLA members were that if they surrendered they ran the risk of having acts of revenge perpetrated against themselves and their families by neighbours or Hezbollah men. They were also certain that they would face prosecution by the Lebanese government for crimes against the state, including treason, which could carry a death sentence. While refuge in Israel might be an option for some, the scope and dimensions of the assistance that would be extended to them by the Israelis had not yet been established as the Israeli army started to demolish certain military posts in the 'Security Zone'.

The Party of God exploited these apprehensions in several ways. On the one hand, flexing its muscle as the power on the ground in the area, leniency was promised to any SLA foot soldier that defected before the full withdrawal took place. This was an important and understandable tactic that party leaders were employing in their psychological battle with the Israeli army and the SLA. On the other hand, according to knowledgeable sources that requested anonymity, senior Lebanese government officials were privately irritated with such out-of-turn posturing by Hezbollah.

At the same time, attacks against Israeli soldiers and SLA fighters in the 'Security Zone' were stepped up. Roadside ambushes of passing patrols were particularly effective along the long corridor linking the large Christian town of Jezzine to the 'Security Zone'.[1] Although most of the trees on both sides of the main artery were cut down and the asphalt was ripped up to uncover hidden mines and roadside bombs, guerrilla attacks were still taking a toll for reasons to be described later. SLA defections in that locale thus became a serious matter for the Israelis in 1999 and it soon became obvious that the Jezzine area, including some 22 villages with a population of about 4,000, could no longer effectively be held. When four military posts were closed down in that area in April and May and no Israeli troops were introduced to strengthen the sector, as had been done many times in the past when combat intensified along that front, it was clear that evacuation of the town of Jezzine and the rest of the area was imminent.

On 1 June 1999, the SLA militia began a disorderly withdrawal, explained by Commander Antoine Lahd as an attempt to save Jezzine from a slow death. Lahd warned against 'the deployment or infiltration of those that call themselves a resistance' since the Israeli attacks that would follow would provoke a definitive exodus of the population.[2] He therefore called for the immediate deployment of the Lebanese Army to guarantee the security and dignity of Jezzine's inhabitants during and after the evacuation of his troops.

As it transpired, the army was neither brought in nor Hezbollah kept out. The issue of sending the army to the border area to protect inhabitants from reprisals by Hezbollah's fighters had been heatedly debated among government officials and Christian political and religious leaders for months before the Jezzine evacuation. While the latter were naturally concerned over possible harm to co-religionists, insinuations that Hezbollah would threaten the southerners formerly under Israeli control were hardly credible. After all, the Christian villages of Saidun and Amal had been evacuated for more than a year before Jezzine was abandoned, and no security incidents had occurred there. Furthermore, it was only logical that if Hezbollah desired more defections, the last thing leaders and field commanders would allow would be any incident involving their fighters and local inhabitants. Another reason for Hezbollah to take important steps to protect Christian and Shiite inhabitants in formerly occupied areas was related to me by a Hezbollah partisan who was studying medicine at the American University of Beirut. This individual said that, as those who would soon be 'liberated' would be choosing their representatives in the 2000 parliamentary elections, the last thing Hezbollah would want to do is alienate them and thus lose their votes!

While security incidents could not be entirely ruled out, the real motivation of the Christian opposition leaders was more the hastening of the departure of Syria's troops. The sooner the presence of the Lebanese Army could be firmly established in the former 'Security Zone', they believed, the sooner it would be absolutely clear that Lebanon no longer needed the Syrian Army in the country to help re-establish its authority. Since that would clearly undermine Hezbollah's role along the border and thus threaten the foreign policy being implemented, the authorities stuck to their position that beefing up the internal security forces in the region would provide sufficient security to the inhabitants.

As the SLA began abandoning checkpoints and posts around Jezzine, an ad hoc system of dealing with the chaotic situation emerged. For its part, Hezbollah kept the pressure on those who were trying to regroup at other locations, taking great care not to subject the evacuated villages to incoming fire from the Israelis covering the retreat. While this was happening, SLA members who wanted to turn themselves in generally accompanied the local priest to a church. There they awaited the arrival of the government security forces that would take charge of them. A favourable security report from Jezzine MP Nadim Salem and former MP Edmond Rizk indicated that this system was working smoothly. That helped calm apprehensions about the risks involved in surrender. After a meeting with 100 surrendering militiamen in Jezzine, Salem and Rizk announced that they had received assurances from the state and from the resistance that the security of these men and others who turn themselves in was guaranteed. They indicated that they themselves were not worried about eventual problems.[3]

Defections picked up speed as the SLA militiamen realized that it was safe to surrender. However, the question of how safe Jezzine's inhabitants felt without the army present was one of interest. According to some residents that were interviewed by a Lebanese daily newspaper, the most important issue was not one of fear of Hezbollah or Amal fighters, but that the region would be open to anyone that wished to enter. They indicated that as it was, if problems arose, contacts could always be made with Amal and Hezbollah leaders to solve them, but an influx of outsiders might cause difficulties that could not be so easily resolved.[4] Although this was not explained, the villagers were most likely apprehensive of random harassment by individuals and groups who might blame them for collaboration with the enemy during the years of occupation. The mayor, who was also interviewed, indicated that he thought that the 280 soldiers who had been posted at nearby Homsiyyah for many years could take over the checkpoints of Bater and Kfarfalous to control comings and goings to and from the region and that some internal security agents would reinforce Jezzine's seven gendarmes and the seven posted in the nearby town of Sfaray. The mayor thought that if this could be managed, there would be no need to send army units.[5]

In a visit to Jezzine soon after its evacuation, I had to show special authorization and my passport at the army post at Bater and undergo a thorough inspection of my car before being allowed to proceed. The security system set up was apparently working very well and those I spoke with in the town were going about their business unperturbed, relieved, as one said, to see the end of a long nightmare.

The manner in which Hezbollah harassed the departing SLA troops and left the government to handle those who wished to surrender – each party again functioning on its designated track – established the basic procedures that would be taken when future SLA surrenders occurred. The message it sent to the SLA was: 'You may safely surrender and you will be taken into custody by the state. If you do not surrender, then you have to take your chances with the resistance.'

On 24 June, in response to stepped-up Hezbollah activity as SLA units made their way to the large town of Marjayoun and other points to regroup, Israeli warplanes bombarded two electricity transformers – one in the northern part of the country near Tripoli – to try to force the government to rein in Hezbollah. However, as in 1993 and 1996, this tactic failed to get results and the ruined equipment was quickly replaced through the generosity of Saudi Prince Alwaleed bin Talal, whose mother is Lebanese. The Israeli raid was most likely undertaken not because positive political results were expected from Beirut, but because the Barak government thought that some action was needed to show the public that everything possible was being done to try to relieve the pressure their troops and the SLA were experiencing from Hezbollah.

As withdrawal from various posts continued, Hezbollah ceased efforts to prod defections by offering clemency and instead published a manifesto in which 'the worst torments to traitors' were promised. It could be inferred from this statement that Hezbollah and not the government would later be dealing with collaborators. Yet, despite the Party of God's posturing and apparent disregard of the state's authority to mete out justice, there was no negative reaction from Lebanese government officials. Apparently the two actors had switched to the carrot and stick routine, where the state dangled the carrot of imprisonment in government jails and fair and individual trials in military courts for any militiaman who surrendered, while Hezbollah promised hell to the recalcitrant.

Who should be punished for cooperating with the Israelis and what penalties should be received after surrender was an issue that surfaced at this time. Hezbollah MP Mohammed Raad had raised the issue previously in parliament in January 1998, a year before defections began. At that time Raad proposed that exemptions from the Penal Code be made if militiamen quit their organization under their own impetus within three months following promulgation of the law. However, the issue had not been decided. Now, however, calls for a general amnesty of SLA militiamen began to arise from some quarters. The head of Parliament's Administration and Justice Committee, Shaker Abu Suleiman, explained that if exemption from the sanctions required by the Penal Code for collusion with the enemy were to be granted, it would nevertheless first be necessary to investigate these individuals and judge them before a state tribunal could grant them amnesty.[6] As it later transpired, militiamen of the Jezzine area and all others who turned themselves in afterwards, were transported to Roumieh Central Prison near the capital, where they awaited individual investigation of their cases. They were then brought before military judges who excused some individuals outright and meted out light fines and/or two or three years of imprisonment to most of the ordinary SLA foot soldiers who appeared before them. Those charged with serious crimes received years of forced labour as punishment. As of summer 2001, approximately 1,200 men had faced judgment and Hezbollah officials were complaining that some of these men were being allowed to reintegrate into the South too easily.

The judicial process established was nevertheless not free of criticism. Amnesty International levelled charges at the government that the trials were hasty and ill prepared and that torture was being used to elicit information from some detainees. For its part, Hezbollah was blamed for sometimes interceding when SLA members were being taken into custody. Their response was that their operatives were the only ones who knew which of the SLA soldiers were double agents and which were not and which ones might be expected to provide information that was vital to future operations against the enemy.

These security gaps received surprisingly little public attention, most likely because it was generally felt that the established process was protecting most of the prisoners from immediate harm and was probably as good as they could expect given their collusion with the enemy. For their part, the SLA officers were not about to chance this system of justice and most had taken refuge with their families in Israel or had already made their way to the West.[7]

## HIGH-TECH, LOW-TECH JIHAD PAYS OFF

Hezbollah's plan was to stampede the Israelis and the SLA into as disorderly and as costly a withdrawal as possible by imposing casualties that further eroded the troops' morale and increased domestic pressure for their departure. Strategists therefore aimed at clever operations that would emphasize Hezbollah's implacability and long reach and demonstrate the enemy's vulnerability. What sorts of actions would successfully propagate those images while still allowing the Party of God to disclaim charges of terrorism?

An operation that had been successfully carried out in 1997 was the sort now required. At that time, Hezbollah communications experts were able to uncover Israeli plans to infiltrate a squad of men into Lebanon under cover of darkness. The elite force of Israeli naval commandos, who may have been on a mission to kidnap or assassinate a Party of

God figure, were surprised as they were making their way inland near Sidon. Lying in wait in a grove of banana trees, Hezbollah fighters annihilated them as they approached.

The impact of this action on the Israeli government and public, as well as on the Arab world, was heightened by the fact that the incident had been captured on videotape by a Hezbollah camera crew that was there with the guerrillas to record the ambush. Israeli military reporters were apparently severely embarrassed by the broadcast of the video on television, since their own reportage had been severely restricted by the Israeli army. Since the Lebanese government had been carrying out a campaign to brand the Israelis rather than Hezbollah as terrorists for years, the fact that Israeli operatives had been caught red-handed while on a presumed assassination or kidnapping mission inside Lebanon was quite a propaganda coup.

When asked by a reporter to explain how this operation had been achieved, a Hezbollah spokesman said off-handedly: 'We just penetrated Israeli intelligence, that's all.'[8]

Actions of a similar impact began to take place in the early months of 2000. One was the assassination, on 30 January 2000, of Colonel Akl Hashim, the SLA's second highest-ranking officer, while he was at home in Marjayoun, a large town in the 'Security Zone'. This action, carried out despite heavy security precautions in the SLA heartland, provided further evidence of Hezbollah's skill and its enemies' weaknesses. A week later, on 6 February, Hezbollah's operatives carried out an ambush that resulted in several Israeli soldiers wounded and the death of the Israeli medic who was tending them. The footage of the depressing incident appeared over and over on Israeli news broadcasts. Then, only three weeks later, a roadside bomb killed Brigadier General Eretz Gerstein, the top Israeli military liaison officer to South Lebanon, as his car passed it in a military convoy. Hezbollah again recorded the incident and rushed the video to Beirut, where it was copied and featured on all the regional news broadcasts. Hezbollah was pressing home the point that any Israeli military personnel on Lebanese soil was fair game and that even high-ranking officers were not safe. Lebanese friends with whom I watched the recording of this operation on the evening news expressed surprise about the pinpoint accuracy of the explosion that demolished Gerstein's vehicle, since it was known that Herculean efforts were being made by SLA troops to sweep the roadsides for the hidden explosives that had taken such a toll on their patrols.

As a result of these kinds of operations, Hezbollah's other tactics became the object of great public interest. In an interview given to a weekly news magazine, Sheikh Nabil Qaouk, Hezbollah's chief of military operations, indicated that the Party of God was continuously trying to devise new uses for its weaponry.[9] One example he gave was that of an old Soviet T55 tank (probably one acquired from Syria) that was hidden in a cave and used to fire sporadically at Israeli positions. He said it took Israeli troops months to find the tank, since it was never driven and did not show up on Israeli heat sensors. Other tactics Qaouk explained involved the use of remote-controlled anti-tank rockets, which can be steered in flight. These were directed into the small openings of the concrete bunkers that dotted the Israeli-Lebanese border. Hezbollah's fighters also learned how to jam Israel's radar and closed-circuit TV monitors. At the same time, Hezbollah had perfected what Qaouk, considered the mastermind of these operations, called clever 'low-tech' methods of guerrilla warfare. One of these was the use of artificial boulders, which could be bought for landscaping purposes at $15 each, into which roadside bombs were inserted. Explosives were also placed among the low branches of trees rather than on the ground where SLA fighters would be looking for them. Herds of sheep were often used to throw off Israeli heat-sensing equipment while the guerrillas changed their positions or attempted to momentarily distract Israeli and SLA lookouts while certain activities were carried out.

Qaouk made the point that a large part of the resistance's success was due to the fact that the men under his command could melt away into a sympathetic population after operations: 'While the Israelis were exposed – we were not,' he said. Moreover, by limiting firing that could draw counter-fire, Qaouk explained, 'we were able to keep the cards in our hands, and to carry out the small battles in which we had the advantage'. From this discussion, it seemed that Hezbollah was applying well-known guerrilla warfare tactics to achieve its military strategy, although the Israelis labelled the acts against their military personnel and the SLA as terrorism.

The use of Katyusha rockets, Qaouk added, was always very carefully considered and these weapons were fired only in response to Israeli attacks that took a toll on Lebanese civilians. I observed that since this was a very important part of the strategy to combat an image of Hezbollah as wantonly attacking Israeli civilians, it was critical that only Hezbollah and not Amal or any other group be in control of these weapons.

There was one other point that Qaouk emphasized as an important Hezbollah asset and that was that 'the Israeli soldier didn't believe in the struggle. He knew he was implementing a failed policy'. As a result, he noted, with only about 500 field operatives active at any one time, Hezbollah over the years wore down its adversaries and finally brought about the collapse of what had been a corps of 1,500 well-armed Israeli regulars and 2,500 SLA militiamen. Qaouk's report omitted any reference to Iran's assistance in supplying the weaponry necessary for this war of attrition, as well as Syria's help in securing the support of the Lebanese government, both also vital to the campaign against Israel and the SLA.

## GUERRILLA WARFARE IN THE COMMUNICATIONS AGE

By fielding an increasingly effective media team to videotape the general situation in the South and the daily attacks launched against the enemy, Hezbollah's television station, al-Manar, became the favoured source of information for those who wanted to closely follow events in the South. While other Lebanese broadcasters and foreign television journalists could only record Israeli/Hezbollah skirmishes from safe positions well behind the lines, Hezbollah cameramen, as noted above, often filmed right at the confrontation point. This left no doubt about what tactics were being used against the Israelis and backed up Qaouk's report that Hezbollah's targets were military personnel inside Lebanon, not innocent Israeli civilians. Besides the obvious damage to the enemy's morale, the television coverage also boosted Hezbollah's national, Arab and Islamic revolutionary images to all-time highs in a region searching for heroes.

The extent to which this might be true in Lebanon was brought home to me one night after the evacuation of Jezzine when I was returning by car to my home in West Beirut. On one side of Charles al-Khoury Boulevard a noisy parade of captured Israeli vehicles – tanks, armoured personnel carriers and trucks – draped with the Hezbollah colours and ridden by jubilant fighters – was cranking along. Swarms of young men on motorcycles waving Hezbollah's yellow banners wove in and out of the crowd following it. Traffic on my side of the highway had come to a complete standstill as many motorists abandoned their vehicles to see the amazing sight. One enthusiastic motorist who had pulled over and got out of his car apparently thought he should explain what was happening to the foreigner. 'This is the first time I remember that there has ever been a victory over the Israelis to celebrate in this part of the world!' he said.

A similar Hezbollah cavalcade was reported to have gone straight through Achrafieh, the Christian quarter of the capital, where it apparently met with a more restrained reception. I asked one of my Hezbollah students why he thought the jubilant partisans had done that when they knew their parade would not get the reaction given it in the Muslim quarters of the city there. He said they may have thought that since Hezbollah's feats against the Israelis and the SLA constituted a national victory, why should one sector be exempt from the celebration? Looked at from another perspective, however, it might simply have been impossible for Hezbollah partisans to resist cruising the district where the Israeli invasion had been so warmly received in 1982, in Israeli vehicles.

The struggle in South Lebanon was changing some minds about Hezbollah. Whereas the Israelis had previously capitalized on the 'David image' as opposed to the Arabs' Goliath, Hezbollah was widely perceived in Lebanon and elsewhere in the region as having now put the shoe on the other foot. As a result of its dogged little war in South Lebanon, the Party of God was being recognized as possessing the invincibility that only Israeli commandos had previously enjoyed.

However, the leaders never short-changed the religious meaning of their jihad activities for their national liberation importance. One way this could be seen was the way in which Hezbollah dealt with the deaths of fighters in action. Unlike armed groups that try to minimize or even hide their losses to maintain an image of military strength, Islam's celebration of martyrdom in righteous wars against infidels meant that Hezbollah's casualties were given high exposure on al-Manar TV, mentioned often in speeches and sermons and featured on roadside posters. This approach also meant that the extent to which Hezbollah partisans were committed to God and country on the southern battlefield was constantly reinforced for public consumption at home and across the border. All of these activities strengthened Arab and Muslim support for the Party of God's militant activities and fortified the image Hezbollah was trying to convey to the Israelis, the SLA and the world – that of righteous fury backed up by unassailable national rights.

## DIPLOMACY AND THE ISRAELI WITHDRAWAL

As Hezbollah was applying its end game in the field, the Lebanese authorities were sparring with Israeli officials over the conditions under which the former would finally withdraw all its troops south of the Lebanese border. Predictably, the Israeli authorities continued to seek guarantees for the safety of their troops and members of the SLA as more and more military posts were abandoned in the 'Security Zone'. They were urging the Lebanese government to have the army move in immediately to ensure that order was maintained in the evacuated zone so that their northern border would remain calm. A probation period of some six to nine months was suggested, during which time the Lebanese Army backed by the UN peacekeeping force in place in South Lebanon would cooperate with the Israeli occupation troops. This arrangement would have ended Hezbollah's jihad activities and was flatly rejected by the Lebanese government on the basis of the wording of Security Council Resolutions 425 and 426. These resolutions demanded unconditional withdrawal of Israeli forces and stipulated the measures that must be taken to verify their retreat. Beirut officials also reiterated the now-familiar line that it was out of the question – in fact, political suicide – to rein in an active resistance, which had recently been gaining more legitimacy as the enemy suffered more and more losses. However, it was also made quite clear that security guarantees might be in order if agreements on the return of all Arab land occupied by Israel could be achieved. This was the 'land for peace' option. Failing this – in other words, since a state of war would still be prevailing – Lebanese leaders asked why they should make Israel's retreat easier and why they should protect Israel's northern border for it.

Hassan Nasrallah weighed in on this debate by drawing a parallel between the behaviour of the Lebanese resistance and that of the Vietcong. He pointed out that the operations Vietcong guerrillas had been undertaking against American forces in Vietnam had not ceased while the Paris negotiations between North Vietnamese and American representatives were taking place. He also emphasized that there was no guarantee that Israel would indeed withdraw from *all* occupied territory and that this could not be ascertained until withdrawal actually took place. During this period, the Hezbollah leader remarked, it was clear and right that resistance activities should not be restrained.[10] For his part, Sheikh Qaouk kept his organization's relentless and muscled image to the forefront of this quarrel when he shot out that 'even if negotiations *were* held and regardless of their results, Hezbollah will force Israel to withdraw in catastrophic conditions, under fire, so no further attacks on Lebanon will ever be contemplated'.[11]

The adamancy with which the Lebanese government refused to 'help' the Israelis depart became grist for more than one propaganda mill. The Israelis, who had ignored all Security Council resolutions calling for their departure from Lebanon for more than two decades, now made much of the fact that their intended move was fully in compliance with those resolutions. They branded Lebanon's position an obstruction of the international will as expressed in those resolutions. They also tried hard to strum chords of sectarian fear by suggesting that when their troops departed, the 'terrorists' would rush into the villages that had enjoyed SLA and Israeli protection and wreak revenge on the inhabitants as collaborators. Despite the fact that nothing like that had happened after the Jezzine withdrawal and others, they seemed to be using images of the atrocities that had taken place between Christians and Muslims in some areas during the Lebanese civil war to buttress their argument that the 'terrorists' must be replaced by the Lebanese Army.

Arguing along similar lines but without applying the terrorist stereotype to Hezbollah, Maronite Christian political and religious leaders had been stepping up their own campaign to send the army to the South since the Jezzine evacuation. Their position and the strong support it gained from the community's traditional ally, the French,[12] caused a great deal of disgruntlement within government, leftist and

Muslim circles and seemed to widen the old sectarian chasm that had so disastrously divided Lebanon during the civil war.

Hezbollah leaders were aware that continued military activities along the Israeli/Lebanese frontier rested very heavily on the ethical behaviour of their fighters. Altercations between villagers and Hezbollah partisans had to be prevented at all costs as they could easily be branded terrorism or religious fanaticism and used to demand Hezbollah's removal from the border area. Therefore, Hezbollah members were ordered to demonstrate strict discipline in any dealings with the locals in the former 'Security Zone'.

Seeking to allay Christian villagers' fears of mistreatment by Hezbollah, Party of God leaders adopted several measures to deal with that problem. For some time before the Israeli retreat began, in press conferences and interviews, they had invoked tenets of Islam and Christianity regarding mutual tolerance and understanding to demonstrate their peaceful intentions toward the southern population. Now, to demonstrate that they held no grudge against the southern Christians, Hezbollah leaders also let it be known that they considered the civilian population as having been held hostage to a few misguided individuals and in no way to blame for the Israeli occupation. At one press conference, Nasrallah explained Hezbollah's position on this issue as follows: 'Whether Muslim or Christian, the majority of people in the "Security Zone" are an oppressed people... they are our kin and we fight for their freedom.'[13] These conciliatory positions also served to further the Party of God's image as a national resistance organization that respected the security and rights of all citizens.

As the long-awaited final Israeli pull-out drew near, Hezbollah and the Lebanese authorities were each handling the specific tasks allotted to them and were also reinforcing each other's positions when it seemed useful to do so. At all times during this charged and fairly chaotic period, they were fully in line with the foreign policy Syria had been orchestrating for the past decade.

## THE END OF THE 'SECURITY ZONE'

While the Israelis prepared for what they considered their final withdrawal in May, defections continued to gut the SLA. The Shiite component had completely collapsed in the central sector of the 'Security Zone' and, after 200 SLA militiamen turned themselves in to the Lebanese authorities in early May, it was also crumbling in the western part. By Monday 22 May, the occupation zone had split in two and SLA militiamen in both parts were on the run. Eyewitness accounts and television coverage allows the following picture of that chaotic day to be recreated.

As news spread of the imminent departure of SLA soldiers from various villages, villagers who had been expelled from the 'Security Zone' over the years waited as close as they could get to their villages to go home. In many instances, despite warnings from UN officials, they began surging toward their villages before the SLA soldiers had completely evacuated them. In one such case, some 500 jubilant villagers entered Houla ahead of throngs of Hezbollah and Amal fighters whose military activities against the departing SLA and Israeli troops were thus cancelled by their presence. According to an eyewitness account of the day's activities along one of the main roads in the area, this particular crowd then decided to keep moving toward Markaba, a village a few miles to the north. There, however, the SLA had not yet abandoned the checkpoint they held at the entrance to the village. As the crowd approached, SLA men feverishly blocked the road with a mound of earth. Five Israeli Apache helicopters then appeared and began strafing the road ahead of two teenagers on bicycles who were leading the ragtag advance. Israeli Merkava tanks came into sight and took up positions near an artillery piece aimed at Markaba. The helicopters continued strafing the road north of Markaba to deter villagers from approaching while new SLA lines were set up at the entrance to another nearby village, Addaysah. At the same time, heavy explosions began to be heard as retreating SLA fighters started blowing up cement bunkers and outposts along this route.

At another point, a crowd that had assembled near a burning tank that had been exploded by missiles fired from a helicopter found the Israelis determined to block their advance on Meiss al-Jabal. According to the accompanying reporter, they retreated a bit when a tank round exploded nearby and heavy machine-gun fire broke out, but remained ready to move forward jeering and taunting the Israelis. Further down the same road, two Lebanese civilians were killed by tank shells and three others by machine-gun fire as they tried the same manoeuvre. Some 21 other Lebanese civilians were wounded in the day's events. While fighting was reported around Tyre as Hezbollah harassed retreating SLA troops and met tank fire, there were nevertheless no casualties there.[14]

These incidents were reported in detail to shed light on the nature of the day's events. The Israelis and SLA partisans wanted to get out quickly and safely and only engaged in rearguard skirmishes. For its part, Hezbollah couldn't do much to punish its enemies on their way out of Lebanon, because crowds of villagers running ahead of their fighters in many areas got in the way. There were no instances of fleeing Israeli troops surrounded and punished and no vendettas. On the other hand, a lot of taunting and posturing on the part of Hezbollah, Amal and the public took place and this caused casualties. By evening, villagers and Lebanese combatants were busily sorting through the piles of abandoned Israeli materiel left behind and happy children were videoed swinging from the guns of abandoned tanks or dancing around waving the Lebanese flag. The spontaneous reaction of the returning villagers was captured on film and used to support the government's contention and Hezbollah's that the national resistance was very popular. The celebration of Israel's departure continued for weeks, only reinforcing that impression.

The most emotional of the events, however, was undoubtedly the liberation of Lebanese prisoners that had been held at the detention centre at Khiam. Built by the SLA and Israelis to hold captured members and sympathizers of Hezbollah and other political opponents – some of whom were young women – the facility was a loathsome symbol of the occupation. On 23 May, when hordes of villagers and guerrilla fighters entered the prison compound and began to sledgehammer the iron doors of cells and freeing those incarcerated, emotions were at their highest level. Al-Manar TV was there broadcasting these events live.

Some of the people whose releases were covered had been detained for more than ten years and had no idea what was happening. When two of the captives, who were father and daughter, stumbled out of their cells into the daylight and embraced, the attending crowds went wild. I was watching that scene on television with neighbours, and there wasn't a dry eye in the room. Plans are now under way to convert the former prison complex into a physical and psychological rehabilitation centre for former detainees.

The following day I went south, along with what seemed to be most of the Lebanese population. Thousands of passenger cars, taxis, trucks and buses jammed with jubilant flag-waving passengers crept along the bomb-cratered roads near the border. People swarmed over the rubble of Israeli-SLA bunkers that had been blown up by the evacuating forces, searching for 'souvenirs'. The Khiam detention facility, its main gate draped with Hezbollah banners and manned by partisans in uniform, was thronged with people and encumbered by Japanese, Spanish, German and other media caravans setting up equipment near al-Manar TV's central location. Visitors peered into the empty cells and climbed up and down the steep stairs of the prison. Some tots wore guerrilla outfits and carried toy guns. Elsewhere, at the entrance of some villages I drove through, crowds lined the street ready with rose petals, candies and rice to toss at local sons and politicians whose arrival was expected imminently. Some were making their returns after absences of more than 20 years.

Along the border fence, crowds were already gathering to taunt and throw stones at the Israeli soldiers manning observation towers on the other side. A visit to the Fatima gate – the former main point of passage between Lebanon and Israel – and the casting of a stone in defiance of the Israelis became a rite for almost all visitors to the border area. Unfortunately, this behaviour later resulted in the death and injury of several people whose more strenuous efforts drew the fire of Israeli soldiers. As a result of this hubbub, Israel turned a strip of some 500 metres wide on its side of the border into a military zone. The Clinton government reportedly gave Israel $5 million to execute this project – funds originally earmarked for a similar project on the Lebanese side where the Lebanese Army was to be on guard.

Those who could not go to the South during the wildest days of celebration could take advantage of al-Manar TV's extensive television coverage of events there. Talk shows and interviews emphasized Hezbollah's role in the event being celebrated as well as the role Islam played in their victory.

## RESISTANCE CHALLENGES AND THEIR RESOLUTION

Now what would happen? The world soon learned that Israel's withdrawal had not put an end to Syria's 'state/resistance' policy by eliminating Hezbollah's combat role in the South. This fact was broadcast from Beirut the very day of the Israeli pull-out when, in a speech addressed to the nation, President Lahoud declared that this victory was still not enough to realize the comprehensive peace desired. For that to occur, he said, Israel must return all Arab lands, including Lebanon's Shebaa Farms region, a strip of water-rich territory 25 kilometres long and eight wide that constitutes about two per cent of Lebanon's total area.[15] Why had the Israelis not evacuated Shebaa at the time of their withdrawal?

The quick answer to this question is that they were not required to evacuate Shebaa as part of Security Council Resolutions 425 and 426, although the Lebanese authorities took a different view of this rather complex situation. Here is how the dispute over the mountainous and largely undeveloped area came about. Indications are that Shebaa has always been part of Lebanon; however, at the beginning of the 1960s, Syria had deployed security agents in the district to try to prevent cross-border smuggling. When the area was captured by Israel during the 1967 Arab-Israeli war there was a Syrian military presence there rather than a Lebanese one.

The United Nations position on the Shebaa issue is based on the fact that the area had to be treated differently from the rest of the 'Security Zone' since it was under UN jurisdiction initiated by agreement of Syria and Israel to disengage in 1973. At that time, the adversaries asked the Security Council to dispatch a UN Disengagement Observation Force (UNDORF) to the area, and in 1974, by Resolution 350, the force arrived and remained in place. In 1978, after the Israeli invasion of Lebanon and when Resolutions 425 and 426 were enacted, the United Nations

Interim Force in Lebanon (UNIFIL) was created to cover another part of the border area. In order not to overlap with UNDORF, Shebaa was excluded from UNIFIL's area. Here it must be remembered that in 2000, the UN was not actually setting the international borderline between Israel and Lebanon but was tracing a 'blue line' between the two countries using maps as references to establish the line of Israeli withdrawal. The 'blue line' excluded Shebaa as being a separate case. It had come under UN jurisdiction when Syrian troops were fighting Israel and the agreement to disengage was between those two states at the time, so, regardless of whether it was Lebanese land or not, it was decided that it would have to fall under Resolution 242. This resolution required Israeli occupied land to be returned to Syria, rather than to Lebanon. The Israeli-annexed Golan Heights falls under that resolution as well. Although Syria declared Shebaa to be Lebanese land and both governments presented documents to that effect, they were not considered by the Security Council as constituting sufficient evidence to establish Lebanon's claim. However, since Israel was occupying that land at present, it was impossible for Syrian and Lebanese experts to enter the area to carry out the topographical work necessary to clearly identify the border between the two countries that would then finish the issue.[16] (See Map 1: Practical Line of Withdrawal)

Lahoud's remark about the Shebaa Farms thus made clear at the outset that the policy guiding state and resistance activities for the last decade had not been altered a jot as a result of what now was being called Israel's *partial* retreat – or more darkly, its political *manoeuvring*. The Shebaa Farms region was considered occupied Lebanese territory and it would now receive the attention of the resistance.

Hassan Nasrallah also stressed this point at a giant rally in the southern town of Bint Jbeil on Friday 26 May. Facing a crowd of some 100,000 people, including Christians and Muslims, he boasted: 'Barak and his government have no other alternative than to withdraw from the Shebaa Farms area and the coming days will prove that.'

Another important part of Nasrallah's speech concerned his organization's solidarity with the state and its implications for the security of the inhabitants, a point also emphasized by Lahoud. As before, the Hezbollah leader underlined the fact that the victory over Israel belonged to all Lebanese citizens and not to any one party, movement, organization or community. On the other hand, lest anyone forget the price Hezbollah had paid for that victory, he noted that the struggle to liberate the South *to date* (my emphasis) had resulted in 1,276 Hezbollah 'martyrs'.[17]

A short time later, I watched the television broadcast of a ceremony held to honour those combatants to which their families had been invited.

Hezbollah's flare for the dramatic was demonstrated when at one point, while Hassan Nasrallah was making the argument for continuing jihad against the Israelis, the 1,276 black-garbed young men who had volunteered to replace the fallen mujahidin silently filed in and were seated before the podium.

As far as the UN was concerned, Shebaa had been properly dealt with in reference to Security Council Resolution 350 of 1974. Since Lebanon had not been in the picture at that time, the Shebaa Farms area would have to be negotiated between Syria and Israel. The issue was less over which state actually owned the area – that would have to be clearly established later – than over who actually constituted the parties to the dispute.

The Israelis approved of the UN's position, since what was important to them was retaining a military presence in the area to prevent cross-border terrorist attacks and they apparently considered themselves a long distance away from negotiating with Syria over Shebaa. Prime Minister Barak explained Israel's willingness to cooperate with the mapping team by saying in an interview that 'a retreat verified by the UN acquires international legitimacy', which helps Israel's position 'in case of an outbreak of violence at the frontier'.[18] The implication of his remark was that any future military activities by Hezbollah against Israeli outposts in Shebaa would be indefensible in light of the UN's stance, and therefore Israel's position, that Hezbollah was a terrorist organization engaging in violence for which there was no tenable justification, would be substantiated.

As in the case of the Jezzine withdrawal, the issue of 'legal' security within the former occupation zone continued to be raised by leaders of the Christian community and others who wanted the Lebanese Army to take over the border area. However, according to the government, there was a question of incomplete withdrawal that would have to be resolved first. Exactly where the frontier between the two countries lay thus became a critical issue. It was to be resolved as a result of boundary verification carried out in cooperation with United Nations mapping teams in accordance with Security Council Resolution 426.

The UN entered the post-withdrawal scene on a negative footing, as far as the Lebanese authorities were concerned, by warning of 'the confessional trap' in the South if the state did not act quickly to fill the vacuum there. Since this remark echoed the statements of Israeli officials and sectarian issues had not surfaced while the Israeli evacuation had been going on, it was considered biased against Lebanon. The position taken by the United Nations on Shebaa was also disappointing to many Lebanese who believed that their country had been railroaded when the withdrawal line was drawn. An editorial in a Syrian daily suggested that what had happened in South Lebanon 'is only Israeli redeployment under the umbrella of the United Nations'. Thus, the writer asked, 'With nothing finally settled, why should the Lebanese Army replace the resistance?'[19]

The Israelis and their sympathizers nevertheless insisted that their withdrawal had fulfilled the requirements of the international community and had been verified by qualified UN officials, so casting doubt on Hezbollah's real motivations in the South. The position taken by some Lebanese journalists and politicians also hinted that the argument advanced by Hezbollah and the Lebanese and Syrian governments on the issue of Shebaa ownership was merely a lame attempt to justify Hezbollah's continuing struggle against Israel. The editor of the French-language daily newspaper L'Orient-le Jour, for instance, asked why the issue of Israel's occupation of Shebaa Farms had only come up now.[20]

Trying to better understand the issues involved in deciding the Shebaa Farms ownership, I consulted a professor of international law on the subject. He said that he found the question of who – or what authority – has the right to challenge boundaries and declare them valid or invalid was an interesting one. His opinion was that when two sovereign states agree that territory belongs to one of them and their presidents declare it several times publicly and put it down in writing it was probably sufficient. Moreover, he also said that the Shebaa Farms case remained hazy not through lack of facts, but because the Lebanese government had not sufficiently marshalled them to make a solid case for ownership.[21] These facts began to emerge when Celina Nasser's report on property ownership in the Shebaa area was published. Researching the Sidon property registry, Nasser found the deeds for Shebaa Farms registered there and not in Syria.[22] Two years later, an Israeli scholar, Asher Kaufman of the Hebrew University's Truman Institute came to a similar conclusion about Lebanon's ownership, based on information he had located in Paris. The maps and documents relating to Shebaa Farms he found were produced during the period the French held mandates over Lebanon and Syria. One document for instance, provided detailed information on the agreement worked out over a water dispute in the area. In the document, the area is referred to as part of Lebanon. Moreover, the French colonial officials reported that Shebaa residents paid their taxes in Marjayoun, Lebanon. The editorial that reported Asher's work took the Lebanese government to task for the sloppy case it presented to back its claim two years earlier, expressing chagrin that it had taken an Israeli to dig up the records that proved Lebanon's claim.[23]

At any rate, in May 2000, Beirut backed up its claim with the facts to hand and produced Damascus' testimony that the land in question was not Syrian. Since there was no doubt that the Israeli presence in Shebaa was illegal, then forcing their troops to evacuate the area could, according to the Lebanese authorities, be defended as national resistance. Since the Israelis clung to the position that their military presence was needed in the Shebaa area, since the sparseness of population and rough nature of the district made terrorist border infiltration a real possibility, the stage was set for the post-withdrawal conflict to begin.

The question was whether Lebanon's position was credible enough to ward off international pressures led by Israel and the USA to sanction it for non-compliance with a UN decision. Beirut's obstinacy on this issue would obviously facilitate continued military activities along the border by Hezbollah, a group considered by the two countries as a terrorist organization. This question became very important when the USA announced it would pursue terrorists and impose sanctions on any government that failed to halt their activities after the September 11 catastrophes 15 months later.

The pressure on Beirut to send the army south soon lessened. French Foreign Minister Hubert Vedrine, for instance, indicated in an interview in Paris in early June that 'the situation at the frontier is more stable than had been foreseen'.[24] A number of SLA soldiers and their families who had fled to Israel in May then came back across the border and encountered no difficulties. It became obvious to all concerned that the Lebanese government would not change its position, and that security was better than had been envisaged. The internal and external hubbub over sending the army south therefore receded.

As Hezbollah officials received congratulations from delegations of businessmen, journalists, trade union members and Lebanese notables from all walks of life, as well as official Arab delegations for their victory, there was no doubt that they were living their finest hour. Yet Hezbollah's continued jihad rested on whether or not the government reached agreement with the UN over whether Israel had left Lebanon completely or not.

During the month of June, Beirut complained of some 14 Israeli violations of its territory, including the fact that the Israelis had placed the source of the Wazzani River within a barbed wire fence about a dozen yards from the designated frontier *on their side* and were continuing to pump water from it. I spoke to a family I knew from a nearby village about this issue and members told me that the Israeli designation was erroneous because they remembered that before the civil war the frontier was about two or three kilometres from the Wazzani's source and could not even be seen from it.

Issam Khalifah, a professor of history at Lebanese University and an expert on Lebanon's waters and frontiers, confirmed this information in an interview with Agence France Press. He noted that, according to the frontier between Lebanon and Palestine established in 1923 by an agreement known as the Paulet-Newcombe Accord, the frontier is indeed three kilometres (about two miles) to the east of the Hasbani River and thus from the source of the Wazzani. (See Map 2) After the armistice agreement between Lebanon and Israel in 1948, he noted, Lebanese and Israeli teams under supervision of the UN established a definitive tracing of the frontier, dated 12 December 1949. This agreement also confirmed that the source of the river is three kilometres from the frontier. Accordingly, the villages of Ghajar and Nakheili that are occupied by Israel, are also well within Lebanese territory.

Emphasizing the importance of this water resource, Khalifah observed 'each year the Wazzani furnishes dozens of millions of cubic metres (mcm) of water that spill into the Hasbani River'.[25] Settling this particular boundary violation is thus a priority for Beirut but possibly less so for water-scarce Israel.

Hassan Nasrallah took a very high-handed approach to the quarrel over the placement of the 'blue line' and alleged Israeli violations such as the one described above when UN Secretary-General Kofi Annan visited him. At the meeting, the Hezbollah leader bluntly told Annan: 'For us the 'blue line' being traced means nothing... we demand that the UN act quickly on Israeli violations. We will not wait long for international efforts to end these violations and, as we have done in the past, we will work to liberate the smallest parcel of our land.'[26] The fat was in the fire.

Israel's disquiet over the quarrel taking place on its northern border was well expressed in a *Jerusalem Post* article that raised the spectre of a continuing Hezbollah jihad now waged just a few yards away from Israeli settlements. The writer observed that Hezbollah was now getting its hands on the villages that Israel fed, watered and electrified, and that since these locales were in urgent need of services, Hezbollah would soon be installing its medical, educational and religious institutions in them. The writer further predicted that the Party of God's presence along the frontier would lead to a state of permanent tension there and that Barak bore sole responsibility for the withdrawal, which he qualified as 'a failed adventure'.[27]

Some Israeli military men were equally disgruntled by Barak's decision to withdraw Israeli troops from Lebanon. Brigadier General Shlomo Brom, former head of Israeli strategic planning, for instance, had remarked in 1999 that the occupation should be continued until a peace treaty with Syria was reached.[28] While admitting that the Israeli military's vulnerability in Lebanon would be reduced following the withdrawal, he said that that would be at the expense of the civilians and towns in northern Israel. In his view, the abandonment of the 'Security Zone' would permit Hezbollah to operate right along the border. That would increase the range of their guns and enable them to more easily pound the settlers with artillery fire. Brom observed that, while that did not constitute an existential threat to Israel, such attacks would still be extremely painful for any Israeli government. Thus he concluded that '20 or 30 military dead per year as a result of Hezbollah's guerrilla activities' was little compared to the consequences of putting the whole northern population at the mercy of Hezbollah. For his part, Chief of Staff Lt Shaul Mofaz indicated that withdrawal constituted 'an unreasonable risk verging on a gamble'.[29]

The fact that the whole northern population of Israel – some million people – was indeed under Hezbollah's guns after May 2000 and that there also remained areas occupied by Israel that could still be resisted by Hezbollah, constituted an important strategic setback for Israel and an important victory for Hezbollah and its sponsors, Syria and Iran. Since shelling of northern Israeli settlements had occurred in the past, the scenario expressed by the generals was not far-fetched. In fact, in a 1999 survey carried out by the municipality of Kiryat Shimona, a village whose location had placed it within the range of attacks from Lebanon over the previous 30 years, it was found that one out of every four residents indicated willingness to relocate in order to distance themselves from these perils.[30]

The interesting question was how the new situation might be used by either side to advance its interests in the deadly little struggle due to continue along Israel's northern frontier.

# Chapter Ten

---

# Hezbollah's Standing
# After the Collapse of
# the 'Security Zone'

---

T he year following the Israeli withdrawal and immediately preceding America's war on global terrorism was exceedingly important for Hezbollah, for parliamentary elections were to take place and the effects of its improved tactical position along the frontier with Israel would be tested.

Ever conscious of their organization's standing and image at home and abroad, Hezbollah leaders hoped the electorate would richly reward them with votes for their performance against the Israelis a few months earlier. If that happened, those results could be read as a mandate for continuing resistance activities. This was important because, as we have seen, some Lebanese had been willing to accept the United Nation's finding that the Israeli withdrawal had been complete and demanded that the regular Lebanese army replace Hezbollah at the border. Israel and the USA had also demanded that the 'terrorists' leave the area. A high vote tally would go far to counter the idea that Hezbollah's military activities may have lost some of their support after the 'Security Zone' collapsed.

It was also hoped by Hezbollah that the new government formed as a result of the elections would assign the same priority to the resistance as previous ones had. This government would face a new strategic situation along the border with Israel now that the 'Security Zone' had collapsed and a far smaller percentage of Lebanon's land mass remained under occupation. Thus its focus might well be placed elsewhere, for instance on the country's dreadful economic plight. If resistance was no longer a priority and Hezbollah's battlefield exploits resulted in new Israeli retaliations, would the 'state track' be manned with as much vigour as previously? And if not, how would that affect the support and popularity Hezbollah counted on to shield itself against the terrorist label?

Another vital election in the offing – Israel's in spring 2001 – was another unknown factor as far as calculations about the resistance's staying power were concerned. Here the question was whether a new man in the driving seat could do any better than his predecessors had in stopping the 'terrorists'. What if that new man was Ariel Sharon – the man who had chased the PLO fighters from the border area 19 years earlier? Of course, no one could foresee the really big event of the year 2000, the outbreak of the Palestinian *intifada* in September, or guess the critical effect it would have on new resistance opportunities for Hezbollah.

One thing was sure for Hezbollah watchers like myself: the months following the Israeli withdrawal would yield some very important information about where the struggle was going and how Hezbollah was fixed in terms of popular support and continued government backing, as it became the target of America's most stringent efforts ever to close it down after 11 September 2001.

## PARLIAMENTARY ELECTION PAY-OFFS

Since Hezbollah was at the zenith of its popularity in summer 2000, it was widely believed that its candidates would do very well indeed in the forthcoming parliamentary elections. In fact, there were rumours that the Party of God might even achieve a cabinet seat in the post-election government. But how much could the Party of God expect to capitalize on its popularity under the rules of Lebanon's confessional electoral system? Could Hezbollah accept a ministerial portfolio without jeopardizing the 'rules' under which the resistance and the state operated?

Ironically, it was concern for resistance unity that once again limited Hezbollah's opportunity to score against its rival, Amal, and therefore amass more parliamentary seats than it had previously held. In 'resistance areas' – the South and Bekaa-Hermel provinces – competition between Amal and Hezbollah would again be forbidden. The question of a cabinet portfolio, however, was a possibility. There was considerable buzzing about how it would look for Lebanon to have a fundamentalist minister in the cabinet and, in addition, a cabinet member that belonged to an organization that was on the US State Department's terrorist list. One MP I spoke with on this subject said, off the record, that he personally thought a ministry portfolio for Hezbollah would be the best possible way 'to thumb our noses at the United States position on Hezbollah'. Another, however, thought it wouldn't do Lebanon's image much good.

As it turned out, Hezbollah leaders ruled out a cabinet position for various reasons. When questioned about the possibility of joining the government in 1998, Sheikh Naim al-Qassim indicated that since Hezbollah did not have the means to achieve its policies, it preferred not to seek any part in the government.[1] This response reflected Hezbollah's reasoning that more gains could be had from pursuing *jihad-al-siyassa* (political jihad) as part of the opposition than from complete integration – a place in the cabinet – in a non-Islamic government. However, that was not the only reason a ministerial post had been ruled out. Qassim also remarked that joining the cabinet was not foreseen while Lebanon was still menaced by Israel. Although he did not explain his remark, we know that any convergence of the parallel tracks allotted to the state and the resistance by Damascus (such as the resistance's incorporation into the government would bring about) would certainly confound the policy, which directs the struggle against Israel. Previous chapters have shown that portrayal of the resistance as unstoppable by Lebanese officials and machine-like in its commitment to jihad had reaped considerable political rewards for Syria. Those rewards lay in the capacity to draw world and especially Israeli attention to the fact that Damascus was the only power that held some sway with the fundamentalist guerrillas – and therefore Israel would be well advised to negotiate with Syria.

With a cabinet post therefore ruled out, victories at the polls and an increased number of seats for Hezbollah in the legislative chamber would be the only way the party could reap the rewards of its jihad activities and thus substantiate their popularity. There was only one setback: electoral competition was again restricted to prevent clashes between Amal and Hezbollah partisans in areas where most of the Shiite seats were at stake. Despite the obstacles, however, the extent of the Party of God's popularity in 2000 could be demonstrated by counting the number of votes won by Hezbollah as compared to its allies on the same ticket in 'resistance areas' – the Bekaa and the South – and elsewhere. Good scores could be considered a reward for the efforts the Party of God had expended to force the Israelis out of their self-declared 'Security Zone'.

## THE SOUTH AND THE BEKAA REWARD HEZBOLLAH

Predictably, the Hezbollah-Amal lists swept the Bekaa and the South. This was facilitated by the commanding political influence and capacity of both parties to serve mass populations. Moreover, they were able to attract popular candidates from other parties, from important families and from independent ranks to join their electoral tickets. But how did Hezbollah's candidates fare compared with Amal's and others?

Since the South has been considered Berri's fief for years, his candidates might have been expected to be the big vote-grabbers on the joint list. It will be recalled that Berri's lists had had the edge over

Hezbollah in the municipal elections two years earlier. In Tyre, his list had totally wiped out Hezbollah's. This was not the case in 2000, however. Four seats are contested by Shiites in this historic city and on the list jointly formed by Amal and Hezbollah the latter's candidate, Abdallah Qassir, out-polled Amal's Mohammed Abdul-Hamid Beydoun by 196,056 votes to 176,555. In his home district of Zahrani, Berri himself had only taken 183,450 votes. The Party of God's Mohammed Fneish did better than that in Bint Jbeil, taking a stunning 200,840 votes to Amal's Ayub Humayid's 174,190. The same trend was found in Nabatieh, where Hezbollah deputy Mohammed Raad scored a significant 201,901 votes against Amal member Abdallatif Zein's 173, 891. The Party of God finally had some incontestable evidence that it had penetrated Berri's domain. This trend was also found in Bekaa-Hermel, where Hezbollah is at home.

A source close to one of the politicians allied with Amal confided that he thought it was normal that the electorate favoured the very popular Hezbollah leaders on the lists. 'Voters,' he said, 'had probably wanted to show the United States and Israel that Hezbollah's popularity had not declined after the Israelis had been expelled.' How would Hezbollah candidates fare in districts where the competition was open?

## ELECTIONS IN THE CAPITAL

In the Beirut area, several anecdotes clearly showed how Hezbollah's status had been enhanced by events in May. In an unprecedented move, Druze leader Walid Jumblat, a Hariri ally, assiduously courted the Party of God to strengthen his list for the Baabda-Aley election. However, Hezbollah MP Ali Ammar turned his back on the opportunity to join the stronger of the district's two main tickets and instead accepted a slot on the list sponsored by Jumblat's Druze rival, Talal Arslan. Ammar easily defeated the Shiite candidate that Jumblat had enlisted. An important point, however, is that to balance his list, Arslan had awarded the second Shiite place on the ticket to Amal's Salah Harakeh, who also won the seat, but with fewer votes than Ammar had received. The need to attract all Shiite votes to this ticket had destroyed Hezbollah's chance to win an extra parliamentary seat.

Hezbollah, however, scored the more impressive win in the Beirut elections, where Hariri fielded a complete list for each of the three designated city districts. His candidates swept the field, taking 18 of the 19 seats contested. Significantly, Hezbollah's Mohammed Berjawi was the only candidate running on a competing list to break the Hariri lockout. Contesting the only Shiite seat in District 2, Berjawi was the big winner there with 28,691 votes. Closest to him was a former MP and minister of the interior, Syrian Orthodox Christian Bishara Mirhaj, with

26,482 votes. The Shiite seat on the District 3 list was won by Hariri's ally, Nassir Kandil, president of the National Audiovisual Council. Hariri himself was elected with 34,820 votes in District 1.

The Party of God had again achieved the largest party bloc in the legislative chamber but, as before, this was only nine of the 128 deputies. It can therefore easily be seen that even at the peak of its popularity, Lebanon's proportional system and the rules imposed by Syria, which restrict competition between the Shiite rivals, prevent any fundamentalist sweep that could unbalance or damage Lebanon's pluralist system. In a way, however, the system works very well for the resistance – Hezbollah's greatest concern – since its built-in limitations on the expansion of the party's political influence removes apprehension over a fundamentalist sweep yet provides the diverse confessional votes needed to underline Hezbollah's broad popularity in the country. This strengthens the legitimacy that surrounds the Party of God's continued actions against the Israelis in the South.

## THE GUNS VS. BUTTER CLASH

Hariri's victory and resultant return to power were widely considered to reflect the citizens' hopes that as an internationally known businessman, a hands-on politician and a noted diplomat, he could turn the sagging economy around by launching visionary programmes and by securing international financial support for Lebanon. His pursuit of that mandate, however, brought him into an open clash with the Party of God. How did this crisis occur and what did it mean for resistance solidarity and continuity?

Since 1998, unfavourable international credit reports and economic statistics on Lebanon had combined with high unemployment rates and rising prices to convince the Lebanese that Hariri was the only man who could save their country's economy. There was thus an overwhelming response when he asked the voters to give him the political muscle he needed in parliament by voting in his whole electoral team. Hezbollah's breakthrough against Hariri's Shiite candidate in Beirut – the only defeat registered by that list – was therefore very impressive.

When President Lahoud polled the newly elected deputies a month after the elections, 106 cast their votes for Hariri as prime minister. Unsurprisingly, Hezbollah MPs withheld their support and became part of a group of only 22 deputies who opposed his appointment. The relationship had never been a warm one and it was about to get a lot chillier.

I have pointed out in preceding chapters how incipient tensions between the Lebanese government and Hezbollah lay close to the surface at all times as a result of the guerrillas' freewheeling activities and how those tensions had to be carefully controlled. A case in point was the quarrel that erupted on 16 February 2001 between the Prime Minister and Hezbollah. Ironically, the dispute was *not* sparked by Hezbollah's reactions to massive Israeli retaliations against targets in Lebanon, as had happened several times before. This quarrel arose when one of the Party of God's operations against the Israelis collided with a mission undertaken at the same time by Prime Minister Hariri. At that time, Hariri was in France with nearly his entire cabinet in search of foreign investments and economic aid. The trip was something of a showcase for the Prime Minister. It was widely viewed as economically critical for the government's programme. Hariri was expected to make good use of his personal friendship with French President Jacques Chirac, other key French leaders and members of the international community to achieve positive results. In a sense, this trip put the Hariri government's credibility with the Lebanese public that had elected him, on the line.

The Prime Minister's task was not an easy one, since part of his job was to reassure potential investors and donors that the conflict in the South was under control and that the kind of calm political climate that was essential for economic growth and development could be expected. Hariri was therefore prepared to answer difficult questions about why his government had not firmly re-established security in the South by sending the army there to maintain order. Many viewed this move as essential so that massive Israeli retaliations against his country's infrastructure could be definitively ruled out. At a press conference, Hariri deliberately played down the possibility of this threat by observing: 'Beirut does not wish to give Israel any provocation at the frontier, and Lebanon and Syria are in agreement on that issue.'[2]

One day later, however, while the Lebanese delegation was still in Paris, it was shocked to learn that Hezbollah fighters had fired an anti-tank missile at an Israeli patrol in the Shebaa Farms area, killing one soldier and wounding two others. The operation was carried out in the name of the 'Islamic Martyrs'.

There is always speculation over the particular 'message' such attacks and their timing are meant to convey, and in this case it was observed that this was the first attack since Prime Minister Ariel Sharon had taken office on 6 February and that it had occurred shortly before US Secretary of State Colin Powell's tour of the Middle East. Thus the attack might have been undertaken as a little reminder to the allies that the Assad government was still waiting to begin 'land for peace' negotiations with Israel. However, another much more provocative rationale for the incident also surfaced. Hezbollah leaders were thought to have taken umbrage at Hariri's Paris statement that his government was against 'provocations' at the border. Miffed at the Prime Minister's use of the term 'provocation' to describe the resistance/jihad and angered over the fact that the statement violated the 'rules' by abrogating the government's obligation to demonstrate full support for the resistance at all times when conducting affairs of state, some believed that Hezbollah might have deliberately timed the operation to embarrass Hariri.

In Paris, the Prime Minister did his best to cover the military attack by qualifying it as a legitimate blow against occupation forces, but egg was on his face. Before leaving for Lebanon he quickly undertook all kinds of contacts to try to avoid further reactions by the Israelis who had immediately responded by pounding the outskirts of villages near the Shebaa Farms with artillery.

The debate in the Lebanese parliament over the disastrous timing of the Hezbollah attack was heated and made headlines in the daily newspapers. Some deputies claimed that regulation of this particular incident was not enough and that there must be some general agreement over what was to be done about the Shebaa Farms case. One MP asked how the government could allow one party to make such serious decisions when the economic fate of the entire nation hung in the balance. Other critics questioned whether the resistance should be engaged in recovering the Shebaa Farms at all, since whether or not they belonged to Lebanon or Syria had not been determined to everyone's satisfaction. The issue of sending the army to the South and calming the border was brought up again. While most deputies understood the reason that that option had been ruled out and continued to support it, some argued that at the very least Hezbollah should inform the government when an attack was imminent.

Hassan Nasrallah quickly responded to these criticisms by verbally attacking the MPs and cabinet members who had criticized the resistance's timing and accusing them of a lack of patriotism. This type of public brouhaha was exactly what the Damascus government had tried so hard to contain since it obviously gave comfort to the enemy and ammunition to those who opposed Lebanese-Syrian foreign policy coordination.

Stung by Nasrallah's attack on his patriotism, Hariri was reported by the fascinated press corps to have prepared what could have been a tough response to Nasrallah, or even his resignation. However, before giving his press secretary the go-ahead to make this message public, Hariri must have thought it prudent to touch base first with the powers that be in Beirut and Damascus. After a quick visit to President Emile Lahoud, whose commitment to Syrian-Lebanese foreign policy coordination is rock solid, Hariri then went to Damascus to confer with Bashar al-Assad. According to press accounts, on his return to Beirut he stopped in the Bekaa to meet with the head of Syrian military intelligence in Lebanon, Major General Ghazi Kenaan, and then had another talk with Lahoud. The unpublished communiqué was then withdrawn.

Some analysts I spoke to about this affair believed that Hariri had come close to resigning over what he perceived as intolerable interference in the affairs of state or even deliberate defiance by Hezbollah. Whatever the reason was, however, he obviously felt insulted as things stood. It looked as if the state-resistance deal was finished before the Damascus meeting. Nevertheless, the next day, back in his office, the Prime Minister received a cordial visit from Mohammed Raad, Hezbollah's parliamentary bloc leader, and political advisor Hussein Khalil, as if nothing at all had happened between their leader and Hariri. The reporters present observed that the three men interacted pleasantly and that Hariri had told his guests that he was convinced that the incident in the South was not meant to embarrass him personally. For his part, Raad assured the Prime Minister that the operation against Israel was carried out, as always, on an opportune basis and had no ulterior motive whatsoever. In short, Damascus seems once again to have interceded in a Hezbollah-government crisis to bring the parties back on their respective tracks.

This tiff has been discussed in some detail for several reasons. First, it illustrates the kind of discord Israel had vainly tried to sow between the Lebanese government and Hezbollah when air strikes far removed from the South were launched against Lebanon's infrastructure. However, an important reason the Israeli strategy had failed in the past, according to the Lebanese official position, was that a large portion of Lebanese territory was still being occupied and resistance was generally agreed to be a governmental priority. In 2001, however, with Israeli troops concentrated only in the very lightly populated Shebaa Farms area and a few other points along the border, and at a time when dismal reports about the public debt and unemployment filled the news, Lebanese public and government attention had shifted from politics to economics. Thus, this flap came closer than ever before to derailing the arrangement between state and resistance.

As we shall see later, this contretemps did not pass unobserved by US foreign policymakers who would try to stir up just such a controversy over economic issues to try to cripple Hezbollah as part of the war against global terrorism.

Nevertheless, in spring 2001 Assad once again let the Lebanese political class know where their priorities lay by strictly holding Hariri to his commitment and apparently convincing him not to make his communiqué public. The struggle in the South was apparently not to be compromised for any reason.

This incident illustrates the strong backing Damascus continued to provide Hezbollah if a tussle with the Lebanese authorities over its on-going struggle against the Israelis threatened to spill over into the public realm. The message was very clear, the Lebanese government on its own or by rallying public support or external assistance is to take all steps that will reflect positively on the resistance and facilitate its military mission under all circumstances. In any event, as far as popular and government support were concerned, in 2000–2001 the resistance seemed to be on firm ground for the foreseeable future and was seeking ways to exploit the strategic advantage it had gained from Israel's evacuation.

## NEW RESISTANCE OPPORTUNITIES

Immediately after the tumultuous events of May 2000, small groups of three or four Hezbollah fighters armed with assault rifles began patrolling the withdrawal line established by the UN between Lebanon and Israel and ignoring it where Shebaa was concerned. Shipping containers had been moved into place to serve as observation posts and checkpoints near the old passages between Lebanon and Israel and were dotted around and between the posts manned by UN observers on duty in the area. From these stations, Hezbollah presently controls all movement on area roads and checks the identity of any person approaching the gates, which were closed after Israel's evacuation. Hezbollah also maintains offices in two beach resorts previously exploited by SLA militiamen at the coastal town of Naqoura, where the headquarters of the UN force is also located. Since the only means of passage between Israel and Lebanon is located there under UN supervision, Hezbollah is able to monitor the return of SLA members and their families who sought refuge in Israel and also stop SLA partisans from escaping to Israel.

With parliamentary elections around the corner, electoral campaigning appears to have led Hezbollah to opt for a lull in the armed struggle during late summer 2000. However, on 7 October, straight after the elections, it was business as usual for the party's fighters. On that day, three Israeli soldiers on patrol in the Shebaa Farms area were abducted by Hezbollah guerillas. Ten days later, Hassan Nasrallah announced that a Hezbollah operative had lured electronics specialist Elhan Tannenbaum, a retired colonel in the Israeli reserves, into Lebanon and then had him arrested by party security forces. Apparently Tannenbaum had met a member of the Party of God in Switzerland and was deceived into thinking he would be willing to cooperate with Israel as a double agent. According to Nasrallah, Tannenbaum's detention was meant to raise the morale of Lebanese detainees in Israeli prisons. It was reported that when US Secretary of State Madeleine Albright later met with Bashar al-Assad and asked him to pressure Hezbollah to release the four captured Israelis, he told her: 'This party [Hezbollah] has serious social power and is within its rights.'[3] These were almost the exact words Assad's father had used when US Secretary of State Warren Christopher asked him to intervene to halt Hezbollah's Katyusha fire during Israel's Grapes of Wrath military operation in 1996.

Meanwhile, the border fence – and particularly the Fatima Gate through which Israeli partisans and others regularly entered and exited Israel – remained volatile. By 2001, at least a dozen Lebanese civilians had been killed there and more than 40 others wounded as a result of rock-throwing incidents that had drawn Israeli fire.

These incidents have been presented to illustrate the several types of activities Hezbollah engaged in along the border to keep the issue of Israeli occupation alive and the military on the alert in 2000. In 2001, however, resistance opportunities were expanded, and ironically, this was partially the result of several of Prime Minister Ariel Sharon's policies.

Recognizing that solidarity between Hezbollah and the Lebanese government could not be shaken by any attempts to set the two actors at each other's throats, when the next Hezbollah attack occurred on an Israeli border outpost Sharon, who had taken office in February 2002, tried a new strategy. On 15 April, he ordered Israeli fighter planes to destroy a *Syrian* radar installation located at Moudeirej, a mountainous area overlooking the Bekaa Valley. The facility was levelled and several soldiers at the site were killed. This attack had considerable implications since it breached the détente system that had prevented direct conflict between Israeli and Syrian forces in Lebanon for more than two decades. It was therefore viewed with consternation in international circles as well as within Lebanon and Syria. Following the raid, Foreign Minister Shimon Peres warned that as long as Syria had an important number of troops in Lebanon and was calling the shots there, it bore responsibility for what happened along the border.[4] In other words, Syria rather than Lebanon would be the target of Israeli retaliations if Damascus would not rein in Hezbollah.

A similar attack was ordered by Israel on 2 July, 48 hours after Hezbollah had again opened fire on Israeli troops in the Shebaa Farms. This time an Israeli air-to-surface missile destroyed a Syrian radar station in the Bekaa Valley near the Rayak Air Base. Three Syrian soldiers and a Lebanese were wounded. As news of the raid circulated, apprehension rose over whether Damascus might respond to this attack and, if so, how that could affect Lebanon. The answer was provided soon after the Israeli attack had taken place, when more than 80 rockets were fired by Hezbollah at an Israeli listening post on the occupied Golan Heights and at two other Israeli positions in the Shebaa Farms area. The listening post was put out of commission and 23 Israeli soldiers were wounded.

The immediacy and strength of Hezbollah's tit for tat response indicated that it had been planned in advance and was probably meant to convey a very strong message to the Israelis about the new Sharon policy. A joint communiqué by Syrian Foreign Minister Farouk al-Sharaa and his Lebanese counterpart, Mahmoud Hammoud, suggested why Hezbollah had responded to the attack by emphasizing the foreign policy coordination between the two governments. The communiqué warned that the episode jeopardized the stability of the entire region.[5]

A few days later, House Speaker Nabih Berri, in his capacity as a senior official of the Lebanese government, further explained Hezbollah's response to the recent Israeli attack by stating that the resistance had established a new policy and that from now on any attack against the Syrians, in Lebanon or *in Syria* (my emphasis) would also be viewed as aggression against Lebanon. 'This gives us the right to respond *against all Israeli settlements*. These are the new rules of the game and the time when Israel can impose its own rules on us is over,' he said.[6]

No further incidents of that nature have since taken place, but the issue of Israeli occupation of the Syrian part of a divided Lebanese village near the Shebaa Farms arose soon after and seemed to offer Hezbollah the potential for a further expansion of resistance activities under the new policy. The story on the village of Ghajar goes as follows. Midway through the 1967 war, the Israeli Army had advanced into the Golan Heights and north into a strip of land controlled by the Syrian Army that included Ghajar. The troops halted south of Ghajar since, according to old British Mandate maps, the village was inside Lebanon. Nevertheless, a delegation of villagers who asked for complete integration with Lebanon at that time was refused because Beirut did not wish to antagonize its neighbour over a land dispute. A tacit agreement was then brokered under which Ghajar was effectively sealed off from Lebanon by a security fence and a minefield that ran around the northern, or Lebanese, part of the village. The Israelis occupied what had apparently been determined to be the Syrian sector. No internal barrier was set up to divide the village and, from what can be learned of the situation, cross-border drug smuggling and access to business and educational opportunities in Israel for both sets of villagers generated relative affluence in Ghajar in comparison with neighbouring hamlets wholly inside Lebanon. Thus, by exception, Ghajar came under Israeli control.

The UN mapping team that carried out the border delineation in 2000 established that, indeed, one third of this village lies inside Lebanese territory and the other two thirds fall within Israeli-occupied Syrian territory. Lebanese Ghajar was generally ignored while the struggle against Israeli occupation in other areas raged during the past decade. This situation changed in August 2001, however, when Indian UN peacekeepers manning a gate in the old fence at Abbasiyya, about a kilometre and a half away from Ghajar, relocated to a newly built observation post 200 metres to the south. Suddenly the gate to Ghajar was open and anyone could drive into the village.

Among the first to arrive were Hezbollah fighters who planted party flags at the north-west and north-east corners of the village. These men were followed by an influx of reporters, adding to the tension of the villagers, who hoped that their town could remain free of an Israeli security fence. According to press reports, the villagers are not burning for reunion with Lebanon, although they are reluctant to admit that.

Soon after, the director of Hezbollah's field operations, Sheikh Nabil Qaouk, and a delegation of some 200 partisans showed up and ostentatiously strolled down the main street of the Lebanese part of Ghajar toward the Israeli troops in the other part. This must have looked like a Middle Eastern version of *High Noon* to the villagers, who were reportedly watching the amazing scene from the roofs and balconies of their homes. Israeli soldiers in the Syrian part of the village remained on high alert during the short visit, which seemed to convey the message that under the recently announced resistance policy, Ghajar's Syrian sector might now be ripe for liberation.

A week later, on 21 August, Hezbollah began stationing men at the north-east entrance and barring people from entering Ghajar. Reporters trying to visit were told that they needed written permission to enter from Hezbollah's media office in Beirut. When asked what was going on they were told 'Hezbollah is taking its own measures in the area'.[7]

The presence of the Party of God in the same village as Israeli soldiers was certainly not reassuring to either the residents or the Israelis. In fact, discussions immediately began in Israel about sealing off the Syrian part with a security fence or abandoning Ghajar altogether, leaving it fully under Lebanese jurisdiction. An analyst writing in the Israeli daily *Yediot Ahronot* indicated that the reason a troop withdrawal might be necessary was because Hezbollah operatives could now infiltrate Israel via the village with 'unbearable ease'.[8]

Ghajar is but one example of the many problems along the Israeli-Lebanese border that, as a result of historical frontier ambiguities and the present tense situation between Hezbollah and the Israeli army, might result in Hezbollah's further resistance activities. In an interview with a local newspaper, Kofi Annan's personal representative to Lebanon, Staffan de Mistura, listed many of those disputes, emphasizing the ones in most pressing need of solution. Some are presented below so that the nature and complexity of the issues involved can be understood.[9] The residents of Abbasieh, for instance, were driven from their homes in the 1967 war when Israeli troops occupied the tri-border (Lebanon-Syria-Israel) pocket. According to the

UN official, the village was then destroyed, the buildings were bulldozed and dynamited, the cemetery desecrated and the area sown with land mines. After the mapping operation in 2000, about 20 per cent of the original village area was on the Lebanese side of the line according to the residents and some began building new homes on the Lebanese sliver. De Mistura reported that now they were all complaining that the Blue Line unfairly prevented them from accessing their original properties on the other side of the border. He also noted that Hezbollah leader Nasrallah had referred to Abbassieh's plight a number of times in recent speeches.

Another territorial dispute raised by both the Lebanese government and Hezbollah, the UN official noted, concerned the so-called 'Seven Villages', whose residents became Lebanese following the creation of the state in 1920 but ended up in Palestine four years later. This was due to an agreement between the Mandate powers, Britain and France, on how Palestine's northern frontier with Syria and Lebanon should be demarcated.

In 1948, during the first Arab-Israeli war, the residents of the villages at issue, who had originally been Lebanese and then became Palestinian nationals, fled their homes and took refuge in Lebanon. Some purchased Lebanese nationality immediately and the rest were granted citizenship in 1994. The Lebanese authorities have declared that the return of those villages that came under Israel's control after 1948 is one of seven demands that that country must meet in return for permanent peace with Lebanon.

Of far more pressing concern, however, according to de Mistura, is the potential for future tension between Israel and Lebanon over the use of water from the Hasbani River that flows down the western flank of the tri-border area, and passes Ghajar. This river feeds into the upper Jordan and runs into the Sea of Galilee, Israel's largest supply of surface water. The Wazzani springs beside Ghajar are the only source of water for the river during the dry summer months. As an example of the potential for conflict between Israel and Lebanon generated by this water source, de Mistura described an incident that had already caused problems between the two states. According to the UN official, when the Lebanese Council for the South – a state developmental agency – installed a small pump and a pipeline ten centimetres in diameter to supply drinking water from the Wazzani springs to a nearby village, Israel immediately warned that unchecked pumping could spark a war. The seriousness of this challenge by the Israeli authorities can be better placed in perspective when it is recalled that an attempt by Syria in the 1960s to divert the Hasbani away from Israel led to military confront-ations that actually culminated in the 1967 Arab-Israeli war,[10] the war in which Syria's water-rich Golan Heights was annexed. Further emphasizing the touchiness of the Wazzani Spring water issue, de Mistura noted that the 1955 Johnston Agreement on regional water sharing, an agreement that was never fully ratified, allocated Lebanon 35 mcm per year of water from the Hasbani. However, he added, although Lebanon is not believed to be using more than ten mcm per year now, this was still enough to provoke a threat from its neighbour.[11]

Nine months after de Mistura's warning, what was then tantamount to a tempest in a teapot assumed the makings of a major new conflict between Israel and Lebanon. This is because Lebanon's Council of the South, the government agency in charge of reconstruction and development, has plans to pump 10,000 cubic meters of water per day from the Hasbani to supply 60 villages in the South. Israel says that will cut the flow of river water it receives by 30 to 50 per cent and Prime Minister Sharon flatly stated on 10 September 2002 that diverting this water was a cause for war.[12]

Speaking for the Lebanese government, Nabih Berri said that threats would not deter Lebanon's rightful use of the waters that arise on its land, a reference to the source of the Hasbani, the Wazzani Springs. For his part, Sayyed Hashem Safieddine, the head of Hezbollah's Executive Council, condemned the threats and warned Israel that if it tried to use force to block the project, the Islamic Resistance 'will cut off the Israelis' hand'.[13]

The point being raised here, however, is not one of Israel's bellicosity toward Lebanon over water usage rights, but the availability of other disputes that might require resistance on Hezbollah's part should Israel eventually decide to withdraw from Shebaa or Ghajar.

## ALL THE WAY TO JERUSALEM?

Hezbollah began turning its attention towards what it could do to assist the Palestinian uprising when it began in September 2000. At that time, its television station, al-Manar, started coverage of the conflict by using Palestinian correspondents and cameramen who were on the scene. Its goal was threefold: to bring live coverage of the struggle that was taking place in historic Palestine into homes and offices right around the Arab and Muslim worlds, to mobilize widespread support for resistance efforts and to send a message of faith and hope to those engaged in the struggle against Israel based on their organization's own successful struggle against Israeli occupation in South Lebanon. Those specifically targeted for assistance were the fundamentalist organizations Hamas and Islamic Jihad. It will be remembered that these Palestinian groups share the Party of God's firm conviction that the only way to deal with the Israelis and return all of historic Palestine to the Muslims, is by militant jihad.

To achieve the goals of its new media campaign, news reportage of the daily battles in Israel and Palestinian areas was interspersed with inspirational messages, views of Jerusalem's al-Aqsa Mosque, Islam's third holiest shrine, and brief scenes of Hezbollah operations against the Israelis in South Lebanon. The latter were cast in a heroic light and accentuated by martial music and male choruses that proclaimed God's greatness.

From a few hours daily at the outset, news coverage expanded in 2001 to almost 24 hours a day. The names of Palestinians who had died in the intifada and were considered martyrs were continuously flashed along the bottom of the screen and updated as new deaths occurred. Messages aimed at demoralizing the Israeli public and the military establishment were also aired. One short clip shows photos of Israeli soldiers killed in battle. An empty frame with a question mark in it appears among the portraits. 'Who will be next?' the Hebrew caption reads.

In an interview with Hassan Ezzeddin, Director of Hezbollah's new Media Department and a member of the party's politburo, I learned that television clips in Hebrew began in 1996 and soon became more numerous and varied.[14] A special bureau now monitors the Israeli media and gathers information that might be useful for the purpose of psychological warfare. The bureau is headed by a Hezbollah fighter who was captured and imprisoned by the Israelis in 1986 and learned Hebrew in order to talk with his guards. When he was released from captivity in 2000 as the result of a prisoner exchange worked out between the contending sides, he was placed in charge of al-Manar TV's Hebrew section. That section, set up to monitor Israeli communications, is now preparing to present the daily news in Hebrew in a manner similar to the English-language programme with Arabic subtitles that was initiated in 2001. Ezzeddin believes that this kind of 'proactive' approach, as he described it, is the first of its kind in this part of the world. Some investigation of his claim indicated that it was correct. I found that no other Arab government or organization has used modern satellite communications to reach Israeli citizens directly, pointing out the negative consequences of their government's policies toward Arabs and Palestinians and trying to influence their opinions. This was a new form of interference in the Arab-Israeli conflict. Would Hezbollah limit itself to propaganda and psychological warfare or would it be expanding its campaign against the Israelis by offering the Palestinian mujahidin more tangible help?

Hassan Nasrallah announced the answer to that question on 29 September, only a few days after the World Trade Center and Pentagon attacks had taken place. Speaking at a giant rally to commemorate the first anniversary of the Palestinian intifada, Nasrallah said that Hezbollah was preparing itself to provide *'direct interference'* (my emphasis) to support the intifada. This drew an enthusiastic response from the audience estimated to be about 10,000 strong.

Since the Hezbollah leader did not elaborate on this critical announcement, I sought out Field Commander Nabil Qaouk and asked him for his understanding of what 'direct interference' in the intifada meant. After some words about the important role presently being played by Hezbollah's media, and some probing on my part, he got to the point, although obliquely. According to the spare and somewhat taciturn cleric, 'it is contingent upon all the Arab leaders to look to see what resources they can contribute to the Palestinian struggle since they will take the brunt of it if a forced exodus like the one previously perpetrated by the Zionists in 1948 takes place'.[15] In this context, he referred to Hezbollah as a major Arab resource and the actual spearhead of the resistance against Israeli occupation of Arab land. From these words I gathered that we were about to witness a new stage in the Middle East struggle in which Hezbollah would have an even more controversial role.

Although the Sheikh would not be drawn on exactly what was being contemplated, it was not hard to see how the Israeli-Lebanese frontier might be heated up or otherwise used to give the Israeli army something else to think about if military operations against the Palestinian uprising intensified. American and Israeli strategists would therefore have to work out a means by which this grave security risk for Israel could be stopped in its tracks.

# Chapter Eleven

# The Terrorism vs. Resistance Controversy

The publication of America's annual terrorist list receives broad coverage but generates only mild reaction in Lebanon, despite the fact that Hezbollah's name is always on it. This bored reaction is understandable since no really damaging measures were taken by the US government against Beirut, Damascus or Tehran to try to get these governments to curb Hezbollah. Furthermore, most Lebanese believed that Hezbollah's resistance role had been solidly grounded for years.

After the September 11th attacks on the World Trade Center in New York and the Pentagon in Washington DC, this complacency changed to apprehension almost overnight. Osama bin Laden and his al-Qaeda organization were rapidly fingered as the perpetrators of the catastrophes and were targeted for immediate reprisals. However, the Bush administration announced it would actively seek ways to find and punish terrorists 'wherever they were hiding'. Government officials declared that the US State Department's annual terrorist list would serve as the reference for the anti-terrorist campaign being launched. Thus, the pursuit and punishment of individuals and organizations on America's blacklist became declared policy that could have important, perhaps painful, consequences for host and supportive countries. Many individuals I consulted at the time believed that Lebanon's lengthy quarrel with the Israelis and the Americans over Hezbollah's terrorist or resistance status might finally be coming to a head and thought that the USA was about to initiate pressure of some kind on Beirut to close Hezbollah down. A central question for the Bush administration, however, was whether the Lebanese authorities would comply.

## LEBANON, SYRIA AND IRAN: WILLING PARTNERS IN THE ANTI-TERRORISM COALITION?

The Bush administration had almost immediately decided that gathering as broad a coalition of nations as possible would be the best way to pursue the global war on terrorism. That strategy was based on evidence that groups such as al-Qaeda had cells located in many countries. If those cells were to be destroyed, the cooperation of coalition partners would be essential. Moreover, the coalition strategy could lessen the anticipated backlash of a unilateral American response and soothe any ruffled feathers. Central to the strategy would be to involve most if not all Muslim countries in the Middle East and Asia as active partners in the coalition. American policymakers hoped that this strategy would demonstrate that the fight against international terrorism was in no way spurred by any hostility toward Islam. Thus the thrust of America's global war against terrorism would be understood as directed against those who, according to Bush administration officials, had perverted Islamic principles and values by taking the lives of innocent civilians, a deed prohibited by all religions and abhorred by all civilized societies.

Dozens of countries were thus presented with a number of American demands regarding terrorism and a list of terrorist organizations operating within their borders. Each was asked to indicate what it could contribute to the war against terrorism and was warned that if it did not join the coalition it would be considered an opponent and treated accordingly.

This American stance provoked a good deal of consternation among countries that had links to some of the individuals and organizations designated by the USA as terrorists. Most countries found themselves forced to choose between the political expediency of cooperating with the dominant world power and their strategic need to maintain support for client organizations on the US blacklist.

Among the countries that found themselves in this dilemma were Iran, Syria and Lebanon. Iran had been portrayed as the very epitome of fundamentalist evil ever since the Islamic Republic saw the light of day and Hezbollah was considered its terrorist arm. Besides sponsoring Hezbollah, Syria showed its ill intent as far as the USA was concerned, by hosting ten Palestinian organizations involved in the intifada, including Hamas and Islamic Jihad, the fundamentalist groups that employ suicide-martyrdom attacks against Israeli civilians. At the time, Lebanon's Hezbollah, however, seemed most dangerous. Lebanon's support for and operational coordination with Hezbollah had received tacit acknowledgement by the American anti-terrorism campaign, presumably because it was considered powerless to resist Syrian manipulation. In any case, toward the end of September 2001, all three governments were waiting to see what they would be asked to do to fight terrorism and how much they could promise without scuttling or gravely weakening the foreign policy that they had been pursuing against Israel by supporting Hezbollah's jihad.

Some of Washington's immediate requests met with cooperation from these three countries. For instance, when asked to share information on known terrorists with Interpol and other intelligence agencies and governments, all three readily consented to handing over individuals on the American list that they considered to be 'real' terrorists and that could be found within their borders. In Syria's case, this cooperation balanced against that country's firm demand for return of the Golan Heights from Israel and its support for the Palestinian militants left a confusing picture for US officials trying to determine whether Syria belonged in the 'with us' or 'against us' category laid out by Bush.

Yet, where Hezbollah was concerned, Syria as well as Lebanon and Iran took exception to America's demands. These countries and other Arab and Muslim states insisted on considering Hezbollah as a legitimate resistance organization. In the case of Lebanon (sensing where the tension with the USA over the distinction between terrorism and resistance might lead next), the authorities began putting their case for Hezbollah's right to use violence against the Israelis in South Lebanon together by referring to legal precedents and international conventions.

## BEIRUT'S POSITION ON HEZBOLLAH AS A RESISTANCE FORCE

The question of whether the use of violence is justified for resistance purposes actually first arose after the Second World War, when the process of decolonization was under way in many countries. The International Court and legal scholars at that time had agreed that decolonization was essential and that the natural outcome of the process would be the self-determination of the inhabitants involved. In this respect, all efforts, including the use of military force to achieve self-determination were considered legally acceptable, as were actions by states to assist colonized people struggling to rid themselves of foreign overlords. Another related precept of international law is that only self-defence warrants the use of threats or violence and makes these acts legal. All other use of force is illegal.[1] Article 2 of the United Nations Charter incorporates this idea by stipulating that no state is permitted to use force against the political independence or territorial integrity of another state. Defending against such an act is therefore considered a legitimate use of violence that can be assisted by other states.

On the subject of resistance, the legal regulator in force is Geneva Convention 4, of 1949. This convention protects civilians under illegal occupation by a foreign power and stipulates that if the occupying power persistently violates this convention, the civilians can announce civil disobedience. If further provoked they may use military force – again in the spirit of self-defence.[2] In this respect, all resolutions issued by the United Nations Security Council after the 1978 Israeli occupation of South Lebanon, have considered Israel as an occupying power and called for its immediate withdrawal referring to the Fourth Geneva Convention. The Lebanese government was therefore prepared to argue that armed resistance by Hezbollah in the South is clearly a recognized right.

The Israeli government, on the other hand, had been countering this argument for years by declaring that its occupation of Lebanon, since 1978, did not seek the expansion of its national boundaries and was not permanent. Spokesmen had pointed out time and again that by establishing the 'Security Zone' in South Lebanon their country's only aim was to protect Israeli citizens from cross-border attacks. They argued that if the Lebanese government assumed its responsibility by sending the Lebanese Army to control Lebanon's border area, there would be no need for the Israelis to be there. Since that had not occurred, they said, it was up to the Israelis themselves to provide the protection their citizens needed against Palestinian terrorist attacks up to 1982 and against those kinds of attacks perpetrated by Iranian-backed Hezbollah from 1985 on.

At this point, another look at this loaded concept – terrorism – is helpful. There seems to be wide agreement amongst legal scholars and experts that terrorism is a rational political strategy whose aim is 'to demonstrate a state's vulnerability or impotency, gain authority, and attract attention for its aims by violent acts generally perpetrated against innocent individuals'.[3] According to the US State Department's definition, 'terrorism is the deliberate and systematic murder, maiming and menacing of the innocent to inspire fear for political ends'.[4] Causing widespread and deep fear is therefore the agreed objective of terrorist acts. With this definition in mind it is worthwhile taking a closer look at how the war in southern Lebanon has taken place.

The simple dynamics of this conflict can be summarized as follows. Hezbollah fighters launched attacks on Israeli and SLA troops within the 'Security Zone' and then quickly drew back into nearby villages within or at the edges of the Zone, since they anticipated that their opponents might refrain from shelling them in those locations. This is a known guerrilla tactic, which calls on the local population to accept the risk of counter-attacks as an integral part of the resistance. In essence, civilians thereby become human shields for the fighters. Considered as military 'deceit' or a 'perfidious act of war' in the 1977 Hague Regulations on Rules of War and the Fourth Geneva Convention, this tactic is prohibited.[5] At any rate, when this happened the frustrated Israelis and their SLA allies very often responded by shelling the areas in and around those villages. When Israeli shells hit villages and caused civilian casualties *outside* the 'Security Zone', Hezbollah considered the incident a direct violation of the mutual understanding it had with the Israelis to limit attacks to military targets within the 'Zone'. As a result, Israeli settlers would then come under Katyusha fire from Hezbollah gunners in a tit for tat response. As we have seen, a general flare-up of violence sometimes then ensued. The question posed here is whether any of this skirmishing can be considered terrorism. Did Israeli officials and military strategists consider it in this light?

In 1992, Hezbollah sent shells into Israeli villages in the Galilee panhandle. Speaking to journalists after a meeting with settlement leaders in November of that year, President Yitzhak Rabin conceded that Hezbollah had not fired on them without provocation from the Israeli army. The rocket attacks, he noted, had never been directed at Israeli population centres 'as targets in themselves'. Instead, he said, they were launched in response to Israeli operations against Hezbollah in South Lebanon. The reporter called this admission 'a startling departure from the Israeli line, which insists on portraying Hezbollah as a force dedicated to mindless terror'.[6]

But this was not the only discussion of Hezbollah tactics worthy of note. In an interview, Israeli General Shlomo Gazit, former Commander of Military Intelligence, said that during the period that led up to the 1992 flare-up, Israel, not Hezbollah, had broken the tacit rules of engagement established between the forces. He noted that these rules only permitted the targeting of military objectives within the 'Security Zone'. 'We need to say it again and again,' the general observed.

> Hizbullah did observe the 'rules of the game' for a long period. They refrained from shelling Israeli territory and from infiltration. They limited their operations to the 'Security Zone'. It was our retaliation for their skilful strikes at our soldiers *inside the zone* [my emphasis; a reference to the deaths of five soldiers by roadside explosives], that made them escalate the fighting. We [first] bombed and shelled many targets in Lebanon, including some far to the north. Only then did Hizbullah retaliate by shelling some Israeli localities – with no casualties.[7]

Gazit noted that this action was Hezbollah's way of passing a message that Israel should refrain from breaching the rules of the game in the future. 'The problem lies at our door,' he concluded.

These remarks indicate that Israeli military leaders did not perceive the Hezbollah attacks as designed to strike wide fear in the northern Israeli population, demonstrate their country's impotence, take it over or call attention to its aims – the definition of terrorism presented above. Rather, they believed that Hezbollah had used its rockets to send a message to the Israeli military establishment, not the civilian population, that 'rule breaking' would not be tolerated.

We have seen in an earlier chapter that this behaviour on Hezbollah's part was not an isolated incident. Reviewing the Party of God's tactics in a 1998 policy study on the use of air power in guerrilla warfare published by Tel Aviv's Begin-Sadat Center for Strategic Studies, military analyst Schmuel Gordon included this statement: 'Only when the Israeli Defense Force escalates its activities, do they [Hezbollah] launch rockets toward towns and villages beyond the border into Israel.'[8]

Writing two years ago about the implications of an Israeli withdrawal from Lebanon, Israeli strategic analyst Gal Luft commented on the absence of any terrorist activity along the Lebanon-Israel border saying that:

> The last infiltrations [sic] and brutal attacks on civilians took place before the 1982 Israeli invasion and were carried out by the PLO operating from South Lebanon... Hizbullah's attitude toward infiltration is enigmatic. It has never been involved in any attempt to cross the border.[9]

The remarks quoted above contrast dramatically with official Israeli comments about Hezbollah that are designed for western consumption. As we know, in those statements the Party of God is almost always referred to as a terrorist organization, the implication being that terrorism is presently its modus operandi in South Lebanon.

The Israeli comments also reinforce the view I expressed earlier that Hezbollah made an early strategic decision to exclude terrorist tactics from its jihad against Israeli occupation and stuck to it. Their strategy focused instead on pre-empting the American and Israeli position on terrorism. This position has it that if Israel's enemies do not stand up and fight against them in a conventional military manner, then these irregular forces are branded as terrorists for using non-conventional tactics that the Israelis are hard pressed to overcome.

However, from a purely practical point of view, targeting Israeli civilians simply does not serve the objectives of Hezbollah's mission, which is to keep constant pressure on the Israeli government in order to move it toward the negotiating table. That would generate public and international outcry that would effectively bury the 'land for peace' issue. Moreover, widespread moral outrage elicited by terrorist attacks might also have prompted more destructive military raids against Lebanon and Syria, a predicament that could have affected the broad-based support enjoyed by Hezbollah in both countries and jeopardized the anti-Israel campaign.

Therefore, as an irregular force determined to insulate itself from the terrorist label applied by two potent military powers, Hezbollah leaders adopted the tactics of guerrilla warfare instead. As defined by the United

States Air Force: 'A guerrilla force is a group of irregulars organized along military lines to conduct military and paramilitary operations in enemy-held, hostile, or denied territory.'[10]

Another characteristic of guerrilla groups, according to Christopher Harmon, an expert on terrorism and guerrilla warfare, is that they 'display some visible identification, at least at the point of using a weapon'.[11] In other words, unlike terrorists who take great pains to disguise themselves as civilians in order to strike them more effectively, guerrillas wear battle dress. In Hezbollah's case, the fighters wear camouflaged uniforms like most soldiers in modern armies do today. Some also wrap the traditional chequered Arab headdress, the *kefiyyah*, around their heads. Harmon also makes the point that the French resistance, which he apparently considers a guerrilla force, took no civilian hostages and murdered no German women during their operations against the Nazis in the Second World War.

Considering the definitions and facts presented above, it is clear that Hezbollah's present objectives and tactics conform quite closely to those of guerrilla fighters operating in or near 'denied or enemy-held territory'. In that sense, the military objective would be to remove the enemy and retrieve the 'denied territory' as efficiently as possible.

These points constitute the basis of the Lebanese government's defence of Hezbollah as an authentic Lebanese resistance organization that uses guerrilla tactics to liberate national territory. In so doing, the Party of God therefore has its blessing.

## THE US-ISRAELI POSITION: HEZBOLLAH AS TERRORIST ORGANIZATION

Irrespective of the position of the Lebanese government, a considerable body of information exists that implies the terrorist nature of Hezbollah, both in its early stage of inception and recently regarding its international activities.

When America's 'Most Wanted Terrorists' list was published on 10 October 2001, three individuals who were allegedly members of Hezbollah – Imad Fayez Mugniyeh, Hassan Ezzedin and Ali Atwa – were among the 22 men listed. Mugniyeh, was alleged to be the mastermind behind terrorist attacks against the USA in the 1980s, from car bombings to kidnappings, while Hassan Ezzedin had already been indicted by a US court along with Mugniyeh for staging the 1985 hijacking of TWA flight 847 and murdering a US Navy diver who was on that flight. Ali Atwa, an accomplice who missed the flight, was captured by the Greek authorities and then released to meet the hijackers' demands.

The prominence given to Mugniyeh after September 11th in news reports and interviews suggested that he would be the focal point of

America's pursuit of Hezbollah as a terrorist organization. For instance, in a CNN presentation that aired in early October 2001, it was claimed that Mugniyeh was actually the world's arch-terrorist and that his fingerprints might even be on the World Trade Center and Pentagon disasters since the way the explosives were delivered in that attack resembled the method used in Beirut terrorist acts in the 1980s. In both cases, ordinary means of transportation – cars, trucks and now commercial airliners – had been driven in suicidal missions into buildings full of people. The fact that the Beirut blasts were directed against political and military targets – the US Embassy during an alleged CIA meeting and the Marine and French army barracks – whereas the New York and Washington ones were aimed at maximum loss of civilian life was not considered during the broadcast.

In addition, it was mentioned in the CNN presentation that Mugniyeh might have been in contact with bin Laden's organization and been involved in training sessions in Lebanon in the early 1990s. This interview also made mention of the two Saudi blasts that killed US military personnel in 1995 and 1996 and suggested Hezbollah's involvement – if only indirectly – by connecting Mugniyeh to these operations. The presenter, CNN's Mike Boettcher, also pointed out that attacks on US embassies in Tanzania and Kenya were also suspected to have been the work of this criminal, who had already been fingered as a suspect by the Argentine authorities for blasts in 1992 and 1994 against the Israeli Embassy and a Jewish Community Center in Buenos Aires that left 144 dead.

According to Magnus Ranstorp, who was interviewed by Boettcher for the programme:

> There was a massive intelligence effort to locate Mugniyeh for over 20 years and until bin Laden popped up on our radar screens, Imad Mugniyeh was the master terrorist... he is the very opposite of bin Laden. He has skills, is more professional, and operates as a faceless terrorist. We don't know what he looks like or where he is... He is truly dangerous, and if there was an alliance between Mugniyeh and al-Qaeda it would be the worst possible scenario.[12]

As further support for the American case for Hezbollah's terrorist nature, US intelligence reports indicated that Mugniyeh remained active in Lebanon after Hezbollah became part of the Lebanese political establishment.

Clearly, further elaboration of who Imad Mugniyeh is and how he relates to Hezbollah is important here because he has been identified by the USA as the pre-eminent terrorist in that organization.

According to one of my informants, Mugniyeh is a Lebanese Shiite from South Lebanon, who was born in Tir Dibba, a village overlooking the Mediterranean Sea, in 1962. He began training with Yasser Arafat's Fatah commandos in the mid 1970s. During this period, Fatah was engaged in cross-border skirmishes with the Israelis. It is reported that Mugniyeh collaborated closely with Palestinian chieftain, Salah Khalaf, known as Abu Ayad – who, in those days, headed the Fatah secret service. It seems that he maintained his close ties with Abu Ayad until the latter's death in Tunis in 1991.

As we know, during the late 1970s and early 1980s the charismatic and much respected cleric, known to his followers as *al-ulama* (the Religious Scholar), Sayyed Mohammed Hussein Fadlallah became prominent on the Lebanese politico-religious scene. Fadlallah's preaching at the Bir al-Abed Mosque in Beirut supposedly impressed Mugniyeh, like many other young Shiite men in the early 1980s. (Information cited by Magnus Ranstorp in Chapter 2 indicated that Mugniyeh was Fadlallah's bodyguard at one point, although that fact was not confirmed or denied by the individual with whom I was talking.) While in the dahiyeh, according to my informant, Mugniyeh met Mohsen Rafiqdost, the man who later became head of Iran's Guardians of the Revolution. Rafiqdost was on a mission to help Fatah mobilize and train Shiites for action in South Lebanon. Impressed by the success of the Iranian Revolution and bereft of the Palestinian structure within which he had formerly operated after the Israeli invasion of 1982, Mugniyeh turned toward Ayatollah Khomeini's version of political Islam, finally committing himself, along with his partners, to continued actions against the Israelis as Islamic mujahidin.

Was Mugniyeh a member of Hezbollah? Considerable circumstantial evidence has surfaced in Arab, Israeli and international press services that point to a functional role performed by Mugniyeh in the activities carried out by the Party of God. For instance, at the time of the anti-American attacks in the early 1980s, the name 'Community of Hezbollah' or Hezbollah was being applied to many small and disorganized groups that actually did not answer to any central local command or organization, but apparently took their orders directly from Tehran.[13] According to American sources, Mugniyeh played an important role in the activities of these quasi-organized groups that eventually fused into Hezbollah. Despite their shadowy nature and the highly volatile and confused situation on the ground at that time, Ranstorp cites local news sources published between 1989 and 1991 that led him to believe that 'Mugniyeh headed the Party of God's central security apparatus with Abd al-Hadi Hamadi and was chiefly responsible for Hezbollah's hostage-taking activity of foreigners [sic]'.[14] This may have made it very difficult for the USA to accurately pin culpability on Mugniyeh. However, although no concrete evidence linking Mugniyeh to the attacks against the US Embassy and the Marine and French barracks has been presented, informal reports and rumours continue to make the rounds in Beirut intelligence and press circles that the organizing brain behind these violent anti-American activities was indeed Mugniyeh and a closely-knit group of operatives working with him.

It was also rumoured at the time of the West Beirut catastrophes that Mugniyeh and this small group were receiving the necessary logistical support and training required for such well-planned operations from America's adversaries in the region at the time, Iran and Syria. For its part, American intelligence was convinced that there was an Iranian connection in all the anti-American activities that were taking place in Lebanon. For instance, a number of the American citizens kidnapped in West Beirut were reported to have been transported to Iran during their captivity. Accordingly, there was good reason to believe the rumours circulating in Beirut at the time regarding Mugniyeh and this small group.

Tehran made the strategic decision to become directly involved in the Arab-Israeli struggle during Rafiqdost's tenure as head of Iran's Revolutionary Guards. As a result, Iran's Guardians of the Revolution set up training camps in Baalbek in the 1980s. According to intelligence sources, Rafiqdost called upon his comrade-in-arms, Mugniyeh, to assist in the coordination between the Revolutionary Guards and the locals responsible for the recruitment and organization of those being trained at these camps. The various Islamist organizations cohered around the Shiite mullahs mentioned in previous chapters and, in due course, most of these organizations and the fundamentalist clerics were integrated into the Party of God.

According to American intelligence sources, Mugniyeh played a key recruitment and organization role during that period. However, whether he had an official position in the leadership structure of Hezbollah or simply maintained a coordinating role remains an open question to this day. Another scenario may be that during that period, the Party of God recruited Mugniyeh into a leadership position.

American officials appear to be convinced that the cadres that were trained, indoctrinated and organized into Hezbollah at these Baalbek camps were responsible for perpetrating the attacks on American military, diplomatic and civilian targets in Lebanon at the time. They seem to be certain that Mugniyeh played a key role in meting out Iranian revenge on American personnel and interests and that he remains one of Hezbollah's key operatives today. However, US intelligence agencies do not appear to have been able to uncover or have found it inconvenient to provide any reliable evidence to support these insights.

For its part, Hezbollah has consistently denied the existence of any relationship with Mugniyeh, direct or indirect. As a matter of record, from the time of the party's inception, all Hezbollah officials have emphatically denied ever knowing a person *by the name of* Imad Mugniyeh. The apparent avoidance of this issue is clear in an answer to a recent question about the party's relationship with Mugniyeh. The response of a Hezbollah senior official was that Mugniyeh had never held a position in their organization, and was, in Deputy Secretary General Naim al-Qassim's words, 'only a name'.[15]

Such denials feed the well-grounded suspicions of American officials who claim that they possess hard evidence that Mugniyeh played a major role for Rafiqdost in the Baalbek operation. This is because the evidence said to be available makes it impossible for any member of Hezbollah's present leadership to deny knowing Mugniyeh, since all of them are known to have been intimately involved with the day-to-day functions of the Baalbek training camps.

Accordingly, in the autumn of 2001, American intelligence sources claimed that Mugniyeh was not only a member of the Party of God, but that he actually headed Hezbollah's intelligence agency, with or without title, and is still occupying that position under the alias of Jawad Noureddin. As proof of this allegation, it is pointed out that when the photographs of recently elected members of Hezbollah's highest council were published, Noureddin's name appeared without a picture. The implications of this piece of information, if true, could be very damaging for Hezbollah since evidence of an early and unbroken relationship between the Party of God and Mugniyeh could furnish grounds for direct American action against Hezbollah.

In an attempt to verify the American position on Noureddin as Mugniyeh, I interviewed a former Hezbollah press liaison, who happens to be a graduate student in the Political Science Department at the American University of Beirut, about this contention. He confirmed that Noureddin is indeed an intelligence official and former resistance leader, but that he is not Mugniyeh. He explained the absence of a published photo of this man by the fact that no military organization publicizes the face of an intelligence officer. 'After all,' he said, 'how well known was Russian President Vladimir Putin's face when he was the head of the KGB?' On Mugniyeh's fate or whereabouts he claimed to have no information.

In any case, Washington pressed ahead with its case against Hezbollah being a terrorist organization. Through official security contacts with the Lebanese government, they claimed that Mugniyeh was presently in Lebanon and demanded that Beirut find him and turn him over to them. American officials were hoping that once Mugniyeh fell into their hands, the interrogation that would follow would provide the hard evidence required to link him to Hezbollah. Consequently, the Party of God could then be held responsible for all the terrorist activities alleged to have been perpetrated by Mugniyeh.

In their response to the US demands, the Lebanese authorities indicated their willingness to fully cooperate on matters of terrorism. They also pointed out that the present Lebanese government authority could not be held responsible for the events of the lawless period of the 1980s, during which Mugniyeh allegedly perpetrated his terrorist crimes. In real terms, the American demand was diplomatically and expertly sidestepped by the Lebanese government. The known response was that their assistance was impossible, since Mugniyeh and his associates were not in Lebanon and hadn't been in the country for years.

While the Mugniyeh issue was a non-starter in Lebanon, as the Bush administration must have known it would be, it served the policy being developed by the American administration of calling up the shocking terrorist incidents of the 1980s and perpetuating their connection with Hezbollah. By arousing anti-Hezbollah passions in the USA and elsewhere, Washington hoped to frighten the Lebanese government and free its hands in dealing with this terrorist scourge once and for all. In this respect it was not too difficult for Americans and other westerners who had shared the misery of the hostages' families during the long years of their captivity, to support Washington's view of Hezbollah and its aims. Many Americans I knew were absolutely convinced that Hezbollah was indeed behind all the crimes it had been accused of and were still outraged that the organization had never been made to answer for them. A young woman from Arizona once told me: 'No matter what they [Hezbollah] are doing today, resistance or not, they have blood on their hands.'

In an interview with the Lebanese Broadcasting Companyrecorded on 10 January 2002, National Security Advisor Condoleeza Rice gave an example of how raising the events of the 1980s and perpetuating their connection with Hezbollah was being put into practice. First she linked the Party of God with other fundamentalist organizations remarking: 'George W Bush said you can't be against al-Qaeda and continue to support the terrorism of Hamas and Hezbollah.' Then Rice went back to the past, saying 'These are organizations with long histories. Hezbollah does have other functions – we understand the social part – but Hezbollah has terrorist functions that have resulted in the death of Americans and there are terrorist acts that continue to take place.' Hezbollah was still carrying out 'traceable' terrorist activity she said. Dismissing the argument that Hezbollah has grown less extreme since the mid 1980s, she remarked: 'We have a saying in the United States that a leopard can't change its spots. It's extremely important for

Hezbollah, if it really doesn't wish to be considered a terrorist organization, to stop engaging in terrorism.'[16]

The 'traceable' terrorist activity was probably a reference to a recent Israeli allegation that Hezbollah was involved in arms smuggling to Palestinians involved in the intifada. At a press briefing on the same day as the broadcast of Rice's interview, US State Department Spokesman Richard Boucher referred to that incident as follows: 'We think the weight of evidence is compelling with respect to Iran's and Hezbollah's involvement in the vessel *Karine A*'s arms shipping operation.'[17] This incident, in which Mugniyeh's name also came up, is discussed further in the next chapter.

References to Mugniyeh as master terrorist and warnings to Hezbollah to change its ways were a major part of the US strategy against fundamentalist terrorism emanating from Lebanon, but by themselves these tactics could not accomplish America's goal to sideline Hezbollah. Another method had to be found.

# Chapter Twelve

# America's Half-Hearted
# War Against Terrorism

The Americans had an axe to grind with the Lebanese government in the Mugniyeh issue and its connection to Hezbollah and now, with the war on terrorism issue in hand, a broader mandate to pressure Beirut to move against Hezbollah was available. Yet, from all accounts, covert pursuit of Mugniyeh and his cohorts had been going on for years and needed no special mandate to continue. America's war on terrorism seemed to incorporate Israel's. It was therefore widely felt in political circles in Washington, Arab capitals and others that Israel was behind the reinvigorated US campaign against Hezbollah and had specifically requested the Bush administration to include that organization in its anti-terrorist policy. From the Israeli perspective such a development would be very important, since the US government could then be further encouraged to threaten or sanction Lebanon for protecting Hezbollah within the context of its war against global terrorism. American support on this issue might very well reap positive results for Israel since Lebanon's government would obviously have to think long and hard before refusing the demands of the world's only superpower. Washington might thus succeed in stopping Hezbollah where Tel Aviv had failed. Moreover, for Israeli strategists, the timing of such an American initiative could not be better. Since the Palestinian intifada had completed its first chaotic year in September 2001 and was clearly out of control, the last thing Israeli strategists needed at this critical juncture in the struggle was the opening of another front with Hezbollah on their northern frontier. The Bush administration certainly understood Israel's apprehensions and therefore decided to try to accomplish its ally's objective to get Hezbollah out of the picture. At the same time, there may have been some discussion among members of the Bush foreign policy team about how an effort to help Israel might be rewarded by some voters in the November 2002 midterm elections. These rewards could be especially important in the Florida gubernatorial race where the President's younger brother, Jeb, was running for re-election.

With the decision taken to help their ally out, US policymakers then had to decide how best to achieve it, keeping in mind the priority they had assigned to building and holding together the Arab/Muslim coalition believed necessary to insure military success against al-Qaeda and the Taliban in Afghanistan.

## THE ANTI-TERRORISM CAMPAIGN IN LEBANON

The plan that US advisors came up with was to push the Lebanese authorities to cripple Hezbollah by threatening unilateral sanctions. This policy, however, was designed in a way that would not seriously destabilize or punish Lebanon. The sanctions threatened were economic in nature and entirely credible given US influence in international financial institutions and with western donor countries. Moreover, given Lebanon's precarious economic state, the means chosen to accomplish the goal were well calculated. The following incidents involving US Ambassador Vincent Battle, Lebanese leaders and National Security Advisor Condoleeza Rice are an illustration of how the USA played that game.

Since an important strategy developed to fight the war against global terrorism involved interrupting the flow of funds to terrorist organizations and closing down their financial transactions, Washington made use of that strategy to demand that the Lebanese government freeze Hezbollah's bank accounts. When this demand was turned down by Prime Minister Hariri on the basis of the Party of God's resistance rather than terrorist status, American officials then began a kind of 'good cop/ bad cop' routine to try to pressure the Lebanese government into taking the desired steps. For example, it seemed obvious from his remarks after presenting his government's demand to Prime Minister Hariri on 7 November that Ambassador Battle was playing the role of the 'good cop'. He explained to reporters that when he had asked for the freezing of Hezbollah's accounts he had not used the word 'immediately' and that since 'this action undoubtedly required a lot of research on the part of the Central Bank, it would be an extremely long and technical exercise'.[1] From these words, it could be taken that the Ambassador was trying to moderate the political impact of the request or even offering a way around the diplomatic impasse by suggesting that, with some finessing on the part of the Central Bank director, the required investigation might easily be dragged out or even forgotten. Unstated was the phrase 'if the authorities would "help" rein in Hezbollah'.

Shortly after this incident, when nothing had been done on the subject, Condoleeza Rice took up the 'bad cop' task. In a televised interview with ABC, Rice launched an indirect threat at Beirut by saying: 'Lebanon's efforts to reinvigorate its economy and advantageously integrate itself into the global economy will remain thwarted if Beirut doesn't respond to America's demands.'[2] This statement caused great consternation in Lebanon, as will be seen later. However, interestingly, quiet discussions between Beirut and Washington were under way at the same time to assist in Lebanon's economic recovery and to encourage friends and allies to lend support during the Paris II Economic Conference of 2002. Similarly, as Ambassador Battle went about his diplomatic duties, there were no hints in his speeches or press conferences of any coldness between his government and Lebanon. This behaviour made it look as if American anti-terrorist policy had been established by policymakers who had said: 'Let's push the Lebanese government a little and see how far we can get.'

Well aware that there was not much real chance of ending Hezbollah's jihad against their ally through the steps they were willing to contemplate at the time, and that the road to Hezbollah's cancellation as a fighting force led to Damascus, Bush advisors probably reasoned that the right pressure carefully applied to the Lebanese government might at least produce a welcome lull in the skirmishing along Lebanon's southern border for their ally and that would be a plus.

## LEBANON'S RESPONSE

The Lebanese authorities, of course, could not be sure of America's end game, yet they were well aware that there was a lot at stake in this diplomatic stand-off. Thus they made strong efforts to cement public and international support for their position that Hezbollah was a resistance movement rather than a terrorist group and therefore could not be touched. Since the USA was essentially trying a new version of the failed Israeli policy discussed in Chapter 8 – that is, leaning on Beirut to stop Hezbollah – the Lebanese officials were taking the same steps to counter that policy; that is, rallying citizens' support of the official line. However, this time they had to reassure the Lebanese public that their position on Hezbollah as resistance organization could stand up to America's pressure rather than Israel's and that no negative repercussions would befall Lebanon as a result of this stance on the terrorism vs. resistance controversy.

In meetings with members of the Maronite Christian League in early November, President Emile Lahoud sought to do just that, reassuring them that, just as national unity had brought about the liberation of South Lebanon from Israeli occupation, solidarity would now protect

Lebanon from the upsets registered in many countries after the September 11th attacks. Lebanon was able to face the developments taking place on the international scene with immunity, he said, since the policy adopted toward the resistance by Lebanon had been consistently pursued for years and was nothing new.[3]

This appeal for national unity yielded important results. Religious dignitaries and politicians of all stripes got on the bandwagon to defend Lebanon's right to resist occupation. Maronite Cardinal Nasrallah Butros Sfeir's contribution was particularly welcome, since he spoke for many Christians who opposed Syrian policy in Lebanon. When asked as he was leaving for an ecumenical conference in Rome whether he thought Hezbollah was a terrorist organization, the Catholic prelate replied: 'These men are Lebanese citizens trying to free their country from foreign occupation; we all thank them for their efforts.'[4] Even former President Amin al-Gemayel, the man whose government had been assisted in its efforts to fight off leftist militias by the American battleship *New Jersey* in 1984, described the branding of Hezbollah as a terrorist organization as 'heresy'.

On the other hand, top Muslim religious leaders required more control than mobilization on the part of the government. At a spiritual ceremony, these clergymen were actually considered too passionate in their denunciations of America's terrorist hunt, and they were subsequently requested by Beirut to temper their remarks. To make sure things did not get out of hand at this tense time, security was increased at mosques to ward off any possibility that Friday sermons might lead to anti-American demonstrations that could raise further tensions between Beirut and Washington.

While President Lahoud was trying to manage public fears and secure strong popular support for the government's position on Hezbollah's resistance status, Prime Minister Hariri began the shuttle diplomacy for which he had become so well known over the years. His travels took him to European, Arab and Muslim capitals. At the Organization of Islamic Countries (OIC) meeting in Doha during the first week of October, some of his efforts were rewarded. Representing the 1.2 billion Muslims of the world, the foreign ministers present crafted a final resolution deploring the terrorist attacks in the USA and agreeing that 'any attempt to link Islam with terrorism, and any confusion of terrorism with the right of peoples – *notably the Palestinians and Lebanese* [my emphasis] – to legitimate defense and resistance to Israeli occupation is totally rejected'.[5] The message to the United States government was that members of the world's largest faith were on the resistance side of the controversy and if the Muslim governments represented at the conference were to remain in the coalition against terrorism, America would have to think twice about any action designed to cripple Arab resistance groups. The Arab and Muslim 'streets' would not tolerate a passive position on the part of their governments if American actions against those groups took place.

While the Lahoud government was manning the diplomatic track, officials of the Central Bank and parliamentarians were preparing positions designed to avoid Washington's demands for the freezing of Hezbollah's accounts. These positions were both announced on 8 November. The Central Bank's argument was that the demand had come from the United States of America and not from the United Nations and was therefore not binding. The brief noted that the measures adopted in September to fight international terrorism were endorsed within the context of UN Security Council Resolution 1373 and were to be considered at a meeting in spring 2002. At that time, Council members would consider whether those steps had been adequately taken on a country-by-country basis. Interestingly, in recognition of the subjectivity of the term terrorism, each state would be asked to present and defend its own definition of that term. As I saw it, that provision meant that Hezbollah would be home free, since it would not be difficult for Beirut to prove that land was still occupied by the Israelis and that the Party of God was presently resisting that occupation. Furthermore, as it could not be proven that the Party of God had engaged in any activity that resembled terrorism during its struggle with the Israelis in the South, no sanctions could be applied on that score either.

The Central Bank officials also noted that since the demand to freeze Hezbollah's accounts did not originate from the International Court of Justice, whose requests are also binding internationally, it had no force. A third reason for the Bank's rejection of the American demand stemmed from the fact that it was not the result of an internal criminal invest-igation, which would have required the Central Bank's intervention.

Finally, to put the icing on cake for the Lebanese position, it was pointed out that there are no bilateral agreements between the USA and Lebanon that prescribe the conditions for 'the freezing of bank accounts that would be undertaken at the request of one of the two parties'. It seemed as if the USA would have to rebut these arguments one by one, or be accused of unjustifiably bullying a member of the international community. To date no action has been taken on this issue.

At this juncture, we should keep in mind that this give and take on Hezbollah's status had been confronted on previous occasions in policy and diplomatic actions relevant to Israel's occupation of southern Lebanon. A case in point is the information contained in the report prepared by Lebanese Parliament's Joint Committee. In this report, it was argued that the April 1996 understanding to which Israel, France,

America, Syria, Lebanon and Hezbollah were party, clearly indicated the resistance status of the latter.

As noted previously, Beirut considered that the USA had committed itself to a de facto recognition of Hezbollah as a resistance organization when it inked the points that constituted that agreement. After the massive Israeli retaliatory raids in 1996, it was thought prudent by France and the United States, as well as by those directly involved in hostilities, to set the rules of engagement down in writing. The position of all parties to the April 1996 understanding was that this agreement formalizes the tacit 'rules of combat' that had formerly governed Israeli-Hezbollah battlefield behaviour.

From a diplomatic and strategic standpoint, this was a clear victory for Hezbollah and its supporters since the April accord sought to restrain Israeli retaliatory actions that Prime Minister Rabin and several Israeli generals had once represented as unfair. Furthermore, by setting up a monitoring group and placing observers from the signatory states on the scene in South Lebanon to report any violations of the agreement, it was given additional weight. Lastly, in recognizing Lebanon as a legitimate combatant, its military arm, Hezbollah, could no longer logically be categorized by Washington as a band of mindless terrorists.

Consequently, the Lebanese parliamentarians affirmed that the international agreement recognized the legitimate right of their country's resistance against Israeli occupation. The report also noted that one of the stipulations of the 1989 Taif Accord was that all measures should be taken to free Lebanon from foreign occupation. In this framework, any activity undertaken for this purpose, or any organization working toward this end, is both constitutional and legitimate, and automatically enjoys the approval of the USA, which helped hammer out that agreement.

The report of the Joint Committees further noted that in April 1998, Lebanon had signed an agreement with other Arab states that distinguished between terrorism and armed combat against foreign occupation and that the treaty holds its signatories responsible for supporting and defending resistance organizations against accusations of terrorism. That treaty states that three features characterize a resistance force: a distinctive ideology; the fact that its militant activities take place only within national borders; and that its attacks are aimed exclusively at military targets. These characteristics, the report stated, fully described Lebanon's national resistance.[6]

While this diplomatic activity was going on in Beirut and Damascus what was Hezbollah doing about the terrorism vs. resistance controversy?

## HEZBOLLAH'S DEVELOPING RESISTANCE ROLE

While the diplomatic confrontations between Washington and Beirut over the terrorist vs. resistance controversy were running their course, Hezbollah stuck to its resistance agenda by latching onto violations of Lebanon's air space by Israeli reconnaissance planes – an opportunity to remind all concerned of its resistance/liberation responsibility. This military posturing involved the use of archaic and ineffective anti-aircraft artillery and at times rockets against sophisticated American-supplied warplanes and Israel's fortified positions in the Shebaa Farms region.

Hezbollah's activities were being recorded by the UN contingent deployed along the Lebanon-Israel border, and this was documented on 4 October 2001, right after President Bush made his well-known 'declaration of war on terrorism'. As described by the UN's de Mistura, the action went as follows: 'The day began with 12 Israeli violations of Lebanese airspace which included sonic booms over Beirut and the northern capital, Tripoli.' He continued:

> Hizbullah anti-aircraft guns opened up each time the planes flew over the border, however the over-flights continued with impunity throughout the day. Towards the end of the afternoon, however, Hizbullah began firing anti-tank missiles at the Israeli outpost at Rousat al-Alam, in the Shebaa area, and sent it up in flames. The Israelis returned fire but no casualties were reported.[7]

Were the artillery teams sending a political message? No doubt about it, in my view. Sure enough, that evening Hasan Nasrallah appeared on al-Manar TV and during the course of an interview tersely observed that Hezbollah's resistance mission would continue irrespective of what else was going on in the rest of the world.[8] This was a clear audiovisual message to the American administration, backed by action shots of the day's events on the programme's news segment of how Hezbollah regarded stigmatization by the war on terrorism campaign.

As Israeli over-flights continued on an almost daily basis and drew ineffectual ground fire from Hezbollah each time, I asked Hezbollah senior official Hassan Ezzeddin why his party continued to fire at planes with such hopelessly ineffective weapons. His response was:

> We are a guerrilla resistance group and no such group possesses the assets to defeat a modern air force – it's impossible. But does this mean we should sit with our arms folded as the Israelis fly back and forth across our country creating sonic booms that terrorize our citizens? What other state would accept such constant violations without reacting?[9]

Interestingly, a veteran Israeli commentator on Middle Eastern affairs also commented on this Israeli tactic. Voicing his opinion in the daily

Hebrew-language newspaper *Yediot Ahronot*, he indicated that the sonic booms over Beirut reflected 'a self-righteous arrogance' on the part of the Israeli government. Worse still, he noted, some Israeli analysts were now calling Hezbollah's shots at Israeli over-flights a new provocation. 'What are we doing in Lebanese skies long after the withdrawal on the ground?' he asked. 'The over-flights are the provocation and what Hezbollah is doing is the response.'[10]

Putting their heads together to try to stop the incessant over-flights, Hezbollah tacticians came up with a low-tech way of dealing with the problem. They began experimenting with anti-aircraft shells of various calibres to see whether the noise of their explosions could be enhanced. Friends in the South told me that they saw Hezbollah gunners testing shells over the sea. Soon after, when an Israeli aircraft violated Lebanon's airspace and created sonic booms, noisy shells were fired in the air over the settlements in the Galilee panhandle. The sudden blasts of these shells are apparently meant to produce the same nervous reaction among the Israeli population as the sonic booms of the Israeli fighter planes achieve in Beirut and other areas. Shrapnel rains down on the settlements from Hezbollah shells but to date they have caused little material damage and wounded two civilians.

On 26 February, the Israeli military announced a reduction in their surveillance flights as a result of 'intensified reactions' by Hezbollah. A remark of Israeli Foreign Minister Shimon Peres at the time that the Party of God was 'a particularly aggressive and dramatic terrorist group' may have reflected his feeling about the Hezbollah leaders' rather creative responses to Israeli military activities. In any event the 'bangs for booms policy' remains in effect and is sometimes, although not always, accompanied by rocket attacks at Israeli outposts in the Shebaa Farms area.

During the autumn and winter of 2001, the USA had also been urging Syria to halt its aid to terrorist groups and was using some of the same techniques being applied to the Lebanese government for that purpose. For instance, US officials visited Damascus to discuss American economic assistance in autumn 2001, and President Bush and some of his aides also expressed their appreciation of Syria's cooperation in the war against terrorism, describing some positions as positive. At the same time, some positive signals came from Washington regarding the Middle East peace process. A message was sent to Syrian Foreign Minister Farouk al-Sharaa by Colin Powell containing a commitment to reviving the Syrian track of the peace process on the basis of Security Council Resolutions 242 and 238. Then, on 19 November, in a speech given in Louisville, Kentucky, Powell publicly announced the American administration's commitment to finding a solution to the Middle East crisis and stated a 'mutual exchange of land for peace' as one of its goals.[11] These words were what the Syrian and Lebanese foreign policy team had been waiting to hear and a reaction was not long in coming. At a meeting in Beirut nine days later, Syrian Foreign Minister Farouk al-Sharaa and senior Lebanese officials were reported as having agreed that 'while the new American peace initiative was being tested in Israeli and Palestinian areas, Israel should be stripped of any pretext for blaming Syria and Lebanon for violence'.[12] This was a way of saying that the resistance would let up for a while to give Powell's initiative a chance to work. The gesture was probably meant to smooth the way for other positive developments.

At the same time as Syria was being offered this and other inducements to cease all assistance to terrorist organizations, it was also being subjected to thinly veiled threats. For instance, Syria was often mentioned with Iran as a sponsor of terrorism about which 'something would have to be done'. The 'something' was unspecified but had an ominous ring to it since no one knew where the war against terrorism might be launched next. The strength of America's determination 'to smoke the bad guys out of their holes and finish them', to use President Bush's expression, was certainly being clearly demonstrated in the military resources being poured into the hunt for Taliban and al-Qaeda terrorists in the mountains of Afghanistan. Under the circumstances, concerns about whether this US anti-terrorist commitment might soon to be demonstrated elsewhere were not too far-fetched.

Nevertheless, like its Lebanese partner, Syria chose to ignore the American threats. It probably felt that the USA had its plate too full with the Afghani campaign to make good on them. Thus, after a few weeks lull following Powell's announcement, Hezbollah's anti-aircraft batteries again opened up on Israeli reconnaissance planes violating Lebanon's airspace.

## THE PARTY OF GOD AND THE INTIFADA

While Hezbollah's 'bangs for booms' policy served the media battle it was conducting against the Israelis well, its patrons Syria and Iran nevertheless found themselves watching from the sidelines in late March 2002 as Prime Minister Ariel Sharon executed the massive onslaught entitled 'Protective Shield' against Palestinian organizations accused of terrorist acts in the Occupied West Bank territories. Their spectator status soon changed, however, as they began to exploit the unfolding battle in the West Bank with the means available – Hezbollah.

What better time to remind the harassed Israelis and their American patrons that the 'land for peace' issue remained the main objective of Syrian and Lebanese foreign policy? By heating up the confrontation with the Israeli forces in the Shebaa Farms region while a major Israeli military campaign was underway elsewhere, Hezbollah could hit three birds with one stone. First it could enter the intifada battle on the side of the Palestinians as a field combatant, while continuing the media campaign being waged against Israel by al-Manar TV. Then Hezbollah could create enough tension on Israel's northern border to force Israeli strategists to divert military resources directed against the intifada to that theatre. Finally, through these actions, the 'land for peace' proponents would be able to play the standard Arab game of using the Palestinian confrontation with Israel to further their own agenda. Specifically, Hezbollah's vigorous entrance into the confrontation would suggest the possible opening of a broader northern front that would sharply underline to the Israelis the decade-old 'no land no peace' message that the Party of God's military activities along Lebanon's southern frontier were meant to convey to the Israeli authorities. As a result of Israel's preoccupation with the intifada, that message now had far sharper teeth.

Hezbollah's appearance on the intifada scene came as no surprise to Israel's political and military establishment. The first hint of 'direct interference' by Hezbollah in the Palestinian uprising, apart from the media campaign, surfaced in January 2002 when a senior Israeli security official tied none other than Imad Mugniyeh to a shipload of arms on the *Karine A*, supposedly originating in Iran and destined for the Palestinian authority. In describing the incident, Prime Minister Sharon claimed that Arafat had assembled a 'coalition of terror that included Hezbollah', while Condoleeza Rice used the incident to point out that Hezbollah was still involved in terrorist activities, as noted previously. However, since the Sharon government was more interested in using the weapons shipment to further discredit Yasser Arafat, Israel's focus remained on the treachery of the Palestinian leader who talked peace but ordered tons of arms, rather than on Hezbollah. Both Hezbollah and Iranian leaders denied involvement in the incident.

Mugniyeh's name appeared again on 18 March in a report by an Iranian analyst based in London. The report described cooperation between two rings engaged in smuggling arms to the Palestinians from Jordan. Those cited as being involved in the rings were Iranian Revolutionary Guards and 'Hezbollah's intelligence unit run by Mugniyeh under the alias Abbas Noureddine'.[13] To be remembered here is the fact that the individual whose photo was missing in the line-up of members of Hezbollah's Command Council, and who was alleged by US intelligence services to be Mugniyeh, had been identified by my source as a man who bore the same family name – Noureddine – but whose first name was Jawad. In any event, the Jordanian authorities subsequently arrested three Lebanese said to be Hezbollah partisans for smuggling Katyusha rockets into the West Bank.

When called on by the press to comment about this incident, Hassan Nasrallah made no attempt to deny it. In fact, at a memorial service to commemorate the tenth anniversary of Secretary-General Abbas al-Musawi's assassination by the Israelis, he explained the gun-smuggling operation by saying that his organization was trying to establish some sort of balance in the Palestinian-Israeli struggle by supplying 'a very modest weapon to the resistance forces – one that for a powerful army like Israel's is like a water pistol'.[14] The Hezbollah operatives arrested were later released through the intervention of Lebanon's Prime Minister Hariri with the Jordanian authorities.

Whether Mugniyeh is indeed actively involved in Hezbollah affairs as suggested remains an open question, since information on the elusive operative appears to be closely guarded by Israeli and American intelligence agencies. Mugniyeh's participation in Hezbollah's present ranks therefore cannot be ruled out. In any event, the mention of his name during spring 2002 thrummed the chord of the TWA hijacking in 1985 and the Beirut bomb blasts and kidnappings and again brought Hezbollah's terrorist face to the forefront of international attention. As far as the American and Israeli governments were concerned, these two incidents put the lie to Hezbollah's resistance look, since the fundamentalist organization was providing aid to Palestinian groups engaged in maiming and killing Israeli civilians by suicide/martyrdom attacks; a tactic that Hezbollah leaders had expressly encouraged rather than repudiated.

Other indications of Hezbollah's entry into the Palestinian struggle surfaced later the same month when six Israeli civilians were killed in an ambush south of the Lebanon-Israel border, that is, within Israel proper. Tel Aviv immediately launched a furious propaganda campaign against Lebanon and Hezbollah blaming the latter for the terrorist act. The two perpetrators who had been killed in the clash, however, bore no identification and the al-Aqsa Martyr's Brigade, according to the *Jerusalem Post*, later claimed the attack.[15] According to Israeli officials, this group is connected to the Palestinian Authority and has claimed several suicide/martyrdom acts as its work. Several days later, the *Jerusalem Post* reported that it was now thought that Hezbollah might have trained the assailants. Israeli officials then revealed that a place where the border fence could have been breached had been found and a ladder was spotted on the Lebanese side that apparently was used to cross the border without alerting Israeli patrols.[16]

Since the modus operandi of the attack bore resemblance to al-Aqsa's style of warfare rather than Hezbollah's, my attention focused on the training idea rather than on Hezbollah's actual involvement in the attack. A more probable scenario is that Palestinian fighters who came to Lebanon for training were infiltrated into Israel across the Lebanon-Israel border, whose terrain is known to Hezbollah fighters like the back of their hands. During a press conference on 6 March, Nasrallah admitted helping the intifada by training Hamas members.[17]

No further details on the incident have been forthcoming from any source. On the Israeli side, those who died in the attack became part of the daily casualty statistics, while those who carried out the attack – whoever they were – became martyrs to the Palestinian cause. Whether Hezbollah played a part in this incident remains an open question on an official level.

Thus, as the Israelis carried out their hunt for terrorists in the Jenin Refugee Camp, Hezbollah had already demonstrated some aspects of its expanded resistance role. Now, however, it openly entered the intifada struggle. On 30 March, its fighters opened up on Israeli outposts in the Shebaa Farms area with Katyusha rockets, artillery, mortars and SAM 7s – surface-to-air Strella missiles – the latter not quite the antiquated weaponry generally used against Israeli over-flights. The barrage against planes and Israeli military outposts in the Shebaa area continued for 13 days and was anything but the wild-eyed and random action generally held to be the work of terrorists. On the contrary, Hezbollah gunners demonstrated a carefully controlled escalation of the border warfare that was meticulously calculated to fall just short of what the Israelis would consider enough to provoke a harsh retaliation. However, the attacks were intense enough to make Israeli military strategists wonder if they might be seeing the opening of a northern front that could signal the entrance of Syria and Lebanon into the intifada. Israeli strategists were nevertheless in a quandary as to how to respond. If they launched heavy reprisals against Lebanon and/or Syria to try to stop Hezbollah's onslaught, those attacks might cause the Party of God to turn its weapons on Israel's northern settlements from much closer positions than had been the case before Israel's withdrawal in 2000. Such a strategy by the Israeli military would therefore certainly not serve their country's interests at a time when the Sharon government was already taking enormous criticism for the level of destruction its military attacks had caused in the Jenin Refugee Camp, Ramallah and elsewhere in the West Bank.

After Hezbollah attacks had targeted six Israeli military outposts in the Shebaa area on one day and Israeli combat aircrafts had flown countless sorties, bombing and strafing the valleys and boulder-strewn sides of the mountains where Hezbollah's gunners seemed to be located, Israeli Defense Minister Benjamin Ben-Eliezer finally asked US Secretary of State Colin Powell 'to appeal to the highest echelons of the Syrian leadership and point out the dangers involved in the continuation of Hezbollah's terror policy'.[18] US contacts with Syrian and Lebanese leaders then took place.

It should now be easy to imagine the responses received from the leaders with whom Powell spoke. As far as they were concerned, Hezbollah was exercising its legitimate rights as a national resistance force in shelling Israeli military outposts located on Lebanese land. They could therefore not be legitimately restrained, etc., etc. Israeli and American officials countered these arguments by citing the fact that in summer 2000 the United Nations had designated a 'withdrawal line' and confirmed that the Israelis had relocated their troops on the other side of that line, in Israel as it were. Thus they considered that Hezbollah's actions were illegal and must stop immediately regardless of any territorial issues that remained unresolved. This argument of course fell on deaf ears in Beirut and Damascus.

By 11 April, Hezbollah fighters had caused enough damage on Rousset al-Alam military post to rid it of its defenders and storm its ramparts. There the Hezbollah flag was planted and souvenir photos were taken that would typically be added to al-Manar TV's archives. The professionally edited footage of Hezbollah's flag being raised over the Israeli position was broadcast by satellite TV that night. Appearing with scenes of Palestinian youths resisting Israeli tank and troop advances in Ramallah, it demonstrated how the Party of God was fighting side by side with the intifada mujahidin against Israel – the only other Muslim-Arab force to do so. No matter that the Israelis quickly denied the brief takeover of Rousset al-Alam post; a picture is worth a thousand words in this part of the world and, in this day and age, the message gets across and the image lingers. Hezbollah's media experts are keen to keep the party's performance as the 'spearhead of the Islamic resistance' in the foreground because they know that if and when the Party of God needs further insulation against the terrorist label this public relations campaign is a major way of getting it.

## GUARDING THE LEBANESE-ISRAELI FRONTIER

Who could have imagined that Hezbollah would one day find itself in the same position the Israelis had been from the 1970s until 1982 as far as preventing Palestinian attacks and infiltrations into northern Israel from Lebanon? This ironic turn of events came to light as the intifada was escalating in March and April 2002, when the Lebanese authorities announced that they were taking stern measures to stop 'rogue' Palestinian factions from the refugee camps from mounting any 'freelance' attacks across the southern border. This reaction occurred after several Katyusha rockets had been fired at Israel from South Lebanon and Hezbollah leaders had denied any involvement. A resident of Meiss al-Jabal, a Lebanese town near the site of one of those attacks, backed up the Party of God's denial when interviewed by a reporter from a local newspaper. According to this eyewitness: 'When the firing started it appeared to have caught some Hezbollah fighters manning a small observation post opposite the target by surprise.' He said he saw them jump into a Range Rover and give chase as the attackers fled into a nearby valley.[19] What was happening to elicit this behaviour from the Party of God?

As we know, Syria's state/resistance 'rules' require Hezbollah's strict control of any military activities in the border area so there can be no slip-ups in the strategic plan to immunize Hezbollah against terrorist charges. Uncontrolled actions by Palestinians at the border area therefore seriously jeopardized this plan by raising the question of Hezbollah's culpability should Israeli civilian casualties occur as a result.

The upshot of these incidents at the border by so-called 'freelance' operatives was the arrest of several Palestinians and the confiscation of weapons by Lebanese security agents and army troops outside the border area – that is, from the southern refugee camps. Along the border, however, Hezbollah remains in charge and is trying to deny access to any individuals and groups who feel compelled to do their bit for the intifada from that location.

One interesting result of this situation was the announcement that Fatah members from one of the refugee camps in the South had been arrested for their involvement in the cross-border incidents. The explicit reference to Fatah may have been because Palestinians in that group are *not* supported by Syria. This would reinforce Hezbollah's denials that it had anything to do with the Katyusha fire. The case might well be that only Syrian-endorsed Palestinians from *outside* Lebanon are to be assisted by the Party of God.

On the other hand, the round-up of rogue Palestinian 'freedom fighters' suggests that the unusual deaths of Israeli civilians that had allegedly involved a border crossing from Lebanon by ladder, may have occurred because Hezbollah – like the Israeli border guards on the other side of the fence – simply could not detect the presence of the perpetrators and stop them. One thing, however, seems certain: Palestinian groups will not have free rein along the border as was the case in the 1970s and 1980s. If they cannot be made to fit the careful Syrian game plan, their access will be strictly denied by Hezbollah.

This is where things stood in this boiling little corner of the world as of early autumn 2002. To date, the USA has made no formal response to the arguments made by Lebanese Central Bank officials or the Joint Committee of the Parliament to deny America's demands to freeze Hezbollah's bank accounts. Nor has any unilateral US action against Hezbollah, Lebanon, Syria or Iran been taken. For its part, no action has been forthcoming from the UN Security Council regarding reviewing anti-terrorist actions taken by Lebanon to determine whether or not they are sufficient to avoid sanctions.

However, official US spokespersons added new terrorist crimes to Hezbollah's docket in the summer of 2002, with accusations that the Party of God is training al-Qaeda operatives in camps inside Lebanon. Given Syria's known posture toward al-Qaeda activities, it can be stated with confidence that Hezbollah is not involved in any al-Qaeda training camps. On the other hand, since Hamas political leaders have been given safe haven in Syria, the training of fighters from that organization by Hezbollah is quite realistic, if not a forgone conclusion.

In late June, during a lull in the skirmishing along the border, Israel made accusations that Hezbollah was preparing a large-scale attack against the Jewish state. This was based on reports of large shipments of sophisticated weapons from Iran – one of the countries mentioned by President Bush as forming an 'Axis of Evil' with North Korea and Iraq. Reacting to the conclusion drawn by the Sharon government that these weapon deliveries indicated an imminent and large-scale military attack against Israel, President Lahoud claimed that these unfounded allegations were an attempt by the Israeli government to ruin Lebanon's tourist season. House Speaker Berri's version of what he called 'Israeli rumour-mongering tactics' was that it was a way for Prime Minister Sharon to escape criticism for the increasing pressure of suicide/martyrdom attacks and the drastic failure of his April offensive against the West Bank. He added: 'Despite its use of massive force against Palestinian citizens, Israel still needs to promote its image as a small country besieged by Arab terrorist hordes.'[20] The battle for making or breaking Hezbollah's resistance image rages on.

# Chapter Thirteen

# Conclusions and Implications

When the Bush administration went after Hezbollah as a terrorist organization in the autumn of 2001, the governments of Lebanon and Syria came to its defence, insisting that it was a legitimate, national resistance group fighting Israeli occupation. However, this terrorism vs. resistance controversy was nothing new. It had been a bone of contention between Beirut and Washington ever since the first post-war Lebanese government took office in 1990. Today, the confrontation from those on both sides of the issue appears to be escalating and I do not expect a resolution in the near future.

I have shown that pinning the 'terrorist' label on Hezbollah is a matter of major importance for the Bush administration, because the Americans remain convinced that the Party of God was responsible for all the terror attacks against American forces and civilians in Beirut during the 1980s. Consequently, there are old scores to settle. But while the US State Department claims to have solid evidence to support their position, this evidence remains under lock and key, except for what has been leaked or publicly stated regarding alleged master criminal Imad Mugniyeh's relationship with Hezbollah. No party has substantiated the link between Mugniyeh and Hezbollah to this day.

Since the September 11th attacks on the World Trade Center and the launching of America's war on international terrorism, the new profile for the terrorist enemy became any irregular force with global reach that threatens America's interests or those of its allies; for instance, Israel, Pakistan, the Philippines and other countries. As an irregular force fighting Israel, Hezbollah therefore received further certification as a long-standing member of America's list of terrorist organizations. Irrespective of the motivation behind this development, however, as far as the Israelis were concerned, the Americans were drawn into an alliance against the intifada. Hezbollah's manoeuvring to play a role in the intifada battle was therefore categorized as terrorism, since irregular forces seeking the overthrow of a country that was an American ally were involved.

The Bush administration became actively involved in pursuing Hezbollah by flexing its economic muscle against the Lebanese government. If this strategy was successful in getting the Lebanese authorities to freeze Hezbollah's financial transactions and shut down its operations in South Lebanon, this initiative would be followed by a request to find, capture, imprison and turn over Hezbollah leaders and operatives, including Mugniyeh and partners, to the US authorities. With this accomplished, the Bush administration could add another victory against terror in the Middle East to the one claimed against al-Qaeda in Afghanistan.

The Israelis rejoiced. Any American effort to close down Hezbollah was an effort to relieve the terrorists' pressure on Israel's northern border and to head off their direct involvement in the Palestinian intifada. With Hezbollah out of the way, Syria's indirect military involvement would be curtailed and Israel would be able to turn its back on the 'land for peace' formula with little if any concern about jeopardizing its security along the border with Lebanon.

On the other side of the terrorism/resistance controversy, the information that I reviewed and investigated indicated that a determined effort was made by Hezbollah to stay clear of all terrorist activities during the lengthy jihad against the Israelis in South Lebanon. This position, although undeclared, is made clear by the evidence presented in this book. Also clear is the fact that Hezbollah is presently expanding its resistance role firmly backed by its sponsors, Syria and Iran.

Belligerent posturing and rather ritual skirmishing with Israeli troops along the border constitute Hezbollah's main service to the strategy in effect in Lebanon today. However, the potential for more serious activities that could be instigated by the Party of God's two patrons prevents the Israelis from shovelling the 'land for peace' negotiations under the carpet and totally ignoring the issue, as they obviously want to do. Thus, Hezbollah is maintained as a thorn in the northern side of Israel by Syria and Iran, while Israel and America coordinate anti-terrorism policy and action to sideline the Party of God and other irregular operatives in the region.

Realizing that they were the weak link in this strategic confrontation, Hezbollah leaders accordingly developed and implemented a plan of action with the full approval of Iran and Syria that focused on setting their organization up as an authentic and legitimate Lebanese party with a resistance wing. This legitimacy, authenticated by the Lebanese government, blunted the most effective weapon in the American and Israeli arsenals, namely, the terrorist label.

The information I have presented shows how this was done; how a pragmatic group of Lebanese mullahs carefully planned and interwove militant policies toward Israel and cooperative ones toward the Lebanese authorities and other Lebanese groups to achieve their goal. That goal, I discovered, was the immunization of Hezbollah's jihad strategy from just the sort of pressure the USA used against Lebanon in autumn 2001. The leaders' careful study of the situation, however, made them explicitly reject terrorism as a means of ending the Israeli occupation in South Lebanon as they foresaw the danger this tactic would pose to the contemplated jihad strategy. Furthermore, by adopting guerrilla warfare tactics, Hezbollah leaders believed that the party cadres would prove themselves in this conflict against a conventional army as other irregular groups in rural-based struggles had before. They were fully convinced that acts of violence against innocent civilians had no place in guerrilla warfare of this type and this was another reason they were ruled out.

The rigorous application of resistance strategy and guerrilla tactics to achieve continuous casualties among Israeli and SLA troops meant that charges of terrorism that were made on the basis of the common definition of that concept could not be sustained against the fundamentalist fighters by Israel or the USA in autumn 2001 on the basis of any factual evidence. No reports were made by United Nations observers in position along the Israeli-Lebanese frontier, or by any other party, of Hezbollah attacks specifically aimed at maiming or killing Israeli citizens for the purpose of spreading terror. Consequently, those with interests in the region remained unconvinced of America's general position that any irregular forces fighting Israel or itself must be terrorists and that Hezbollah therefore belonged in that category.

However, the circumstantial nature of the case made against Hezbollah by the Bush administration for earlier terrorist acts against American citizens cannot be written off lightly. Neither can the international community forget more recent attacks against Israeli citizens in Argentina that are alleged to have been carried out by Hezbollah operatives. The importance of finding and bringing to justice the perpetrators of these crimes is imperative. However, in the absence of hard evidence, these allegations were overwhelmed by Hezbollah's clean military record in South Lebanon from 1985 on. Their performance against the Israeli military in the 'Security Zone' enshrined the Party of God as an untouchable resistance movement in the Arab and Muslim worlds.

Oblivious to Arab and Muslim public opinion, the USA and Israel nevertheless pressed on with their programme to clip Hezbollah's wings. To American policymakers the aims and modus operandi of the Party of God in South Lebanon are trivial matters when weighed against past terrorist actions and recent irregular activities in the Shebaa Farms region. They did not hesitate to use the pejorative label to blacken Hezbollah's image and try to close it down. However, when the Bush administration threatened sanctions against Lebanon based on what most Lebanese and all government officials considered was a trumped up charge designed to save its ally's skin, local public reaction against the United States initiative and in support of the government's position was intense. That reaction and its echoes around the Middle East constituted a critical element in Beirut's capacity to defy US demands that it take action against Hezbollah.

I have already mentioned that Beirut's long-standing position on Hezbollah's national resistance status had, over the years, been constantly supported and defended against international pressures of various sorts. I also noted that this support was the result of careful consideration and coordination with Hezbollah's sponsors, Syria and Iran. To me, what remains in question is how much of the Lebanese authorities' support for Hezbollah's jihad activities is the result of official conviction and/or coercion by ever-present Syria and, to a lesser extent, Iran.

Hezbollah's policies were certainly designed to make it easier for the Lebanese government to resist American pressure. Through these policies it actively tried to cast off the terrorist image with which it had been saddled since the early 1980s. To change its terrorist face, a great deal of internal political restructuring, as well as media-backed cosmetic surgery, had to be performed. Political restructuring was accomplished by transforming Hezbollah into a mainstream political party. That transformation was followed up by the initiation of a number of policies and programmes aimed at achieving the party's deep integration into the social and political life of Lebanon's multi-confessional and secular society.

The success of this political restructuring owed a great deal to the leadership's nimbleness in appealing to the religious and patriotic feelings of various Lebanese groups. An interesting feature of this ideological flexibility was that although the leaders' deep commitment to Islam and its particular goals were soft-pedalled at times, it was never completely hidden or retracted. This is because Hezbollah's Islamic appeal is a key draw in terms of recruitment and financial support.

The media-backed cosmetic surgery mentioned above was performed to give a new look to 'Hezbollah, the Iranian-backed terrorists' as seen by western society, the international media and to a certain extent by some locals. To display the Party of God's resistance and mainstream party face and ensure it unfettered coverage, the al-Manar television station was established, licensed and positioned with media satellites for worldwide viewing. Within a relatively short period, it was beaming the daily activities of Hezbollah's parliamentarians and administrators as well as the sermons and speeches of its leaders and its battlefield exploits into the homes of ordinary Arabs, Muslims and viewers all over the world. This television coverage provided a contrasting image to that put forward by America and Israel and made it difficult to insinuate that Hezbollah was being shoved down Lebanon's throat by Syria or was merely following Iran's orders. It also went a long way toward immunizing Hezbollah's jihad from the American claim that the Party of God was no different than any other fundamentalist group on the terrorist list to be sidelined or eliminated sometime later. By autumn 2001, Hezbollah's strongest detractors had to acknowledge the party's socio-political contributions to Lebanese life.

Yet, while investigating all Hezbollah's activities since their first appearance on the Lebanese political scene, I noticed their intense concern – perhaps paranoia – with America's terrorism policy initiatives. It looked as if party leaders were convinced that Hezbollah was the principal target of this policy, irrespective of all the other regional groups that had made the infamous list of terrorist organizations. In my view, where there is smoke there is fire. However, the Americans were either unable or unwilling to pinpoint the fire and put it out. This indecisiveness contributes to the USA's inability to sideline or make an impact on Hezbollah's jihad activities to date. The half-hearted strategy of coercing Lebanon to act against Hezbollah that was formulated by Bush administration policymakers is a case in point. The Israelis had tried a much more punishing version of that strategy five times to get Beirut to rein in Hezbollah, yet massive destruction of Lebanon's infrastructure had not changed the government's position toward Hezbollah one whit. True, economic sanctions were chosen by Bush strategists to pinch the Lebanese government where it was sure to hurt the most and push it to comply with America's demands, still, the operative words were 'pinch' and 'push' rather than 'bash' and shove'. Furthermore, these pressure tactics elicited the same results as they had when the Israelis used them. Public outrage made any move by the Lebanese government to comply with America's demands look like knuckling under to superpower bullying. The response from Lebanon was to stall and coordinate its diplomatic response with Syria's. At the same time, government institutions went to work preparing the legal bases of their refusal to freeze the Party of God's bank accounts as demanded by the USA.

America's half-hearted attempt to pressure Lebanon was obvious to me from the start and stood to reason. Where would it get them with Syria exercising its veto power over any action the Lebanese government might take regarding Hezbollah? Washington thus chose to sidestep a confrontation with Beirut and tried some pressure tactics on the Syrians.

Unlike in Lebanon, where only punishment was promised for non-compliance with US demands, the Americans unveiled a carrot and stick routine with Syria. If the Damascus government would disarm Hezbollah, it could receive substantial economic support. If not, it might face possible military action by unspecified forces. As a sweetener, the Americans promised to nudge Israel toward land for peace negotiations with the Syrian government. Like their Lebanese allies, the Syrians were not impressed and ignored the American inducements and threats. This was because, while they clearly recognized the nature of the stick being brandished, the substance of the main carrot – helping Syria regain the Golan Heights – was not specific enough. As that remains the paramount issue for the Assad government it is not difficult to see why, with the unstable conditions prevailing in the region, it would be illogical for Syria to give up its most important tactical asset – Hezbollah – for vague promises on which the American administration might not be able to deliver.

What this means for Lebanon is that it will continue to be buffeted now and then by events unfolding along its southern border. Since the Syrian strategy is continuing and a pattern of skirmishing has been established between the Party of God's militants and the Israeli army in the Shebaa Farms area, there seems to be little possibility that the Lebanese Army will be sent to the border area to replace Hezbollah any time soon. Consequently, Beirut will continue to reject demands by the United Nations, the USA, Israel and other countries to withdraw the fundamentalist fighters so that stability can return to that region. To Israel's enemies, the quest for stability along the Lebanese-Israeli frontier is a euphemism for protection of the Hebrew state. Thus, the tempo of the struggle along the border will continue to fluctuate up and down in accordance with the message Hezbollah sponsors want delivered to the Americans and the Israelis. At the same time, it appears that the present Israeli government has second thoughts about applying the policy of massive retaliation against Lebanon that was previously used to try to stop Hezbollah attacks in the South and is aware that retaliation against Syrian installations or troops could risk Hezbollah gunners opening up on Israel's northern settlements. The strategic advantage Hezbollah fighters gained as a result of Israel's troop withdrawal in May 2000 thus comes into play here. All the makings of a regional disaster are present in this confrontation and it is difficult under the present circumstances to anticipate what may come next.

Consequently, the political state of affairs in the region creates a difficult, if not an untenable environment for America's war on terrorism. Moreover, by applying this policy to Hezbollah, the Bush administration finds itself sucked into an anti-Arab position on the one hand and facing charges of anti-Islamic motivations on the other.

Another very troubling aspect of this situation, for the Americans as well as for the Israelis, is the entrée it gives Iran into regional affairs. It is clear that the Islamic Republic's alliance with Syria and its sponsorship of Hezbollah is an integral part of the Khomeini policy to export the Islamic Revolution. One manifestation of this policy is the support given Hezbollah's Islamist activities in Lebanon that are designed to encourage Islamic discourse and promote the faith. Mosques, religious centres and schools have increased considerably in number over the last decade and the celebration of Ashura, a commemoration of the murder of Imam Hussein, the Prophet's grandson and Imam Ali's son, reached staggering proportions at Hezbollah's massive hall in the dahiyeh in 2002.

The Americans knew at an early stage that Hezbollah, financed by Iran, was behind this surge of interest in Islam in the Lebanese Shiite community. Furthermore, they were also convinced that the activities mentioned above, as well as the network of social and public services established by Hezbollah with Iran's help, facilitated the fundamentalist party's ability to find 'terrorist' recruits. American policymakers also observed this trend in Gaza and the West Bank, where Hamas and Islamic Jihad are operating. To the Bush administration, the spread of Iranian-sponsored Islamic fundamentalism could undermine its whole policy in the region.

Recently, the USA and Israel charged that Iran was practising its policy of exporting the Islamic Revolution by providing financial and material support directly to Palestinian fundamentalist groups. How the Party of God was helping its patron became public knowledge when Jordanian security forces caught members trying to smuggle Katyusha rockets to intifada activists across the northern part of the Israeli-Jordanian border. Similarly, a shipload of arms to the Palestinians, allegedly traceable to Iran and supposedly assisted by Mugniyeh, was considered by the USA and Israel as further evidence of Iran and Hezbollah's interest in involving themselves in the Palestinian uprising. According to the Bush administration, these kinds of actions by Iran fall under the category of state-sponsored terrorism and must be dealt with accordingly. For its part, Iran places Israel's activities toward the Palestinians and America's pro-Israeli bias in the same category.

Strategic goals notwithstanding, my view of the main reason for Iran's unquestionable involvement in this regional strife rests on its leaders' absolute conviction of the religious sanctity of actions taken to liberate Jerusalem from Israeli occupation. Through the centuries, liberating the Holy City from the hands of infidels has inspired similar passion and commitment from Jews and Christian Crusaders alike. The implications of this ideological position taken by the mullah leadership in Iran are that its alliance with Syria and assistance to Hezbollah will most likely continue. This impression is reinforced by the fact that Hezbollah's Hassan Nasrallah enjoys close relations with reformist President Mohammed Khatami, as well as with Islamic hardliner Ayotallah Ali Khameini, Iran's spiritual leader. Both these men have openly praised Hezbollah as a national and Islamic resistance movement since the recent terrorism vs. resistance controversy surfaced. Iranian and Hezbollah leaders see eye to eye on the recovery of Jerusalem and all of historic Palestine for the Muslims and on supporting Palestinian fundamentalist organizations as a means of accomplishing this goal. This implies that, while Hezbollah may be able to assist Iran in that campaign, Iran will not hesitate to make available to the Party of God whatever it might need in terms of weapons and funds to carry out the sacred mission. Recent reports that Iran has been flying weapon supplies destined for Hezbollah in cargo aircraft through Iraq twice a week support that conclusion.

On another more general level, these interactions between Muslim fundamentalist groups called 'terrorist networks' by the Bush administration to thwart or even destroy Israel are believed by some US policymakers and scholars to pose a threat not only to Israel, but also to the West as a whole. If the spread of fundamentalist Islam is not neutralized, so the thinking goes, it might eventually cause a 'clash of civilizations' – Islam vs. Judaeo-Christianity. In this scenario, Hezbollah, perhaps more than any other Middle Eastern group including al-Qaeda, might be the West's number one enemy. Militantly religious, disciplined and skilled in modern communications techniques, Hezbollah leaders, coached by Syria and backed by the important resources Iranian leaders make available, have learned how to put their version of activist Islam across to the Arab and Muslim peoples in ways not likely to be forgotten. It can be assumed, for instance, that radical fundamentalist groups confronting secular governments in Egypt, Saudi Arabia, Pakistan, Indonesia and other countries have not been deaf to the jihad messages transmitted by al-Manar TV, nor blind to the lessons of Hezbollah's long struggle with the region's superpower in South Lebanon.

Hezbollah also connects with other Islamic fundamentalist groups as well as secular Arabs and Muslims in its efforts to fan the flames of the Palestinian revolt, which it believes will inevitably lead to the destruction of the 'Zionist infidels' and the return of all Palestinians to their homeland. Before the present intifada, most people considered this goal unthinkable because of the vast difference in conventional military power and other resources between Palestinians and Israelis. Now, however, Hezbollah's achievements against the Israelis combined with Tel Aviv's failure to quickly control the intifada conflict and the Islamist attacks that some feel pose an existential threat to Israel, an element of doubt has entered the picture.

For these reasons, I do not expect the Bush administration to sidestep the challenge Iran's fundamentalist policy represents to the region or back off from confronting Hezbollah as a terrorist organization. However, it should now be apparent that forcing the Lebanese government into action against the Party of God is a non-starter. Irrespective of the special consideration and flexible handling given Lebanon on issues of regional security and especially those relevant to the war on terrorism, United States policymakers well know that Syria alone can pull the plug on Hezbollah. This the Assad government will not do, however, unless there is something to be gained from it. Some motion by the Israelis to renew 'land for peace' negotiations with its neighbours would probably be a step in the right direction. However, since the present Israeli administration shows little sign of interest in that option, there seems to be no end of the confrontation in South Lebanon in sight. Consequently, the quarrel over Hezbollah's terrorist or resistance face will continue to create waves in the region.

If, however, we take the Bush administration at its word, the days of Hezbollah as a force for change are numbered, although this largely depends on when America and its Arab allies can afford to ignore popular sentiment in the region. To improve the chances of that development happening sooner rather than later, the Bush administration appointed an advertising magnate to a newly created post of undersecretary for public diplomacy and public affairs. The task: to put a better face on American foreign policy. To find out how that could best be done, a senior staff member of the House Appropriation Committee and an assistant to the new undersecretary began informal meetings with opinion moulders in Syria and Lebanon, as well as in Egypt, during August 2002. The question posed by the American visitors was: 'How can America change its negative image of unwavering bias toward Israel at the Arab and Muslim's expense to one of credible regional troubleshooter?' As far as changing Lebanese and Syrian public opinion about American foreign policy objectives in the region is concerned, I think I can safely say that the USA will have as much trouble changing its image as any other player in the Middle East political game, strong public relations campaigns notwithstanding.

In Hezbollah's case, this was demonstrated on 5 September 2002, a few days after Hezbollah had shattered a four-month lull in the Shebaa Farms by shelling two Israeli outposts and wounding three soldiers, one of whom later died. In response to a question about this incident, the US Deputy Secretary of State, Richard Armitage, announced that in his opinion Hezbollah had become even more dangerous than Osama bin Laden's group; that it had in fact 'made the A team of terrorists, maybe al-Qaeda is actually the B team'. 'We are going to go after them just like a high school wrestler goes after opponents. We are going to take them down one at a time,' he said.[1] These comments are among the strongest yet made against Hezbollah by a senior US official and have reignited fears in Lebanon of a military strike against the party, possibly by Israel, following the US-led assault on Iraq of 2003. After a meeting in Beirut with the Lebanese Foreign Minister, US Ambassador Vincent Battle responded to a journalist's question about Armitage's statement by explaining that he also applied the A team analogy to Hezbollah and that his government views Hezbollah 'as a focal point in its campaign against terrorist organizations around the world'.[2] He said that he had been expressing that view to the Lebanese authorities ever since he arrived in Lebanon and presented his credentials one day after the September 11th attacks.

Not allowing these statements to pass unremarked, Hezbollah issued a press statement calling Armitage's statements 'a pack of lies designed to mislead and divert public opinion, in an attempt to justify the US administration's hostile actions'.[3] The announcement further declared that Hezbollah would hold the American administration accountable for any offensive against Lebanon and emphasized that they are 'in full readiness to confront any eventuality and defend our people'.

Exactly one year after the war against terrorism had begun, it was back to square one. But there was, after all, one interesting change. Asked whether Hezbollah's attack was considered an act of terrorism, Battle said that it did 'not fall within the rubric' of terrorism, since Hezbollah had gone after 'combatant targets' and not civilians.[4] That admission, a first from an American official, at last revealed that regardless of what the Party of God was doing in South Lebanon in terms of terrorist or resistance action, the United States of America wanted them out of business.

# Notes

## Introduction

1.    'Jihad', from the Arabic verb *jahada* (to strive), is used here in its familiar military connotation – holy war.

2.    Pluto Press, London, published Amal Saad Ghorayeb's book, *Hizbullah: Politics and Religion* in spring 2002. See also Hala Jaber, *Hezbollah: Born with a Vengeance* (New York: Columbia University Press, 1997) and Magnus Ranstorp's *Hizb'allah in Lebanon: The Politics of the Western Hostage Crisis* (London: Macmillan Press, 1997). See also the following articles and chapters on Hezbollah that appeared in the 1990s: Nizar A Hamzeh, 'Lebanon's Hizbullah From Islamic Revolution to Parliamentary Accommodation', *Third World Quarterly*, 14, 2 (1993), pp.321–37; Judith Harik, *The Public and Social Services of the Lebanese Militias* (Oxford: Centre for Lebanese Studies, 1994); 'Between Islam and the System: Sources and Implications of Popular Support for Lebanon's Hizbullah', *Journal of Conflict Resolution*, 40, 1 (March 1996), pp.41–67; Martin Kramer, 'The Moral Logic of Hizbullah', in Walter Reich (ed.), *Modern Origins of Terrorism: Psychologies, Ideologies, Theologies, States of Mind* (Cambridge: Cambridge University Press, 1990), pp.131–57; 'Hizbullah: The Calculus of Jihad', in Martin E Marty and R Scott Appleby (eds), *Fundamentalisms and the State: Remaking Polities, Economies, and Militancy* (Chicago: University of Chicago Press, 1993), pp.539–56. Eyal Zisser, 'Hizbullah in Lebanon – At the Crossroads', *Terrorism and Political Violence*, 8, 2 (1996), pp.90–110, and Richard Augustus Norton, *Hizbullah of Lebanon: Extremist Ideals vs. Mundane Politics* (New York: Council on Foreign Relations, 1999) briefly review Hezbollah's standing in Lebanon and possible directions as a fighting force.

3.    Giovanni Sartori, *Parties and Party Systems: A Framework for Analysis* (Cambridge: Cambridge University Press, 1976).

4.    Cynthia Lorraine Irwin discusses these problems in *Paramilitary Politics in Parliamentary Democracies: Militant Nationalism in Ireland and Spain*, unpublished PhD Dissertation (Raleigh, North Carolina: Duke University, 1995).

## Chapter 1: Hezbollah's Version of Political Islam

1.    See Juan RI Cole's *Sacred Space and Holy War: The Politics, Culture and History of Shi'i Islam* (London and New York: I.B.Tauris, 2001) for more information.

2.    Fazlar Tahman, 'Islam: Challenges and Opportunities', in Alford T Welch and Pierre Cachin (eds), *Islam: Past Influence and Present Challenge* (Edinburgh: Edinburgh University Press, 1979), pp.318–23.

3.    See John Voll, *Islam: Continuity and Change in the Modern World* (Boulder, Colorado: West View Press, 1982); Robin Wright, *Sacred Rage* (New York: Simon and Schuster, 1985); and Ali EH Dessouki, *Islamic Resurgence in the Arab World* (New York: Praeger, 1982) for further information on the religious revival.

4.    See Hamid Enayat, *Modern Islamic Political Thought* (London: Macmillan, 1982); Panyiotis J Vatikiiotis, *Islam and the State* (London: Croom-Helm, 1987).

5.    R Scott Appleby (ed.), *Spokesmen for the Despised: Fundamentalist Leaders of the Middle East* (Chicago: University of Chicago Press, 1997), p.3.

6.    See Richard P Mitchell, *The Society of Muslim Brothers* (London: Oxford University Press, 1969), p.30. See also Charles Wendell (tr.), *Five Tracts of Hassan al-Banna (1906–1949)* (Berkeley: University of California Press, 1978).

7.    See Ahmad S Moussalli, *Historical Dictionary of Islamic Fundamentalist Movements in the Arab World, Iran and Turkey* (Lanham, Maryland: Scarecrow Press, 1999), pp.37–9 for further details.

8.    Patrick Seale, *Asad: The Struggle for the Middle East* (Berkeley, California: University of California Press, 1988) provides an insightful history of this leader's life and politics. See also Umar Abd-Allah, *The Islamic Struggle in Syria* (Berkeley, California: Mizan Press, 1983).

9.    Fred H Lawson, 'Social Basis of the Hamah Revolt', *MERIP Report*, 9, November–December 1982.

10.   For more on political Islam in Egypt, see Mahmoud A Faksh, *The Future of Islam in the Middle East: Fundamentalism in Egypt, Algeria, and Saudi Arabia* (Westport, Connecticut: Praeger, 1997).

11.   R Hrair Dekmejian, 'Resurgent Islam and the Egyptian State', in Reeva Simon (ed.), *Essays in Honor of J. C. Hurewitz* (New York: Columbia University Press, 1989); and Patrick D Gaffney, 'Fundamentalist

Preaching and Islamic Militancy in Upper Egypt', in R Scott Appleby (ed.), *Spokesmen for the Despised: Fundamentalist Leaders of the Middle East* (Chicago: University of Chicago Press, 1997), pp.257–93, give a good idea of fundamentalist politics in Egypt.

12.   Farzana Shaykh, *Islam and Islamic Groups: A Worldwide Reference Guide* (London: Longman, 1992), p.68.

13.   See al-Sadiq Mahdi, 'Islam, Society, and Change', in John L Esposito (ed.), *Voices of Resurgent Islam* (Oxford: Oxford University Press, 1981).

14.   Judith Miller, 'Global Islamic Awakening or Sudanese Nightmare? The Curious Case of Hassan Turabi', in Appleby (ed.), *Spokesmen for the Despised*, pp.182–224.

15.   See Shireen Hunter (ed.), *The Politics of Islamic Revolution* (Bloomington, Indiana: Indiana University Press, 1988); Vanessa Martin, *Creating an Islamic State: Khomeini and the Making of a New Iran* (London and New York: I.B.Tauris, 2000); and Baqer Moin, *Khomeini: Life of the Ayatollah* (London and New York: I.B.Tauris, 1999).

16.   Hamid Dabashi, *Theology and Discontent: The Ideological Foundations of the Islamic Revolution in Lebanon* (New York: New York University Press, 1993) and Amal Saad Ghorayeb, *Hizbullah: Politics and Religion* (London: Pluto Press, 2002) examine the finer points of the Party of God's ideology.

17.   See Martin Kramer, 'Redeeming Jerusalem: The Pan-Islamic Premise of Hezbollah', in David Manashri (ed.), *The Iranian Revolution and the Muslim World* (Boulder, Colorado: Westview Press, 1990), pp.105–30.

18.   Daniel Brumberg, 'Khomeini's Legacy: Islamic Rule and Islamic Social Justice', in Appleby (ed.), *Spokesmen for the Despised*, pp.16–82.

19.   See Farid el-Khazen, *The Communal Pact of National Identities: The Making and Politics of the 1943 National Pact*, Papers on Lebanon Series, no.12 (Oxford: The Centre for Lebanese Studies, 1992); and Helena Cobban, *The Making of Modern Lebanon* (London: Hutchins, 1985) for details.

20.   Michael C Hudson explains Lebanon's internal problems well in *The Precarious Republic: Political Modernization in Lebanon* (Boulder, Colorado: Westview Press, 1985). See also Kamal S Salibi, *A House of Many Mansion: The History of Lebanon Reconsidered* (London and New York: I.B.Tauris, 1988).

21.   Arnold Hottinger, 'Zu'ama in Historical Perspective', in Leonard Binder (ed.), *Politics in Lebanon* (New York: John Wiley and Son, 1987), pp.85–105.

22.   For instance, Ghassane Salame points out that 43% of the deputies in the 1968–1972 parliament were the sons, grandsons, cousins, etc. of someone who had either been, or still was, a deputy; *Lebanon's Injured Identities: Who Represents Whom During a Civil War?*, Papers on Lebanon Series,

no.2 (Oxford: Centre for Lebanese Studies, 1986), p.22. See also Samir Khalaf, 'Primordial Ties and Politics in Lebanon', *Middle Eastern Studies*, 4, 3 (Summer 1968), pp.243–69; 'Parliamentary Elites', in Landau et al, *Electoral Politics in the Middle East: Issues, Voters and Elites* (London: Croom Helm, 1980), pp.243–71; and Iliya Harik, 'Political Elites of Lebanon', in G Lenczowski (ed.), *Political Elites in the Middle East* (Washington, DC: American Enterprise Institute, 1975), pp.201–20. See also Khalaf, 'Changing Forms of Political Patronage', in Ernest Gellner and John Waterbury (eds), *Patrons and Clients in Mediterranean Societies* (London: Duckworth, 1977).

23.    See Rex Bynen, *Sanctuary and Survival: The PLO in Lebanon* (Boulder, Colorado: Westview Press, 1990); Yezid Sayigh, *Armed Struggle and the Search for State: The Palestinian National Movement, 1949–1993* (Oxford: Clarendon Press, 1997). Elaine C Hagopian explains Maronite Christian radicalization in 'From Maronite Hegemon to Maronite Militancy', *Third World Quarterly*, 11, 4 (1989), pp.101–115.

24.    Marius Deeb, *The Lebanese Civil War* (New York: Praeger 1980); Samir Khalaf, *Lebanon's Predicament* (New York: Columbia University Press, 1987); N Kliot, 'The Collapse of the Lebanese State', *Middle Eastern Studies*, 23 (January 1987); and Joseph Chamie, 'The Lebanese Civil War: An Investigation into the Causes', *World Affairs*, 139 (Winter 1976), pp.171–88.

25.    See A Nizar Hamzeh and R Hrair Dekmejian, 'The Islamic Spectrum of Lebanese Politics', *Journal of South Asian and Middle Eastern Studies*, 16, 3 (Spring 1993).

26.    See Helena Cobban, 'The Growth of Shiite Protest in Lebanon and its Implications for the Future', in Juan IR Cole and Nikki R Keddie (eds), *Shiism and Social Protest* (New Haven: Yale University Press, 1988), pp.138–43.

27.    Elizabeth Picard reviews the economic and political bases of Shiite mobilization in 'Political Identities and Communal Identities: Shifting Mobilization Among the Lebanese Shi'a Through Ten Years of War, 1975–1985', in Dennis L Thompson and Dov Ronen (eds), *Ethnicity, Politics and Development* (Boulder, Colorado: Lynne Riener Publishers, 1986), pp.159–78.

28.    Fuad Ajami, *The Vanished Imam: Imam Musa al-Sadr and the Shi'a of Lebanon* (Ithaca, New York: Cornell University Press, 1986).

29.    For information on the Arab-Israeli wars, see Trevor Nevitt Dupuy, *Elusive Victor: The Arab-Israeli Wars, 1947–1974* (New York: Harper and Row, 1978); Ahron Bregman, *Israel's Wars, 1947–93* (London: Routledge, 2000); and Sydney Dawson Bailey, *Four Arab-Israeli Wars and the Peace Process* (New York: St Martin's Press, 1990).

30. James P Piscatori, 'The Roles of Islam in Saudi Arabia's Political Development', in John L Esposito (ed.), *Islam and Development* (Syracuse: Syracuse University Press, 1980), pp.123–38.

31. Ziad Abu-Amr, 'Shaykh Ahmad Yasin and the Origins of Hamas', in Appleby (ed.), *Spokesmen for the Despised*, pp.225–93. See also Hisham H Ahmad, *Hamas From Religious Salvation to Political Transformation: The Rise of Hamas in Palestinian Society* (Jerusalem: Palestinian Academic Society for the Study of International Affairs, 1994); and Shaul Mishal and Avraham Sela, *The Palestinian Hamas: Vision, Violence, and Coexistence* (New York: Columbia University Press, 2000).

32. For further information, see Said K Aburish, *Arafat: From Defender to Dictator* (London: Bloomsbury, 1998); Barry M Rubin, *The Transformation of Palestinian Politics from Revolution to State-Building* (Cambridge, Massachusetts: Harvard University Press, 1999); and Andrew Gowers, *Behind the Myth: Yasser Arafat and the Palestinian Revolution* (London: WH Allen, 1990).

33. See Graham Usher, 'What Kind of Nation? – The Rise of Hamas in the Occupied Territories', in Joel Beinin and Joe Stork (eds), *Political Islam: Essays from Middle East Report* (London and New York: I.B.Tauris, 1997), pp.339–54.

## Chapter 2: Hezbollah and the Outside World

1. UN forces were sent to the Golan Heights to patrol a buffer zone between the two belligerent states in 1974. Today, 1,048 soldiers are present from Austria, Canada, Japan and Poland.

2. Patrick Seale provides background on Assad's life, ideology and policies, in *Asad: The Struggle for The Middle East* (Berkeley, California: University of California Press, 1988). See also Alasdair Drysdale and Raymond Hinnebusch, *Syria and the Middle East Peace Process* (New York: Council on Foreign Relations Press, 1991).

3. Adeed Daweesha, *Syria and the Lebanese Crisis* (London: Macmillan, 1980).

4. Graham Fuller, *The Center of the Universe: The Geopolitics of Iran* (Boulder, Colorado: Westview Press, 1990) provides an overview and analysis of Iran's modern history and contemporary politics.

5. See William Forbis, *The Fall of the Peacock Throne* (New York: Harper and Rowe, 1980); Ervand Abrahamian, *Iran Between Two Revolutions* (Princeton, New Jersey: Princeton University Press, 1982); and Amin Saikal, *The Rise and the Fall of the Shah, 1941–1979* (Princeton: Princeton University Press, 1980) for further background information on Iranian politics.

6. See Nikki R Keddie, *Iran: Religion, Politics and Society* (London: Frank Cass, 1980); David Manashri (ed.), *The Iranian Revolution and the Muslim*

*World* (Boulder, Colorado: Westview Press, 1990); and Shireen Hunter University Press, 1988).

7.  For accounts of the Gulf War, see Shararam Chubin and Charles Tripp, *Iran and Iraq at War* (London and New York: I.B.Tauris, 1988); John Bullock and Harvey Morris, *The Gulf War: Its Origins, History and Consequences* (London: Methuen, 1989); and Dilip Hero, *The Longest War: The Iran/Iraq Military Conflict* (London: Grafton, 1989).

8.  Patrick E Tyler, *International Herald Tribune*, 19 August 2002, p.3.

9.  See Walid C Khalidi, *Conflict and Violence in Lebanon: Confrontation in the Middle East* (Cambridge: Harvard Center for International Affairs, 1979) for information on the civil war within its regional context.

10. Rouhollah K Ramazani, *Revolutionary Iran: Challenge and Response in the Middle East* (Baltimore, Maryland: Johns Hopkins University Press, 1986), pp.28–35.

11. Farid el-Khazen discusses the PLO's role in Lebanon's disintegration in *The Breakdown of the State in Lebanon, 1967–1976* (London and New York: I.B.Tauris, 2000). See also Rex Brynen, *Sanctuary and Survival: The PLO in Lebanon* (Boulder, Colorado: Westview Press, 1990); and Zeev Schiff and Raphael Rothstein, *The Story of the Palestinian Guerrillas* (London: Vallentine, Mitchell, 1972).

12. Zeev Schiff and Ehud Yaari (eds), *Israel's Lebanon War* (New York: Simon and Schuster, 1984).

13. Avner Yaniv, *Dilemmas of Security, Politics, Strategy and the Israeli Experience in Lebanon* (New York: Oxford University Press, 1984).

14. Ariel Sharon, now Israel's Prime Minister, was taking defensive measures in 2001 to avoid being brought to trial in a Belgium court on charges of alleged involvement in the Sabra and Shatila Refugee Camp massacres raised by 40 relatives of victims. In February 1983, Israel's Kahan Commission of Inquiry found that Israel was not 'directly responsible' for the massacre, but determined that Sharon 'bore personal responsibility'. He then resigned his portfolio but stayed in the cabinet. In late spring 2002, it was determined by the Belgian tribunal that the case against Sharon was not admissible on grounds that he is at present exercising his function as a head of state. The victims' lawyer, Shibli Mallat, indicates that an appeal is being prepared, however.

15. Magnus Ranstorp, *Hizb'allah in Lebanon* (London: Macmillan Press Ltd, 1997), p.91.

16. Ibid. pp.90–1 and p.6. Ranstorp's information is carefully pieced together from press reports from international news agencies such as Reuters and from Arab and Israeli daily newspapers.

17. Robert Fisk provides a detailed account of the Israeli invasion, the actions

of the protagonists and their effects in *Pity the Nation: Lebanon at War* (Oxford: Oxford University Press, 1990).

18.    See Yair Evron, *War and Intervention in Lebanon: The Syrian-Israeli Deterrence Dialogue* (Baltimore, Maryland: Johns Hopkins University Press, 1987) for further details on this interesting arrangement.

19.    Hussein J Agha and Ahmad S Khalidi, *Syria and Iran: Rivalry and Cooperation* (London: Pinter, 1995); Ehteshami and Hinnebush provide a very useful chronology of Syrian-Iranian relations in *Syria and Iran: Middle Powers in a Penetrated Regional System* (London: Routledge, 1997), pp.207–22.

20.    Fouad Ajami, *The Vanished Imam: Imam Musa al-Sadr and the Shi'a of Lebanon* (Ithaca: Cornell University Press, 1986).

## Chapter 3: The Mechanics of Hezbollah's Transformation from Radical Militia to Mainstream Party

1.    See Elie Adib Salem, *Violence and Diplomacy in Lebanon: The Troubled Years, 1982–1988* (London and New York: I.B.Tauris, 1995) for a review of the events that led up to the Taif Accord.

2.    Paul Salem, 'Document of National Accord and Constitutional Amendments', *Beirut Review*, 1, 1 (1991), pp.119–64.

3.    Amal's Berri seems to be a permanent fixture as Speaker of the House, the Syrian Orthodox Christian Murrs, first Michel and now his son Elias, hold the Interior Ministry portfolio, prime ministers Hoss and Hariri, and Maronite presidents Hirawi and Lahoud, the latter a military man, all completely conform with Damascus' criteria.

4.    See Judith Harik, 'Democracy (Again) Derailed: Lebanon's Ta'if Paradox', in Bahgat Korany, Rex Brynen and Paul Noble (eds), *Political Liberalization and Democratization in the Arab World*, V.II 'Comparative Experiences' (Boulder, Colorado: Lynne Rienner, 1998), pp.127–55; and 'Citizen Disempowerment and the 1996 Parliamentary Elections in the Governorate of Mount Lebanon', *Democratization*, 5, 1 (Spring 1998), pp.158–82.

5.    Fida Nasrallah describes and analyses the impact of this agreement in 'The Treaty of Brotherhood, Cooperation and Coordination: An Assessment', in Youssef Choueri (ed.), *State and Society in Syria and Lebanon* (New York: St Martin's Press, 1994), pp.103–11. See also Farid el-Khazin, 'Lebanon – Independent No More', *Middle East Quarterly*, 8 (Winter 2001), pp.43–50.

6.    Political party theorist Giovanni Sartori calls this a process of reciprocal re-legitimization between the transforming radical party and the authorities. Whether the party is able to integrate the political system

hinges on the positive unfolding of this process. See his classic work, *Parties and Party Systems: A Framework for Analysis* (Cambridge: Cambridge University Press, 1976), pp.144–5 for more details.

7.　　See 'Persona Non Grata: The Expulsion of Civilians from Israel Occupied Lebanon', *Human Rights Watch Report*, July 1999.

8.　　Judith Harik and Hilal Khashan, 'Lebanon's Divisive Democracy: The Parliamentary Elections of 1992', *Arab Studies Quarterly*, 15, 1 (Winter 1993), p.50.

9.　　Richard Augustus Norton, *Amal and the Shi'a: Struggle for the Soul of Lebanon* (Austin, Texas: University of Texas Press, 1987).

## Chapter 4: Managing the 'True Believers'

1.　　For a discussion of the motivations of hardline politicos, see Eric Hoffer, *The True Believer: Thoughts on the Nature of Mass Movements* (New York: Mentor Books, 1951). Giovanni Sartori explains how societies become polarized (radicalized) and how some parties eventually accommodate with the governing authorities in *Parties and Party Systems* (Cambridge: Cambridge University Press, 1976), pp.131–145. Herbert Kitschelt, *The Logic of Party Formation: Structure and Strategy in the Belgian and West German Ecological Parties* (Ithaca, New York: Cornell University Press, 1989) talks about how strategic decisions are made within transforming parties, and Cynthia Lorraine Irvin includes an important section in her PhD dissertation, 'Splits in the Ranks', about the arguments between radicals and moderates in Ireland's Sinn Fein and the Basques' ETA over exchanging the bullet for the ballot. See *Paramilitary Politics in Parliamentary Democracies: Militant Nationalism in Ireland and Spain* (Raleigh, North Carolina: Duke University, 1995), pp.57–101.

2.　　The cases of Shaykh Tufeili and Abbas al-Musawi will be discussed later. See Magnus Ranstorp, 'Hizbullah's Command Leadership: Its Structure, Decision-making and Relationship with Iranian Clergy and Institutions', *Terrorism and Political Violence*, 6, 3 (Autumn 1994), pp.303–39, for further information.

3.　　There is some evidence to support the fact that Hezbollah was secretly governed by a supreme religious body instituted by Iran's Fazlallah Mahallati in 1983, and that it was structured like the higher ranks of Iran's own clerical leadership. See an MA thesis in Hebrew by Shimon Shapira, 'Shiite Radicalism in Lebanon: Historical Origins and Organizational, Political and Ideological Patterns' (Tel Aviv: Dayan Center for Middle Eastern and African Studies, May 1987) and Nikola Schahgaldian, *The Iranian Military Under the Islamic Republic* (Santa Monica, California::RAND Corporation, 1987) pp.119–21.

4.      Magnus Ranstorp, *Hizb'allah in Lebanon: The Politics of the Western Hostage Crisis* (London: Macmillan Press Ltd, 1997), p.68; see also pp.69–72 for information on the organization's security apparatus. See also As'ad Abu Khalil, 'Ideology and Practice of Hizbullah in Lebanon: Islamization of Leninist Organizational Principles', *Middle Eastern Studies*, 27, 3 (July 1991), especially pp.394, 395 for an explanation of Hezbollah's organizational dynamics.

5.      Ranstorp, *Hizb'allah in Lebanon*, pp.68–9.

6.      Martin Kramer, 'The Calculus of Jihad', in Martin E Marty and R Scott Appleby (eds), *Fundamentalisms and the State: Remaking Politics, Economies and Militance* (Chicago: University of Chicago Press, 1993), pp.539–56.

7.      *Revue du Liban*, 30 January 1988, p.7.

8.      *Al-Hayat*, 27 October 1989, p.2; also see Magnus Ranstorp, op. cit., p.315.

9.      Rudolph Peters, *Jihad in Classical and Modern Islam* (Princeton: Markus Wiener Publishers, 1996), pp.5–6.

10.     Abdelaziz Sachadena, 'Activist Shi'ism in Iran, Iraq and Lebanon', in Martin E Marty and R Scott Appleby (eds), *Accounting for Fundamentalisms: The Dynamic Character of Movements* (Chicago: University of Chicago Press, 1994), pp.23–4.

11.     Michael C Hudson, 'The Islamic Factor in Syrian and Iraqi Politics', in James Piscatori (ed.), *Islam in the Political Process* (London: Cambridge University Press, 1983), pp.73–97, explains how 'objective conditions' that hinder Islamization actually work. Powerful leaders with strong intelligence and military assets make Islamic expansion in Syria and Iraq impossible and therefore jihad in those countries is self-defeating.

12.     See, for example, the following books by Sayyed Fadallah: *al-Islam wa-montiq al-quwwa* (*Islam and the Logic of Power*), 2$^{nd}$ ed. (Beirut: al-mu'assaasa al-jamiyya lil-dirasat wal-nashr, 1981) and *al-harakat al-islamiyya fi lubnan* (*The Islamic Movement in Lebanon*) (Beirut: Dar al-shira, 1984).

13.     Martin Kramer, 'The Oracle of Hezbollah: Sayyid Muhammad Husayn Fadlallah', in R Scott Appleby (ed.), *Spokesmen for the Despised: Fundamentalist Leaders in the Middle East* (Chicago: University of Chicago Press, 1997), p.84.

## Chapter 5: Squaring Jihad with the General Public

1.      Rudolph Peters, *Jihad in Classical and Modern Islam* (Princeton, New Jersey: Markus Wiener Publishers, 1996), p.63.

2.      Ibid. p.65.

3.      *Al-Safir*, 25 February 1985, p.2.

4.      In an interview with Sheikh Hassan Ezzeddin, a member of Hezbollah's Supreme Council, on 20 November 2001 at Harat Hareik, Beirut, this

letter was mentioned when I asked for organizational by-laws, or a founding charter.

5.   See R Scott Appleby, *Spokesmen for the Despised: Fundamentalist Leaders of the Middle East* (Chicago: University of Chicago Press, 1997), pp.5–6, 406.

6.   See, for example, Mohammed Hussein Fadlallah, 'An Islamic Perspective on the Lebanese Experience', *Middle East Insight*, 6, 1 and 2 (Summer 1988), pp.18–26. Martin Kramer's essay, 'The Oracle of Hizbullah, Sayyid Muhammad Husayn Fadlallah', in Martin E Marty and R Scott Appleby (eds), *Accounting for Fundamentalisms: The Dynamic Character of Movements* (Chicago: University of Chicago Press, 1994), pp.81–181, provides an excellent analysis of Fadlallah's ideology and political impact.

7.   Hugh Roberts, 'From Radical Mission to Equivocal Ambition: The Expansion and Manipulation of Algerian Islamism, 1979–1992', in Martin E Marty and R Scott Appleby (eds), *Accounting for Fundamentalisms*, pp.374–412.

8.   Ziad Abu-Amr, 'Shaykh Ahmad Yasin and the Origins of Hamas', in Appleby, *Spokesmen for the Despised*, p.249.

9.   See Erving Goffman, *Frame Analysis: An Essay on the Organization of Experience* (Cambridge: Harvard University Press, 1974) for an in-depth look at the process and results of framing.

10.  This mantra is repeated in virtually all public speeches and press interviews and is echoed by Lebanese government officials.

11.  Jean-Francois Legrain, 'Palestinian Islamisms as a Condition of their Expansion', in Marty and Appleby (eds), *Accounting for Fundamentalisms*, pp.413–28.

12.  Interview, Lebanese Broadcasting Company (LBC), 12 July 1997.

13.  Interview with Ali Fayyad, Director of Hezbollah's Islamic Research Center, by Amal Saad Ghorayeb, 2 March 1997, Harat Hareik, Beirut. Ghorayeb, a former student of mine, reported this information to me.

14.  *Al-Ahd*, 21 November 1997, p.4.

15.  Ibid. p.3.

16.  Op. cit., Ghorayeb.

17.  Interview with Emile Saliba, Director of the Syndicate of Lebanese Engineers, Bteghrine, 1 August 2000. Not all of the 23,000 registered members are active. It was impossible to determine what percentage of the overall membership were Hezbollah partisans but Saliba indicated that it was not high and that it should be remembered that Hezbollah had only been participating for about ten years.

18.  Interview, Future TV, 12 May 1998.

19.  *L'Orient-le Jour*, 16 August 2001, p.3.

20.  Interview, Harat Hareik, 30 September 1999.

21.     Interview with Muhammad Fnaysh, 'Face to Face', al-Manar Television, 15 January 2000.

## Chapter 6: Serving the *Umma* – Hezbollah as Employer and Welfare Organization

1.      See Judith Harik, *The Public and Social Services of the Lebanese Militias*, Papers on Lebanon, no.14 (Oxford: Centre for Lebanese Studies, 1994).
2.      Ibid. pp.29–30.
3.      Interview with Hajj Hussein Shami in Harat Hareik, 17 August 2001.
4.      Lamia el-Moubayed, *Strengthening Institutional Capacity for Rural Community Development: Two Case Studies from Lebanon* (Beirut: Economic and Social Commission for Western Asia, 1999).
5.      The United Nations Development Programme and the Council for Development and Reconstruction, *Poverty and Gender Profile in the Baalbek-Hermel Region*, vol.1: 'Report' (Beirut: The Consultation and Research Institute, April 1998), ES–2.
6.      Ibid. The information is drawn from a survey of 800 householders in 1996. The margin of error was +/- 3.5 per cent. Inequality in income distribution was as follows: 50 per cent of the population control about 20 per cent of the total income, while 10 per cent control more than 30 per cent. Some 66 per cent of the poor population is below the age of 30 years.
7.      Judith Harik, 'Between Islam and the System: Sources and Implications of Popular Support for Lebanon's Hizbullah', *Journal of Conflict Resolution*, 40, 1 (March 1996), pp.53–4.
8.      The United Nations Development Programme..., op. cit., p.4.
9.      Ibid. pp.2–18.
10.     Syrian dairy products freely crossing the border also mean that those families who had a family cow or two and who could earn a little extra selling surplus milk locally have also lost that capacity.
11.     *Al-Ahd*, 9 June 2000, p.5; and *L'Orient-Le Jour*, 7 August 2000, p.3.
12.     Lamia Moubayed, *Strengthening Institutional Capacity for Rural Community Development*, pp.23–4.
13.     Ibid. p.28.
14.     Ministry of Social Affairs, Government of Lebanon, *The Guide for Donor Organizations for Small Projects in Lebanon* (2001), pp.94–5.

## Chapter 7: The Grass Roots Speak

1.      See Robin Wright, 'Islam's New Political Face', *Current History*, 90 (552), pp.25–8 and 35; Meriam Verges, 'Genesis of a Mobilization: The Young Activists of Algeria's Islamic Salvation Front'; and Rabbia Bekkar,

'Taking up Space in Tlemcen: The Islamist Occupation of Urban Algeria', both in Joel Bienen and Joe Stork (eds), *Political Islam: Essays from Middle East Report* (London and New York: I.B.Tauris, 1997), pp.292–308 and 283–91.

2.     *L'Orient-Le Jour*, 18 March 1998, p.3.

3.     Judith Harik, 'Citizen Disempowerment and the 1996 Parliamentary Elections in the Governorate of Mount Lebanon', *Democratization*, 5, 1 (Spring 1998), pp.158–82.

4.     Interview, al-Manar Television, 16 April 1998.

5.     Hassan Nasrallah, speech at Baalbek, 10 June 1998.

6.     Islamist parties in Sudan, Algeria, Turkey, and Jordan are among those that profited, although not always continuously, from participation in democratic processes in their respective countries. See Robin Wright, *Sacred Rage* (New York: Simon and Schuster, 1985).

7.     Of this list, Christian Deputy Fuad Butros, who was a 'coordinator', observed that there was no accord or political understanding among the men who had put the list together. Each party maintains its political options and strategies but together has demonstrated that it is possible to agree on running the city.

8.     *L'Orient-Le Jour*, 8 May 1998, p.3.

9.     See Elaine C. Hagopian, 'Redrawing the Map in the Middle East: Phalangist Lebanon and Zionist Israel', *Arab Studies Quarterly*, 5 (Fall 1983), pp.321–36.

10.    *L'Orient-Le Jour*, 5 June 1998, p.1.

11.    *Nidaa al-Watan*, 29 May 1998, p.2.

12.    *L'Orient-Le Jour*, 27 May 1998, p.4.

13.    *Al-Ahd*, 29 May 1998, p.8.

14.    *Al-Ahd*, 5 June 1998, p.12

15.    *Al-Ahd*, 12 June 1998, p.4.

16.    See A Nizar Hamzeh, 'Lebanon's Islamists and Local Politics: A New Reality', *Third World Quarterly*, 21, 5 (2000), p.753.

17.    Paul Khalifa, *L'Orient-Le Jour*, 15 June 1998, p.2.

18.    Judith Harik, 'Between Islam and the System: Sources and Implications of Popular Support for Lebanon's Hizbullah', *Journal of Conflict Resolution*, 40, 1 (March 1996), pp.56–7. When religiosity and party preference were correlated, 59 per cent of the Shiites who were highly religious were in Hezbollah's ranks, but a respectable percentage of the moderately religious – 47 per cent – and 23 per cent of the least religious were also Hezbollah supporters. These figures indicated that, in 1993, factors other than religion played a part in Hezbollah's appeal.

19.    Martin Kramer discusses the importance clans play in Hezbollah's

makeup and political considerations in 'The Moral Logic of Hizbullah', in Walter Reich (ed.), *Origins of Terrorism: Psychologies, Ideologies, Theologies, States of Mind* (Cambridge: Cambridge University Press, 1990), pp.131–57. He observes that the loyalty of clans to Hezbollah 'may owe more to intra-clan alliances and rivalries than to Islamic commitment'. I fully agree.

### Chapter 8: The Mechanics of Military Jihad

1. With the exception of an expanded discussion on framing resistance, adjustments that are consistent with a greater focus on Hezbollah and analysis of military events after 1996, this chapter substantially reproduces a study published in *Studies in Conflict and Terrorism*, 20 (1997), pp.249–65, entitled 'Syrian Foreign Policy and State/Resistance Dynamics in Lebanon'.

2. An analysis of the type of strategy and tactics used by Hezbollah appears in the two following chapters.

3. *Middle East Weekly Reporter*, 3664, 27 July 1993, p.8.

4. See *an-Nahar*, 28 July 1993, p.2; *As-Safir*, on page 1, quoted Hezbollah politburo chief Hussein al-Khalil as saying: 'There is great coordination between us and the government. Israel will not be able to drive a wedge into our domestic front.'

5. *As-Safir*, 16 April 1996, p.1.

6. For an analysis of Syria's bargaining strategy in these negotiations, see Mohammed Muslih, 'Dateline Damascus: Asad is Ready', *Foreign Policy*, 96 (Fall 1994), pp.155–60.

7. *An-Nahar*, 22 April 1996, p.2.

8. *As-Safir*, 17 April 1996, p.9; 22 April 1996, p.1.

9. *Middle East Daily Reporter*, 132, 4349, 19 April 1996, p.7.

10. Interview, CNN, 22 April 1996.

11. *L'Orient-Le Jour*, 22 April 1996, p.3.

12. *L'Orient-Le Jour*, 27 April 1996, p.1.

13. *L'Orient-Le Jour*, 29 May 1996, p.5 and 30 May 1996, p.3.

14. Interview with Zuhayr Mansur, project engineer, RC, Beirut, 13 June 1996.

### Chapter 9: The Collapse of the 'Security Zone'

1. Jezzine was never a part of the Security Zone, but was nonetheless under SLA control.

2. *L'Orient-Le Jour*, 27 May 1999, p.1.

3. *An-Nahar*, 1 June 1999, p.1.

4. *L'Orient-Le Jour*, 7 June 1999, p.3.

5. Ibid. p.3.

6.     *L'Orient-Le Jour*, 16 June 1999, p.3.

7.     The officers' families have been returning to their homes in Lebanon in groups of 30 to 40. No security problems have arisen in this regard.

8.     *An-Nahar*, September 5, 1997, p. 1.

9.     Shaykh Nabil Qaouk, interview, *Magazine,* July 7, 1999 pp 4-5.

10.     Al-Manar TV interview, 24 June 1999.

11.     *L'Orient-Le Jour*, 2 July 1999, p.3.

12.     The Maronite Christians sided with the crusaders in their wars against the Muslims and were aided by the French when Mt Lebanon's Druzes carried out massacres in that community in 1860.

13.     Al-Manar TV, 4 April 1999, p.1.

14.     See *L'Orient-Le Jour* and *an-Nahar*, 23 May 2000 issues for accounts of these events and others.

15.     For the full text of Lahoud's speech see the Beirut *Daily Star*, 22 May 2000, p.3.

16.     A thorough discussion of the Shebaa case can be found in Marie Ghantous, *Les Hameaux de Chebaa et le Droit International Public* [The Chebaa Farms and International Public Law] (Beirut: Mokhtarat, 2001). The boundary problems in the Shebaa region are particularly complex since the frontiers of Israel, Syria and Lebanon converge there. Boundaries fixed by Britain and France during the Mandate period and then changed, are part of the problem.

17.     See the Beirut *Daily Star*, 27 May 2000, p.3 for the full text of Nasrallah's speech.

18.     *Jerusalem Post*, 17 June 2000, p.1.

19.     Syrian National Information Agency, 3 June 2000.

20.     See, for instance, the editorial written by Issa Ghorayeb, Editor-in-Chief, *L'Orient-Le Jour*, 2 June 2000, p.1.

21.     Interview with Dr Shafik Masri, Professor of International Law at the American University of Beirut and Lebanese American University, Beirut, 20 November 2000.

22.     Celina Nasser, 'The Shebaa Landowners are Lebanese', *Daily Star*, 15 June 2001, p.3.

23.     *Daily Star*, 28 June 2002, p.1.

24.     *L'Orient-Le Jour*, 8 June, p.3.

25.     *L'Orient-Le Jour*, 2 June 2000, p.3.

26.     *L'Orient-Le Jour*, 21 June 2000, p.3.

27.     *Jerusalem Post*, 2 June 2000, p.2.

28.     Shlomo Brom, *Israel and South Lebanon: In the Absence of a Peace Treaty with Syria* (Tel Aviv: Jaffee Center for Strategic Studies, Tel Aviv University, 1999).

29.  Yavkov Erez, 'Interview with Shaul Mofaz', *Maariv*, 20 September 1998, p.16.

30.  Israel/Wire 1, no.529 (15 July 1999), 'Twenty-five Percent of Kiryat Shimona Residents Ready to Relocate'.

## Chapter 10: Hezbollah's Standing After the Collapse of the 'Security Zone'

1.  Interview with Naim al-Qassim, Radio al-Nour, 30 November 1998.

2.  *L'Orient-Le Jour*, 16 February 2001, p.3.

3.  *L'Orient-Le Jour*, 19 October 2000, p.3.

4.  *Daily Star*, 16 April 2001, p.1.

5.  *L'Orient-Le Jour*, 3 July 2001, p.1.

6.  *L'Orient-Le Jour*, 4 July 2001, p.3.

7.  Related by a personal friend who accompanied the journalists to Ghajar.

8.  *Yediot Ahronot*, 21 August 2001, p.4.

9.  Nicholas Blanford, interview with Staffan de Mistura, *Daily Star*, 10 December 2001, p.3.

10.  See John Bullock and Adel Darwish, *Water Wars: Coming Conflicts in the Middle East* (London: Victor Gollancz, 1993), pp.33–57 for information on the claims of arid Syria, Israel and Jordan on the Jordan River system whose headwaters are located in Lebanon. For further information on the impact of water scarcity on the geopolitics of the region, also see JA Allen and Chibli Mallat, *Water in the Middle East* (London and New York: I.B.Tauris, 1995) and Nina Copaken and Murray Rosovksy, *Rivers of Fire* (Lanham, Maryland: Rowman and Littlefield, 1999).

11.  Because of the current Israeli utilization of all its renewable water resources and the predicted annual water deficit the water-rich area raises questions about Israel's water imperatives. Interests in Lebanon's hydrological resources are well documented in letters from the early Zionist leader, Haim Weitzmann, to various British governmental officials in 1919 and 1920, where he claimed that they were essential to the future of the Jewish 'national Home'. In this respect, after the 1967 war, Moshe Dayan, Israel's military chief, indicated that 'provisionally satisfactory borders had been achieved, with the exception of those with Lebanon'.

12.  *Yediot Ahronot*, 11 September 2002, p.1. Military analyst Alex Fishman writing in the editorial column on 4 September, used the term *casus belli* to describe what he said was Lebanon's intended pumping of 25 per cent of the Hasbani waters. He indicated that Israel was working around the clock through the Americans to get Beirut to stop the project and if that does not help, he writes, 'the seeds of war are being planted right now'.

13.    *Daily Star*, 11 September 2002, p.1.

14.    Interview with Sheikh Hassan Ezzeddin, Director of Hezbollah's Media Department, 20 November 2001, Haret Hareik, Beirut.

15.    Interview with Sheikh Nabil Qaouk, Haret Hareik, Beirut, 1 November 2001.

## Chapter 11: The Terrorism vs. Resistance Controversy

1.    For information on the principle of self-determination, see Ian Brownbie, *Principles of Public International Law*, 4th ed. (Oxford: Clarendon Press, 1992), pp.595–98; IA Shearer, *Starke's International Law*, 11th ed. (London: Butterworths, 1994), pp.111, 113, 333–4.

2.    *The Geneva Conventions of August 12, 1949* (Geneva: International Red Cross, 1949), especially the Fourth Geneva Convention, 'Protection of Civilian Persons in the Time of War', pp.153–214, Articles 7, 8, 47 and 147. Also see Van Glohn, *Law Among Nations*, 7th ed. (London: Allyn and Bacon, 1996), p.475, 608, 664–5.

3.    See John Richard Thackrah, *Encyclopedia of Terrorism and Political Violence* (London: Routledge, 1987); J Mallin, *Terror and Urban Guerrillas* (Miami: University of Miami Press, 1971); BM Jenkins, *International Terrorism: A New Mode of Conflict* (Los Angeles: Crescent Publications, 1975).

4.    US State Department, *Patterns of Global Terrorism 1996* (Washington, DC: GPO, April 1997).

5.    See Louis Rene Beres, 'Israel, Lebanon and Hizbullah: A Legal View', *Midstream*, 42 (1996), pp.2–7. The author cites the Hague Regulations, Protocol 1, Articles 24 and 51 and Article 28 of the Fourth Geneva Convention to make the point that the responsibility for shelling (in this case by the Israelis in the Security Zone) lies with those (Hezbollah's fighters and Lebanon) whose perfidious conduct brought about such shelling.

6.    Peretz Kidron, *Middle East International*, 20 November 1992, p.7.

7.    Israel Shalak, *Middle East International*, 20 November 1992, pp.17–8.

8.    Schmuel Gordon, *The Vulture and the Snake: Counter-Guerrilla Air Warfare – The War in Southern Lebanon*, Security and Policy Studies, no.30 (Tel Aviv: Begin-Sadat Center for Strategic Studies, Bar Ilan University, 1998), pp.12–13.

9.    Gal Luft, 'Securing Northern Israel Following an IDF Withdrawal from South Lebanon', in Patrick Clawson and Michael Eisenstadt (eds), *The Last Arab-Israeli Battlefield? Implications of an Israeli Withdrawal from Lebanon* (Washington, DC: Washington Institute for Near East Policy, 2000), p.96.

10.   US Air Force 1995, *Special Operations: Air Force Doctrine Document 35*

(Washington, DC: Department of the Air Force 9/1997), p.33.

11. Christopher C Harmon, *Terrorism Today* (London: Frank Cass, 2000), pp.192–5.

12. CNN Special, 'America's Wake-up Call to Suicide Terror on a Massive Scale', 6 October 2001.

13. One of the rumours circulating in the aftermath of the kidnappings was that Shiite families, whose relatives were being held by the Kuwaiti authorities for attacks there, were taking westerners hostage for trade.

14. Ranstorp, *Hizb'allah in Lebanon: The Politics of the Western Hostage Crisis* (London: Macmillan Press Ltd, 1997), p.68.

15. Interview, *L'Orient-Le Jour*, 5 October 2001, p.3.

16. Interview with US National Security Advisor Condoleeza Rice, broadcast by Lebanese Broadcasting Company, 11 January 2002.

17. Richard Boucher, press conference, Washington, DC, broadcast by CNN, 11 January 2002.

## Chapter 12: America's Half-Hearted War Against Terrorism

1. *L'Orient-Le Jour*, 8 November 2001, p.1.

2. Interview, ABC Television, 11 November 2001.

3. *L'Orient-Le Jour*, 16 October 2001, p.2.

4. *An-Nahar*, 26 September 2001, p.2.

5. *As-Safir*, 6 October 2001, p.3.

6. *Daily Star*, 9 November 2001, p.3.

7. *L'Orient-Le Jour*, 5 October 2001, p.3.

8. Interview on al-Manar TV news, 4 October 2001.

9. Interview with Hassan Ezzeddin, Director of Hezbollah's Media Department, 20 November 2001, Harat Hareik, Beirut.

10. Guy Bichor, *Yediot Ahronot*, 8 February 2002, p.3.

11. *Daily Star*, 20 November 2001, p.3.

12. *Daily Star*, 29 November 2001, p.3.

13. *Daily Star*, 18 March 2001, p.3.

14. *L'Orient Le-Jour*, 9 March 2001, p.3.

15. *Jerusalem Post*, 12 March 2001, p.1.

16. *Jerusalem Post*, 14 March 2001, p.1.

17. *Middle East Reporter (Weekly)*, 102, 1188, 9 March 2002, p.4–5.

18. The *Daily Star* carried the report 'Hizbullah Tests Israeli Nerves with Cross-border Attacks' on 9 April 2002, p.2. Israeli Diplomats and military observers were cited.

19. *Daily Star*, 15 April 2002, p.2.

20. *As-Safir*, 30 June 2002, p.2.

## Chapter 13: Conclusions and Implications

1.    Armitage's remarks were made at a conference hosted by the US Institute of Peace in Washington, DC and were reported in the *Daily Star*, 6 September, 2002, p.1.
2.    *L'Orient-Le Jour*, 7 September 2002, p.1.
3.    Ibid.
4.    *Daily Star*, 7 September 2002, p.1.

# Select Bibliography

Abd-Allah, Umar, *The Islamic Struggle in Syria* (Berkeley, California: Mizan Press, 1983)

Abrahamian, Ervand, *Iran Between Two Revolutions* (Princeton, New Jersey: Princeton University Press, 1982)

Abu-Amer, Ziad, 'Shaykh Ahmad Yasin and the Origins of Hamas', in R Scott Appleby (ed.), *Spokesmen for the Despised: Fundamentalist Leaders of the Middle East* (Chicago: University of Chicago Press, 1997), pp.225–56

Abu Khalil, As'ad, 'The Ideology and Practice of Hizbullah in Lebanon: The Islamization of Leninist Principles', *Middle Eastern Studies*, 27, 3 (July 1991), pp.390–403

Abu-Lughod, Ibrahim, 'Retreat from the Secular Path? Islamic Dilemmas of Arab Politics', *The Review of Politics*, 28, 4 (October 1966), pp.447–76

Aburish, Said K, *Arafat: From Defender to Dictator* (London: Bloomsbury, 1998)

Agha, Hussein, 'The Syrian-Iranian Axis in Lebanon', in Rosemary Hollis and Nadim Shehadi (eds), *Lebanon on Hold: Implications for Middle East Peace* (London: Royal Institute of International Affairs/Centre for Lebanese Studies, 1996), pp.24–31

Ahmad, Hisham H, *Hamas: From Religious Salvation to Political Transformation: The Rise of Hamas in Palestinian Society* (Jerusalem: Palestinian Academic Society for the Study of International Affairs, 1994)

Ajami, Fouad, *The Vanished Imam: Imam Musa al-Sadr and the Shi'a of Lebanon* (Ithaca: Cornell University Press, 1986)

Allen, JA and Chibli Mallat, *Water in the Middle East* (London and New York: I.B.Tauris, 1995)

al-Rasheed, Madawi, 'Saudi Arabia's Islamic Opposition', *Current History* (January 1996), pp.16–22

Appleby, R Scott (ed.), *Spokesmen for the Despised: Fundamentalist Leaders of the Middle East* (Chicago: University of Chicago Press, 1997)

Apter, David E (ed.), *The Legitimization of Violence* (London: United Nations Research Institute for Social Development, 1997)

Auda, Gehad, 'The "Normalization" of the Islamic Movement in Egypt from the 1970s to the Early 1990s', in Martin E Marty and R Scott Appleby (eds), *Accounting for Fundamentalisms: The Dynamic Character of Movements* (Chicago: University of Chicago Press, 1994) pp.428–89

Aulas, Marie Christine, 'The Socio-Ideological Development of the Maronite Community: The Emergence of the Phalanges and the Lebanese Forces', *Arab Studies Quarterly*, 7, 4 (Fall 1985), pp.1–27

Azar, Edward and Renee E Marlin, 'The Costs of Protracted Social Conflict in the Middle East: The Case of Lebanon', in Gabriel Ben-Dor and David B Dewitt (eds), *Conflict Management in the Middle East* (Lexington, Maryland: Lexington Books, 1987), pp.29–44

———, 'Protracted Social Conflict: Theory and Practice in the Middle East', *Journal of Palestine Studies*, 3, 1 (1978), pp.41–60

Bailey, Sydney D, *Four Arab-Israeli Wars and the Peace Process* (New York: St Martin's Press, 1990)

Beinin, Joel and Joe Stork (eds), *Political Islam: Essays from Middle East Report* (London and New York: I.B.Tauris, 1997)

Bekkar, Rabia, 'Taking up Space in Tlemcen: The Islamist Occupation of Urban Algeria', in Joel Beinin and Joe Stork (eds), *Political Islam: Essays from Middle East Report* (London and New York: I.B.Tauris, 1997), pp.283–91

Bell, Wendell and Walter E Freeman (eds), *Ethnicity and Nation-building: Comparative, International and Historical Perspectives* (Beverley Hills: Sage, 1974)

Ben-Dor, Gabriel and David B Dewitt (eds), *Conflict Management in the Middle East* (Lexington, Maryland: DC Heath and Company, 1987)

Beres, Louis Rene, 'Israel, Lebanon and Hizbullah: A Legal View', *Mainstream*, 42 (1996)

Betts, Robert Brenton, *The Druze* (New Haven, Connecticut: Yale University Press, 1988)

Bregman, Ahron, *Israel's Wars, 1947–93* (London: Routledge, 2000)

Brom, Shlomo, *Israel and South Lebanon: In the Absence of a Peace Treaty With Syria* (Tel Aviv: Jafee Center for Strategic Studies, TIU, 1999)

Brownbie, Ian, *Principles of Public International Law*, 4th edition (Oxford: Clarendon Press, 1992)

Brumberg, Daniel, 'Khomeini's Legacy: Islamic Rule and Islamic Social Justice', in R Scott Appleby (ed.), *Spokesmen for the Despised: Fundamentalist Leaders of the Middle East* (Chicago: University of Chicago Press, 1997), pp.16–82

Brynen, Rex, *Sanctuary and Survival: The PLO in Lebanon* (Boulder, Colorado: Westview Press, 1990)

Bullock, John and Adel Darwish, *Water Wars: Coming Conflicts in the Middle East* (London: Victor Gollancz, 1993)

Carre, Olivier, 'Quelques mots-clefs de Muhammad Husayn Fadlallah', *Revue Francaise de Science Politique* (Paris) 37, 4 (August 1987), pp.478–501

Chamie, Joseph, 'The Lebanese Civil War: An Investigation into the Causes', *World Affairs*, 139 (Winter 1976), pp.171–88

Chaudhary, Muhammed Akram and Michael D Berdine, 'Islamic Resurgence and Western Reaction', *American Journal of Islamic Social Sciences*, 11, 4 (Winter 1996), pp.549–65

Choueri, Youssef M (ed.), *State and Society in Syria and Lebanon* (New York: St Martin's Press, 1994)

Clawson, Patrick and Michael Eisenstadt (eds), *The Last Battlefield? Implications of an Israeli Withdrawal from Lebanon* (Washington, DC: Washington Institute for Near East Politics, 2000)

Cobban, Helena, 'The Growth of Shi'i Protest in Lebanon and its Implications for the Future', in Nikki R Keddie and Juan RI Cole (eds), *Shi'ism and Social Protest* (New Haven, Connecticut: Yale University Press, 1986), pp.137–59

———, *The Making of Modern Lebanon* (London: Hutchins, 1985)

Cole, Juan RI and Nikki R Keddie (eds), *Shi'ism and Social Protest* (New Haven, Connecticut: Yale University Press, 1986)

———, *Sacred Space and Holy War: The Politics, Culture and History of Shi'i Islam* (London and New York: I.B.Tauris, 2001)

Collings, Deirdre (ed.), *Peace for Lebanon? From War to Reconstruction* (Boulder, Colorado: Lynne Rienner Publishers, 1994)

Copaken, Nina and Murray Rosovsky, *Rivers of Fire* (Lanham, Maryland: Rowman and Littlefield, 1999)

Courbage, Y and P Fargues, *La Situation Demographique au Liban* (Beirut: Editions Libanaises, 1974)

Crighton, Elizabeth and Martha Abele MacIver, 'The Evolution of Protracted Ethnic Conflict: Group Dominance and Political Underdevelopment in Northern Ireland and Lebanon', *Journal of Comparative Politics*, 23, 2 (January 1991), pp.128–32

Dabashi, Hamid, *Theology of Discontent: The Ideological Foundation of the Islamic Revolution in Lebanon* (New York: New York University Press, 1993)

Dawisha, Adeed, 'The Motives of Syria's Involvement in Lebanon', *The Middle East Journal*, 38, 2 (Spring 1984), pp.228–37

———, *Syria and the Lebanese Crisis* (London: Macmillan, 1980)

Deeb, Marius, *The Lebanese Civil War* (New York: Praeger, 1980)

———, 'The External Dimension of the Conflict in Lebanon: The Role of Syria', *Journal of South Asian and Middle Eastern Studies*, 12, 3 (Spring 1989), pp.37–51

Dekmejian, R Hrair, 'Resurgent Islam and the Egyptian State', in Reeva Simon (ed.), *Essays in Honor of J. C. Hurewitz* (New York: Columbia University Press, 1989)

_____, *Islam in Revolution: Fundamentalism in the Arab World* (New York: Syracuse University Press, 1985)

Dessouki, 'Ali EH, *Islamic Resurgence in the Arab World* (New York: Praeger, 1982)

Dupuy, Trevor N, *Elusive Victory: The Arab-Israeli Wars, 1947–1974* (New York: Harper and Row, 1978)

Ehteshami, Anoushiravan and Raymond A Hinnebusch, *Syria and Iran: Middle Powers in a Penetrated Regional System* (London: Routledge, 1997)

El-Khazen, Farid, 'Lebanon – Independent No More', *Middle East Quarterly*, 8, 1 (Winter 2001), pp.43–50

_____, *The Breakdown of the State in Lebanon, 1967–1976* (London and New York: I.B.Tauris, 2000)

_____, *The Communal Pact of National Identities: The Making and Politics of the 1943 National Pact*, Papers on Lebanon No.12 (Oxford: The Centre for Lebanese Studies, 1992)

El-Moubayed, Lamia, *Strengthening Institutional Capacity for Rural Community Development: Two Case Studies from Lebanon* (Beirut: Economic and Social Commission for Western Asia [ESCWA], 1999)

Entelis, John P, *Pluralism and Party Transformation in Lebanon – al Kataib, 1936–1970* (Leiden: Brill, 1974)

Erez, Yavkov, 'Interview with Shaul Mofaz', *Ma'ariv*, 20 September 1998, p.16.

Esposito, John (ed.), *The Iranian Revolution: Its Global Impact* (Miami: Florida International University Press, 1990), pp.116–37

_____ (ed.), *Voices of Resurgent Islam* (Oxford: Oxford University Press, 1981)

_____ (ed.), *Islam and Development* (Syracuse: Syracuse University Press, 1980)

Evron, Yair, *War and Intervention in Lebanon: The Israeli-Syrian Deterrence Deal* (London: Croom-Helm, 1987)

Fadlallah, Ayotallah Muhammed Hussein, 'An Islamic Perspective on the Lebanese Experience', *Middle East Insight*, vol.6, nos.1 and 2 (Summer 1988), pp.18–26

_____, *al-muqawwama al-islamiyya: afaq wa-tatallu'a* (The Islamic Resistance: Vision and Prospects) 2nd edition (Bir al-Abd, Lebanon: Lajnat masjid, al-Imam al-Rida, 1986)

_____, *al-harakat al-islamiyya fi Lubnan* (The Islamic Movement in Lebanon) (Beirut: Dar al-Shira, 1984)

_____, *al-islam wa nitaq al-quwa* (Islam and the Logic of Power) 2nd edition (Beirut: Dar al-islamiyya, 1981)

Faksh, Mahmud A, *The Future of Islam in the Middle East: Fundamentalism in Egypt, Algeria and Saudi Arabia* (Westport, Connecticut: Praeger, 1997)

Faour, Ali, 'Migration from South Lebanon with a Field Study of Forced Mass Migration', *ESCWA Population Bulletin*, 21 (1981)

Fisk, Robert, *Pity the Nation: Lebanon at War* (Oxford: Oxford University Press, 1990)

Gellner, Ernest G and John Waterbury (eds), *Patrons and Clients in Mediterranean Societies* (London: Duckworth, 1977)

*Geneva Convention of August 12, 1949* (Geneva: International Red Cross, 1949)

Ghorayeb, Amal Saad, *Hizbullah: Politics and Religion* (London: Pluto Press, 2002)

Gilmour, David, *Lebanon: The Fractured Country* (London: Sphere Books, 1984)

Goffman, Erving, *Frame Analysis: An Essay on the Organization of Experience* (Cambridge: Harvard University Press, 1974)

Goldman, Robert B and A Jeyaratnan Wilson (eds), *From Independence to Statehood: Managing Ethnic Conflict in Five African and Asian States* (London: Francis Pinter, 1984)

Gordon, Schmuel, *The Vulture and the Snake*, Security and Political Studies, 30 (Tel Aviv: The Begin-Sadat Center for Strategic Studies, Bar-Ilan University, 1998)

Gowers, Andrew and Tony Walker, *Behind the Myth: Yasser Arafat and the Palestinian Revolution* (London: WH Allen, 1990)

Guazzone, L (ed.), *The Islamist Dilemma: The Political Role of Islamist Movements in the Contemporary Arab World* (London: Garnet Publishing Company, 1995)

Hagopian, Elaine C, 'Redrawing the Map in the Middle East: Phalangist Lebanon and Zionist Israel', *Arab Studies Quarterly*, 5 (Fall 1983), pp.321–36

_____, 'From Maronite Hegemony to Maronite Militancy', *Third World Quarterly*, 11, 4 (1989), pp.101–15

Hamdi, Mohammed E, *The Making of an Islamic Political Leader: Conversations with Hasan al-Turabi* (Boulder, Colorado: Westview Press, 1998)

Hamzeh, A Nizar, 'Lebanon's Islamists and Local Politics: A New Reality', *Third World Quarterly*, 21, 5 (2000), pp.739–59

_____, 'Lebanon's Hizbullah: From Islamic Revolution to Parliamentary Accommodation', *Third World Quarterly*, 14, 2 (1993), pp.321–37

_____ and R Hrair Dekmejian, 'The Islamic Spectrum of Lebanese Politics', *Journal of South Asian and Middle Eastern Studies*, 16, 3 (Spring 1993)

Harik, Iliya, 'Political Elites of Lebanon', in G Lenczowski (ed.), *Political Elites in the Middle East* (Washington: American Enterprise Institute for Public Policy Research, 1975), pp.214–5

_____, *Politics and Change in a Traditional Society: Lebanon, 1711–1845* (Princeton: Princeton University Press, 1968)

Harik, Judith, 'Democracy Derailed: Lebanon's Ta'if Paradox', in Bahjat Korany, Rex Brynen and Paul Noble (eds), *Political Liberalization and Democratization in the Arab World*, vol.II: 'Arab Experiences' (Boulder, Colorado: Lynne Rienner, 1998), pp.127–55

_____, 'Citizen Disempowerment and the 1996 Parliamentary Elections in the Governorate of Mount Lebanon', *Democratization*, 5, 1 (Spring 1998), pp.158–82

_____, 'Syrian Foreign Policy and State/Resistance Dynamics in Lebanon', *Studies in Conflict and Terrorism*, 20 (1997), pp.249–65

_____, 'Between Islam and the System: Sources and Implications of Popular Support for Lebanon's Hizbullah', *Journal of Conflict Resolution*, 40, 1 (March 1996), pp.41–67

_____, *The Social and Public Services of the Lebanese Militias*, Papers on Lebanon Series, no.14 (Oxford: The Centre for Lebanese Studies, 1994)

_____ and Hilal Khashan, 'Lebanon's Divisive Democracy: The Parliamentary Elections of 1992', *Arab Studies Quarterly*, 15, 1 (1993), pp.41–59

Harmon, Christopher C, *Terrorism Today* (London: Frank Cass, 2000)

Hijazi, Hussein, '"Hamas: Waiting for Secular Nationalism to Self-Destruct", an interview with Mahmud Zahhar, spokesman of Hamas in Gaza, Oct–Dec', *Journal of Palestine Studies*, 24, 3 (Spring 1994), pp.81–8

Hinnebusch, Raymond A, 'The Islamic Movement in Syria: Sectarian Conflict and Urban Rebellion in an Authoritarian-Populist Regime', in 'Ali EH Dessouki, *Islamic Resurgence in the Arab World* (New York: Praeger, 1982), pp.138–70

_____ and Alasdair Drysdale, *Syria and the Middle East Peace Process* (New York: Council of Foreign Relations Press, 1992)

Hollis, Rosemary and Nadim Shehadi (eds), *Lebanon on Hold: Implications for Middle East Peace* (London: Royal Institute of International Affairs/Centre for Lebanese Studies, 1996)

Holt, PM and MW Daly, *A History of the Sudan: From the Coming of Islam to the Present Day* (Essex: Longman, 2000)

Horowitz, Donald L, *Ethnic Groups in Conflict* (Berkeley: University of California Press, 1985), especially Chapter 15, 'Structural Techniques – Lebanon', pp.633–5

Hottinger, Arnold, 'Zu'ama in Historical Perspective', in Leonard Binder (ed.), *Politics in Lebanon* (New York: John Wiley, 1966), pp.85–105

Hudson, Michael C, 'The Islamic Factor in Syrian and Iraqi Politics', in James Piscatori (ed.), *Islam in the Political Process* (London: Cambridge University Press, 1983), pp.73–97

_____, *The Precarious Republic: Political Modernization in Lebanon* (Boulder, Colorado: Westview Press, 1985)

_____, 'The Problem of Authorative Power in Lebanese Politics: Why Consociationalism Failed', in Nadim Shehadi and Dana Haffar Mills (eds), *Lebanon: A History of Conflict and Consensus* (London and New York: I.B.Tauris, 1988), pp.182–99

Human Rights Watch Report, 'Persona Non-Grata: The Expulsion of Civilians from Israeli Occupied Lebanon', July 1999

Hunter, Shireen (ed.), *The Politics of Islamic Revolution* (Bloomington, Indiana: Indiana University Press, 1988)

Irwin, Cynthia Lorraine, *Paramilitary Politics in Parliamentary Democracies: Militant Nationalism in Ireland and Spain*, PhD Dissertation (Raleigh, North Carolina: Duke University, 1995)

Jarrar, Bassam, 'The Islamist Movement and the Palestinian Authority', in Beinin and Stork (eds), *Political Islam: Essays from Middle East Report* (London and New York: I.B.Tauris, 1997), pp.335–48

Jerichow, Anders, *The Saudi File: People, Power and Politics* (Surrey: Curzon, 1998)

Keddie, Nikki R, *Iran: Religion, Politics and Society* (London: Frank Cass, 1980)

_____, 'Iran: Change in Islam: Islam and Change', *International Journal of Middle East Studies*, 11 (July 1980), pp.527–42

Kerr, Malcolm, 'Political Decision making in a Confessional Society', in Leonard Binder (ed.), *Politics in Lebanon* (New York: John Wiley, 1966)

Kfoury, Assaf, 'Hizb Allah and the Lebanese State', in Beinin and Stork (eds ), *Political Islam: Essays from Middle East Report* (London and New York: I.B.Tauris, 1997), pp.136–43

Khalaf, Samir, *Lebanon's Predicament* (New York: Columbia University Press, 1987)

_____, 'Primordial Ties and Politics in Lebanon', *Middle Eastern Studies*, 4, 3 (1968), pp.243–69

Khalidi, Walid C, *Conflict and Violence in Lebanon: Confrontation in the Middle East* (Cambridge, Massachusetts: Harvard Center for International Affairs, 1979)

Khashan, Hilal, 'The Political Values of Lebanese Maronites', *Journal of Conflict Resolution*, 34, 4 (December 1990), pp.723–4

_____, *Inside the Lebanese Confessional Mind* (Lanham, Maryland: University Press of America, 1992)

Khuri, Fuad I, *From Village to Suburb: Order and Change in Greater Beirut* (Chicago: Chicago University Press, 1975)

Kitschelt, Herbert, *The Logic of Party Formation: Structure and Strategy in the Belgian and West German Ecological Parties* (Ithaca, New York: Cornell University Press, 1989)

Klein, Menachem, 'Competing Brothers: The Web of Hamas-PLO Relations', *Terrorism and Political Violence*, 8, 2 (Summer 1996), pp.111–31

Kliot, N, 'The Collapse of the Lebanese State', *Middle Eastern Studies*, 23 (January 1987), pp.54–75

Kramer, Martin, 'The Oracle of Hezbollah, Sayyid Muhammad Hussein Fadlallah', in Appleby (ed.), *Spokesmen for the Despised: Fundamentalist Leaders of the Middle East* (Chicago: University of Chicago Press, 1997), pp.83–181

_____, *Hizbullah's View of the West* (Washington, DC: Washington Institute for Near East Policy, no.16, October 1989)

_____, 'The moral logic of Hizbullah', in Walter Reich (ed.), *Origins of Terrorism: Psychologies, Ideologies, Theologies, States of Mind* (Cambridge: Cambridge University Press, 1990), pp.131–57

_____, 'Redeeming Jerusalem: The Pan-Islamic Premise of Hezbollah', in David Manashri (ed.), *The Iranian Revolution and the Muslim World* (Boulder, Colorado: Westview Press, 1990), pp.105–30

_____, 'Hezbollah: The Calculus of Jihad', in Marty and Appleby (eds), *Fundamentalisms and the State: Remaking Polities, Economies and Militance* (Chicago: University of Chicago Press, 1993), pp.539–56

Landau, Jacob M, Ergun Ozbudun and Frank Tachau (eds), *Electoral Politics in the Middle East: Issues, Voters and Elites* (London: Croom Helm, 1980)

Lawson, Fred H, 'Social Basis of the Hamah Revolt', *MERIP Report*, 9 (November–December 1982)

Legrain, Jean-Francois, 'Palestinian Islamisms: Patriotism as a Condition of their Expansion', in Marty and Appleby (eds), *Accounting for Fundamentalisms* (Chicago: University of Chicago Press, 1994), pp.413–428

Long, David E, *The Kingdom of Saudi Arabia* (Gainesville, Florida: University Press of Florida, 1997)

Luft, Gal, 'Securing Northern Israel Following an IDF Withdrawal from South Lebanon', in Clawson and Eisenstadt (eds), *The Last Arab-Israeli Battlefield? Implications of an Israeli Withdrawal from Lebanon* (Washington, DC: Washington Institute for Near East Policy, 2000)

Ma'oz, Moshe and Avner Yaniv, *Syria Under Assad* (London: Croom Helm, 1986), pp.38–52

_____, *War and Intervention in Lebanon: The Israeli-Syrian Deterrence Dialogue* (London: Croom Helm, 1987)

Martin, Vanessa, *Creating an Islamic State: Khomeini and the Making of a New Iran* (London and New York: I.B.Tauris, 2000)

Marty, Martin E and R Scott Appleby (eds) *Fundamentalisms Observed* (Chicago: University of Chicago Press, 1991)

_____, *Fundamentalisms and the State: Remaking Politics, Economies, and Militance* (Chicago: University of Chicago Press, 1993)

_____, *Accounting for Fundamentalism: The Dynamic Character of Movements* (Chicago: University of Chicago Press, 1994)

_____, *Fundamentalisms Comprehended* (Chicago: University of Chicago Press, 1995)

Miller, Judith, 'Global Islamic Awakening or Sudanese Nightmare? The Curious Case of Hasan al-Turabi', in Appleby (ed.), *Spokesmen for the Despised: Fundamentalist Leaders of the Middle East* (Chicago: University of Chicago Press, 1997), pp.182–224

Mishal, Shaul and Avraham Sela, *The Palestinian Hamas: Vision, Violence, and Coexistence* (New York: Columbia University Press, 2000)

Moin, Baqer, *Khomeini: Life of the Ayatollah* (London and New York: I.B.Tauris, 1999)

Moussalli, Ahmad S (ed.), *Islamic Fundamentalism: Myths and Realities* (Reading: Ithaca Press, 1998)

\_\_\_\_\_, *Historical Dictionary of Islamic Fundamentalist Movements in the Arab World, Iran and Turkey* (Lanham, Maryland: Scarecrow Press, 1997)

Nasr, Samir, 'La Transition des Chiites vers Beyrouth: Mutations Sociales et Mobilisation Communautaire a la Veille de 1975', in CERMOC (ed.), *Mouvements Communautaires et Espaces Urbains au Machreq* (Beyrouth: CERMOC, 1985), pp.85–116

Nasrallah, Fida, 'The Treaty of Brotherhood, Cooperation and Coordination: An Assessment', in Choueiri (ed.), *State and Society in Syria and Lebanon* (New York: St Martin's Press, 1994), pp.103–11

Netanyahu, Benjamin, *Terrorism: How the West Can Win* (New York: Farrar Strauss Giroux, 1986)

Norton, Augustus Richard, *Amal and the Shi'a: Struggle for the Soul of Lebanon* (Austin: University of Texas Press, 1987)

\_\_\_\_\_, 'Lebanon: The Internal Conflict and the Iranian Connection', in Esposito (ed.), *The Iranian Revolution: Its Global Impact* (Miami: Florida International University Press, 1990), pp.116–37

\_\_\_\_\_, 'Lebanon after Ta'if – Is the Civil War Over?', *Middle East Journal*, 45, 3 (Summer 1991), pp.457–75

\_\_\_\_\_, *Hizbullah of Lebanon: Extremist Ideals vs. Mundane Politics* (New York: Council on Foreign Relations, 1999)

Peters, Rudolph, *Jihad in Classical and Modern Islam* (Princeton: Marcus Wiener Publishers, 1996)

\_\_\_\_\_, *Islam and Colonialism: The Doctrine of Jihad in Modern History* (The Hague: 1979)

Picard, Elizabeth, 'The Lebanese Shi'a and Political Violence in Lebanon', in Apter, *The Legitimization of Violence* (London: United Nations Research Institute for Social Development, 1997), pp.189–233

\_\_\_\_\_, 'Political Identities and Communal Identitites: Shifting Mobilization Among the Lebanese Shi'a Through Ten Years of War, 1975–1985', in Thompson and Ronen (eds), *Ethnicity, Politics and Development* (Boulder, Colorado: Lynne Riener, 1986), pp.159–77

Piscatori, James, 'The Roles of Islam in Saudi Arabia's Political Development', in Esposito (ed.), *Islam and Development* (Syracuse: Syracuse University Press, 1980), pp.123–38

Rabinovitch, Itamar, 'Controlled Conflict in the Middle East: The Syrian/Israeli Rivalry in Lebanon', in Ben-Dor and Dewitt (eds), *Conflict Management in the*

*Middle East* (Lexington, Maryland: DC Heath and Company, 1987), pp.97–111

Ramazani, Ruhollah K (ed.), 'The Islamization of Lebanon?', in *Revolutionary Iran: Challenge and Response in the Middle East* (Baltimore: Johns Hopkins University Press, 1986), pp.175–8

———, *Iran's Foreign Policy: A Study of Foreign Policy in Modernizing Nations* (Charlottesville, Virginia: University of Virginia Press, 1975)

Randal, Jonathon, *Going All the Way: Christian Warlords, Israeli Adventurers and the War in Lebanon* (New York: Viking Press, 1983)

Ranstorp, Magnus, 'Hizbollah's Command Leadership: Its Structure, Decision-Making and Relationship with Iranian Clergy and Institutions', *Terrorism and Political Violence*, 6, 3 (Autumn 1994), pp.303–39

———, *Hizb'allah in Lebanon: The Politics of the Western Hostage Crisis* (London: Macmillan Press Ltd, 1997)

Rejewan, Nissim, 'Pax Syrian for Lebanon', *Midstream* (October 1991), pp.9–11

Roberts, Hugh, 'From Radical Mission to Equivocal Ambition: The Expansion and Manipulation of Algerian Islamism, 1979–1992', in Marty and Appleby (eds), *Accounting for Fundamentalism*, pp.374–412

Rubin, Barry M, *The Transformation of Palestinian Politics: From Revolution to State-Building* (Cambridge, Massachusetts: Harvard University Press, 1999)

——— and Judith Colp Rubin, *Anti-American Terrorism and the Middle East* (London: Oxford University Press, 2002)

Saadeh, Safiyah, 'Greater Lebanon: The Formation of a Caste System?', in Youssef M Choueri (ed.), *State and Society in Syria and Lebanon*, pp.62–74

Sachedena, Abdulazziz A, 'Activist Shi'ism in Iran, Iraq and Lebanon', in Marty and Appleby (eds), *Accounting for Fundamentalism*, pp.422–43

Saikal, Amin, *The Rise and Fall of the Shah, 1941–1979* (Princeton, New Jersey: Princeton University Press, 1980)

Salameh, Ghassane, *Lebanon's Injured Identities: Who Represents Whom during a Civil War?*, Papers on Lebanon Series, No.2 (Oxford: Centre for Lebanese Studies, 1986)

Salem, Elie A, *Violence and Diplomacy in Lebanon: The Troubled Years, 1982–1988* (London and New York: I.B.Tauris, 1995)

Salem, Paul, 'Two Years of Living Dangerously: General Awn and the Precarious Rise of Lebanon's "Second Republic"', *Beirut Review*, I, 1 (1991), pp.81–7

——— and Farid el-Khazen, *al-intikhabet al-ula fi Lubnan ma b'ad al-harb: al-arkam wa al-wakii wa al-dalalt* (The First Elections in Lebanon after the War: Numbers, Facts and Evidence) (Beirut: The Lebanese Centre for Research, 1993)

Salibi, Kamal S, 'Lebanon – The Historic Perspective', in Hollis and Shehadi (eds), *Lebanon on Hold* (London Royal Institute of International Affairs/Centre for Lebanese Studies, 1996), pp.1–13

_____, *A House of Many Mansions: The History of Lebanon Reconsidered* (London and New York: I.B.Tauris, 1988)

_____, *Crossroads to Civil War: Lebanon, 1958–1976* (Delmar: Caravan Books, 1976)

_____, *The Modern History of Lebanon* (New York: Praeger, 1965)

Sartori, Giovanni, *Parties and Party Systems: A Framework for Analysis* (Cambridge: Cambridge University Press, 1976)

Sayigh, Yezid, *Armed Struggle and the Search for State: The Palestinian National Movement, 1949–1993* (Oxford: Clarendon Press, 1997)

Schieff, Zeev and Ehud Ya'ari (eds), *Israel's Lebanon War* (New York: Simon and Schuster, 1984)

Schieff, Zeev and Raphael Rothstein (eds), *Fedayeen: The Story of the Palestinian Guerrillas* (London: Vallentine, Mitchell, 1973)

Seale, Patrick, *Asad: The Struggle for the Middle East* (Berkeley, California: University of California Press, 1988)

_____, *The Struggle for Syria* (London: Oxford University Press, 1964)

Shapira, Simon, 'The Imam Musa al-Sadr: Father of the Shiite Resurgence in Lebanon', *Jerusalem Quarterly*, 44 (1987), pp.121–44

_____, 'The Origins of Hizbullah', *Jerusalem Quarterly*, 46 (1988), pp.115–30

Sharara, Waddah, *Dawlat Hizb'allah Lubnan Mujtawa'm Islamiyya* (Hizbullah's Lebanese State: An Islamic Society) (Beirut: Dar al-Nahar, 1996)

Shaykh, Farzana (ed.), *Islam and Islamic Groups: A Worldwide Reference Guide* (Essex: Longman Group, 1992)

Shearer, IA, *Starkes International Law*, 11th edition (London: Butterworths, 1994)

Shehadi, Nadim and Dana Haffar Mills (eds), *Lebanon: A History of Conflict and Consensus* (London and New York: I.B.Tauris, 1988)

Shlaim, Avi, 'Israeli Intervention in Internal Arab Politics – The Case of Lebanon', in L Guazzone (ed.), *The Islamist Dilemma: The Political Role of Islamist Movements in the Contemporary Arab World* (London: Garnet Publishing Company, 1995)

Sidahmed, Abdel Salam, *Politics and Islam in Contemporary Sudan* (New York: St Martin's Press, 1996)

Sivan, E and M Friedman, *Religious Radicalism and Politics in the Middle East* (New York: State University of New York Press, 1990)

Snider, Lewis W, 'The Lebanese Forces: Their Origins and Role in Lebanon's Politics', *Middle East Journal*, 38, 1 (Winter 1984), pp.1–33

Snow, D and R Benford, 'Ideology, Frame Resonance and Participant Mobilization', in B Klandermans, H Kriesi and S Tarrow (eds), *From Structure to Action: Comparing Social Movements Across Cultures* (Greenwich, Connecticut: JAI Press, 1988), pp.197–218

Soffer, A, 'Lebanon – Where Demography is the Fare of Politics and Life', *Middle Eastern Studies*, 18 (1982), pp.197–205

Tahman, Fazlar, 'Islam: Challenges and Opportunities', in Alford T Welch and Pierre Cashin (eds), *Islam: Past Influence and Present Challenge* (Edinburgh: Edinburgh University Press, 1979), pp.318–23

Tufeili, Shaykh Subhi, Interview, *Nouveau Magazine*, 11 June 1993, p.4–6

United Nations Development Programme, *Poverty and Gender Profile in the Baalbek-Hermel Region*, V.1 (Beirut: The Consultation and Research Institute, 1998)

United States Air Force, *Special Operations 1995: Air Force Doctrine*, Document 35 (Washington, DC: Department of the Air Force 9/1997)

United States State Department, *Patterns of Global Terrorism 1996* (Washington, DC: GPO, 1997)

Usher, Graham, 'What Kind of Nation? The Rise of Hamas in the Occupied Territories', in Beinin and Stork (eds), *Political Islam* (London and New York: I.B.Tauris & Co Ltd, 1997), pp.338–9

_____, 'Hizbullah, Syria, and the Lebanese Elections', *Journal of Palestine Studies*, 26, 2 (Winter 1997), pp.59–67

Van Glohn, *Law Among Nations*, 7th edition (London: Allyn and Bacon, 1996)

Vatikiotis, Panyotis J, *Islam and the State* (London: Croom-Helm, 1987)

Vaziri, Haleh, 'Iran's Involvement in Lebanon: Polarization and Radicalization of Militant Islamic Movements', *Journal of South Asian and Middle Eastern Studies*, 16, 2 (Winter 1992), pp.1–16

Verges, Meriem, 'Genesis of a Mobilization: The Young Activists of Algeria's ISF', in Beinin and Stork (eds), *Political Islam* (London and New York: I.B.Tauris & Co Ltd, 1997), pp.292–308

Voll, John Islam, *Continuity and Change in the Modern World* (Boulder, Colorado: Westview Press, 1982)

Williams, Rhys H, 'Movement Dynamics and Social Change: Transforming Fundamentalist Ideology and Organizations', Marty and Appleby (eds), *Accounting for Fundamentalism*, pp.786–834

Wright, Robin, *Sacred Rage* (New York: Simon and Schuster, 1985)

_____, *In the Name of God: The Khomeini Decade* (New York: Simon and Schuster, 1989)

Yaniv, Avner, *Dilemmas of Security, Politics, Strategy and the Israeli Experience in Lebanon* (New York: Oxford University Press, 1984)

Zald, Mayer N and John D McCarthy, *Social Movements in an Organizational Society: Collected Essays* (New Brunswick, New Jersey: Transaction Publishers, 1987)

Ziadeh, S and Elaine Hagopian, 'The Realignment of Power in Lebanon: Internal and External Dimensions', *Arab Studies Quarterly*, 17, 4 (1985)

Zisser, Eyal, 'Hizbullah in Lebanon – At the Crossroads', *Terrorism and Political Violence*, 8, 2 (1996), pp.90–110

Zonis, Marvin and Daniel Bromberg, *Khomeini, the Islamic Republic of Iran, and the Arab World* (Cambridge, Massachusetts: Center for Middle Eastern Studies, 1987)

# Index

Abi Talib, Ali bin (Prophet's cousin and son-in-law) 8

Abi Talib, Hussein bin Ali bin (Prophet's grandson) 199

al-Qaeda 9, 14, 19, 27, 163, 178, 185, 191, 200

Amal Movement (*afwaj al-muqawama al-lubnaniya*) and attack on Lebanese Army 75, 83; and Israel 40–1; and Lebanese National Resistance 41, 46, 51, 137; origins 22; and PLO 51; and reorganization of 109; and rivalry with Hezbollah 51–2, 88, 95, 97, 101–9, 114, 124, 149–51, social services 92

American Embassy bombing ix, 36, 170, 172

American Marine Barracks bombing ix, 36, 170

Annan, Kofi 144

Aoun, Michel 45–6, 53, 85

April Understanding (1996) 122–3, 181–2

Arafat, Yasser 25–6, 34, 186

Assad, Bashar 21, 154–6

Assad, Hafiz 11–12, 21, 31, 38, 40, 117–18

Ashura 199

Atwa, Ali 169

Awdah, Abdul Aziz 25

Baalbek 38–9; Iranian Revolutionary Guards in 55; municipal elections in 108; socio-economic conditions in 86–7

Baath Party, see Syria

Banna, Hassan 10–11, 68

Barak, Ehud 124–5, 144

Bashir, Omar Hassan 13, 15

Battle, Vincent 178, 202

Bekaa Valley, see Baalbek; municipal elections in 107; and Revolutionary Guards in 39; Syrian presence in 38–9

Beirut, East 39, 134; explosion at Lebanese Forces headquarters 35; municipal elections in 107; parliamentary elections (2000) in 150–1; southern suburb (*dahiyeh*) conflict in 51, 83–4, 104; municipal elections in 75–7, 101–4; social services in 83–6

Beirut, West, Battle of 35–8; catastrophes in 27–8, 172; Hezbollah demonstrations in 123, 133; Israeli army in 64–5; multinational force in 36; Syrian troops in 44; see also Israel

Berri, Nabih, and Amal 22; electoral competition with Hezbollah 96–7, 99–109, 148–51; cooperation with Hezbollah 77, 96, 149–50; and Israel 40–1; and PLO 51; political views of 51, 157, 191; and South Lebanon 88, 93, 106–7, 124, 150; and Syria 110; see also Council of the South

bin Laden, Osama 12, 20, 140, 144, 159, 163, 201

Bint Jbeil, municipal elections in 107

Border disputes 143–3, 158–60; see also Shebaa Farms and Ghajar

Brom, Shlomo 144–45

Bush, George W. 165, 178, 183–4, 186, 191; administration, see United States

Cairo Accord 34

Ceasefire Surveillance Committee 122–3, 182

Christian militias 36, 43–4, 67–8, 83

Christian opposition 44–6, 74, 98, 121, 128, 135–6, 141, 180

Christopher, Warren 115, 119, 122, 156

Civil war 3, 17–18, 22, 28, 38–9, 82–3

Council of the South (*majlis al-janub*) 120–1, 160

Dahiyeh, see Beirut, southern suburb

De Mistura, Steffan 158–60, 183

Document of National Reconciliation 44–5

Egypt, crisis of secularism in 12; Muslim Brotherhood in 10–12; peace treaty with Israel, 12

Ezzedin, Hassan 169

Ezzedin, Sheikh Hassan 183

Fadlallah, Mohammed Hussein 22, 37, 60, 171; and Arab Nationalist discourse 70; assassination attempt on 37; on Christian-Muslim understanding 56, 68, 70, 73; and Hezbollah 61–2, 65; on an Islamic Republic in Lebanon 56, 61, 69–70

Fatah 24–5, 34, 73, 171, 190

Fatimah Gate 138–9, 156

France, see 'April understanding'; and assistance for Lebanon 152–3, 179; and bombing of paratrooper headquarters 36–7, 64, 70, 170, 172; and ceasefire negotiations 118; see also cease fire Surveillance Committee; and Lebanese Christians 16, 45, 68, 116, 135; as Mandate power, 17, 30, 159, 144

Fundamentalism 9–10, 23–4; and leaders 69

Gazit, Shlomo 167

Gemayel, Amin 67–189

Gemayel, Bashir 35–6, 44

Geneva Convention 26, 165–6

Ghajar 144, 157–60

Golan Heights 27, 30–1, 38, 47, 125, 140, 156–7, 159, 166, 198

Guerrilla warfare 168–9; see also Hezbollah

Haddad, Saad 35, 41

Hamas, and Hezbollah, see Hezbollah; and ideology and tactics of 24–7, 71–2, 117–8, 164;

and Palestinian Authority 26–7; and PLO 71

Harat Hreik, municipal elections in 75–7

Harb, Ragheb 55

Hammoud, Mahmoud 157

Hariri, Rafik and Council for Development and Reconstruction 100; election strategies of 95–105, 150–1; and friction with Hezbollah 151–4; and support for resistance 119–20, 180, 187; and Solidere 99

Hasbani River 144, 159–60

Hezbollah and advocacy role 52, 89–90; and Amal rivalry 51–2, 82, 92, 99; see 'April Understanding'; charter of 66–9; and confessionalism 67, 197; and election strategies/results, see municipal and parliamentary elections; emergence of 21; and finances of 82; and guerrilla warfare 3, 27–8, 113, 117–18, 128, 131–2, 166–9, 195; and Hamas 188–91; ideology 16–7, 19, 27, 59, 66, 69, 71–2, 196; and *infitah* policy 51–2, 73–8, 101, 136; and internal divisions 56–7; and *intifada* 161–2, 175, 185–91, 200; and Iran 16, 28, 39–40, 52, 81–2, 85, 87, 89–90, 93, 199, 200; as Islamic resistance 69, 71, 124, 134, 199–200; see also charter; and Israeli hostages 155; over-flights 183–84; withdrawal from Lebanon 148–51, 155–62, 195; and jihad 67–8, 71–2, 118, 134; and Lebanese Government, cooperation with 19–20, 76, 83, 85, 89–91, 104, 140; 'deal' with 47–8; tensions with 97, 113–4, 119, 123–4, 153; see Nasrallah, Hassan; and the media 54, 133; see Manar Television; and

National Brigade 73; as National resistance 43, 169; organizational structure 54; origins of 172; popular support for 48–51, 86, 108–9, 133, 138, 148 51; see municipal and parliamentary elections; public and social services of 81–94; see Qassim, Naim; and reconstruction activities, see Reconstruction Campaign; and response to war against global terrorism 183; see Shebaa Farms; and South Lebanese Army 78, 114, 122, 126, 130; and Syria 40; also see Syria

Higher Shiite Islamic Council 22

Hirawi, Elias 119–20

Hostages, Americans held in Iran 32; Lebanon x, 37; Israelis held in Lebanon 155; see Waite, Terry

Husseiniyyas 60

Ibn Abdullah, Mohammed (Prophet) 7–8

Intifada 25–6; see Hezbollah; see Israel

Iran, and Hezbollah 39, 82–3; and Iraq war 32–4; and Islamic revolution 15–17, 21, 24–5, 200; see Khomeini, Ayatollah Ruhollah; and Lebanon 34–8; and Middle East policy 199–200; and Revolutionary Guards 15, 32, 39, 40, 55, 172, 186; and Syrian alliance 33–39; under Shah's regime (see Pahlavi, Mohammed Reza); and war against global terrorism 164–5; and western imperialism 31–32

Islamic Amal 39

Islamic Jihad 25–6

Islamic law (*Sharia*) 16

Islamic Resistance, see Hezbollah

Islamic Resurgence 8–28

Israel, and the annexation of Golan Heights, see Golan Heights; see 'April Understanding'; and Arab wars 23; creation of 23; ideology, see Zionism; and intifada 177, 186, 188, 194; and Lebanese Christian militias 31; and military operations in Lebanon, 'Accountability' 112, 115–16; 'Grapes of Wrath' 112, 117–22, 156; 'Litani' 49, 50, 72, 139, 166; 'Peace for Galilee' 35; over-flights 18, 183–4; and South Lebanese Army, see South Lebanese Army; and Syria, tacit understanding with 39, 93, 118; attacks on Syrian communications installations in Lebanon 156; and war against global terrorism 177–8

Jezzine, evacuation of 127–9
Jihad 57–60; Hezbollah's jihad, see Hezbollah
Jihad al-Binaa, see Reconstruction Campaign
Jordan, arms smuggling from 186, 200; and peace treaty with Israel 30; River basin 159

Katyusha rocket attacks 112, 115, 117, 132, 145, 156, 167, 188–90
Kenaan, Ghazi 153
Khalaf, Salah (Abu Ayad), 171
Khamenei, Ayatollah Ali 16, 56, 200
Khansa, Mohammed 103–4
Khatami, Mohammed 200
Khiam Prison 138
Khomeini, Ayatollah Ruhollah 16–17, 21, 23–4, 32, 53, 55–6, 65, 67–8
Kidnappings, see hostages
Kiryat Shimona 145
Koran 8, 10, 20, 57–8, 81–2, 93

Lahd, Antoine 127
Lahoud, Emile 139, 141, 151, 153, 180–1, 191
Lebanese Army, and avoiding clash with Israeli military 114; and clashes with Amal 83; and cooperation with Christian militias 36, 44; disintegration of 18, 39; defeat of 45; and dispute over sending to border area 4, 48, 78–92, 121, 125, 127–9, 134–5, 139, 141–3, 147, 152–3, 166, 198; and 'Grapes of Wrath' 121; and Palestinian arrests 190; and reconstruction with Syrian help 45; and Tufeili demonstration 60; US assistance to 36–7
Lebanese Forces 44, 77
Lebanese Government, and 'Accountability' operation 115–16; see Berri, Nabih; and 'deal' with Hezbollah 47–8; and 'Grapes of Wrath' operation 112–14; see Hariri, Rafik; and Israeli withdrawal 126, 130–1, 134–6, 142–3; and joint foreign policy with Syria 44, 46–7, 116–22, 164–5, 197–8; see Lahoud, Emile; and position on Hezbollah as national resistance 165–70; and US anti-terrorism policy 178–82
Lebanese militias 22, 31; see Lebanese Forces and Phalange Party
Lebanon, see civil war; confessional political structure of 17–8 63–76, 97, 101, 121, 141; see municipal and parliamentary elections in

Mahalati, Fazlallah 53
Manar Television, intifada campaign 160–1, 186; resistance coverage 72, 116–7, 131, 133–4, 138–9; 'proactive' policy 160–1, 189, 200

Military occupation, see Geneva Conventions and 'Security Zone'

Mofaz, Shaul 145

Mohtashemi, Hojjatoleslam Ali Akbar 55–6

Movement of the Disinherited (harakat al-mahrumin) 22

Mugniyeh, Imad, and arms smuggling 186; and Beirut attacks 172; and Karine A 175; and Fatah 171; and Hezbollah 171, 173, 186–7; and hostages, see hostages; and Lebanon's position on 174; and Rafiqdost 171–2; see TWA hijackings; and US intelligence on 172–4, 187

Municipal elections 75–7, 95–110

Musawi, Abbas 54–5, 59, 187

Musawi, Hussein 22–3, 39, 54–5, 187

Muslim Brotherhood in Egypt 12–3; origins 10; in Palestine 24–5; in Sudan 13–5; in Syria 10–12, 21

Nabatiyeh, municipal elections in 106–7

Najaf and Shiite religious leaders 16, 22, 54

Naqoura 56

Nasrallah, Hadi 72

Nasrallah, Hassan, and Nabih Berri 99; and criticism of Lebanese government 154; and dialogue with Christians 74, 78; and 'direct intervention in intifada' 161; and electoral democracy 98; and gun-smuggling charges 187; and Hezbollah leadership 54–5, 59; ideological flexibility of 57, 71–2, 124; and jihad 124; and political discourse of 62; and public respect for 72–3; on resistance activities after Israeli withdrawal 141 144; on charges of politicizing the resistance 123; on war against global terrorism 183; and Shebaa Farms 140–1

Nasser, Jamal Abdul 10, 12; and influence in Lebanon 18; and union with Syria 11

National Brigade, see Hezbollah

National Movement 51

Oslo Accord 25

Organization of Islamic Countries (OIC) 180

Pahlavi, Mohammed Reza 31–2; see Iran

Palestinian Authority 25; and Bush administration 26

Palestinian Refugees in Lebanon 19; see Sabra and Shatila massacres

Palestine and Zionists 23

Palestine Liberation Organization (PLO), and cross-border attacks ix, 19, 22, 34, 168, 171; evacuation from Lebanon 32; and Iran 34; and Israel 34–5, 48; and Mugniyeh 54, 171; and Syria 34, 39

Parliamentary elections 1992 47, 50–2, 1996 97–8, 2,000 148–51

Peres, Shimon, and 'Accountability' operation 115; and Clinton 117; and 'Grapes of Wrath' operation 117, 122; and Hezbollah 156, 184

Phalange Party 68, 77, 101

Powell, Colin 152, 184–5, 188–9

Qana 121–2

Qaouk, Nabil 131–3, 135, 158, 162

Qassim, Naim 54, 149, 173

Qutb, Sayyed 10–11, 68

Rabin, Itzhak 167, 182

Rafiqdost, Mohsen 171–3
Rasul al-Azam Hospital 61, 83–4, 103–4
Rafsanjani, Hashemi 56–7
Reagan, Ronald 33, 38
'Revolt of the Hungry', see Tufeili, Subhi
Reconstruction Campaign (*jihad al-binaa*) 54, 84, 88–92, 106, 124
Revolutionary Guards, see Iran
Rice, Condoleeza 174–5, 178–9, 186
Rousat al-Alam 183, 189

Sabra and Shatila massacres 23, 36, 64–5, 78
Sadat, Anwar 12
Sadr, Mohammed Baqer 22, 53
Sadr, Musa 22, 99, 105
Salafiyyun 20
Saud, Abdullah bin abdul Aziz 20
Saud, Mohammed Ibn 20
Saudi Arabia Islamic resurgence in 15, 20–1, 24, 34, 44; terrorist attacks in 171–201
Sayyed, Ibrahim Amin 54, 57
Security Council, see United Nations
'Security Zone', elections in 77, 106; establishment of 17, 40; Hezbollah tactics, in see Hezbollah; Israeli evacuation of 112, 126–134, 137–9, 142; Israel's goals in 166; 'rules' of combat in 115, 117, 167–8; and SLA in, see SLA
Sfeir, Nasrallah Bulos 73, 180
Shami, Hussein 85, 93
Sharaa, Farouk 118, 122, 157, 184–5
*Sharia*, see Islamic law
Sharon, Ariel, and attacks on Syrian troops in Lebanon 156; and the intifada 26; and *Karine A* incident 186; and 'Peace for Galilee' mili-

tary operation; and 'Protective Shield' operation 186, 188, 191; and Sabra-Shatila massacres, see Sabra and Shatila massacres; and water pumping dispute 160
Shebaa Farms 139; and Hezbollah attacks on 152, 155–6, 183, 185–6, 188–9, 198; and sovereignty dispute, Lebanon's position on 140, 142–3, 189; Israel's position on 141–2; United Nations position on 139–41
Shiites, doctrine 8–9; in Lebanon, displacement of 19; mobilization of, see Movement of the Disinherited and Amal; socio-economic plight of 18, 83–9; political grievances of 20; and Iran 34–5
South Lebanese Army (SLA), attacks on, see Hezbollah; and Israel 31, 34, 41, 49; legal proceedings against members 129–30; return to Lebanon from Israel 143, 155; surrender of 127–9, 137
South Lebanon, see border disputes; military operations in, see 'Security Zone', Israel and Hezbollah; parliamentary elections in 149–50; municipal elections in 105–7
Soviet Union 17, 22, 31–2; and Arab clients 38, 132
Sudan, Islamic resurgence in 13–15
Suicide/martyrdom attacks 26–7
Sunnite Islam 8–9
Syrian Arab Republic, see Assad, Bashar and Hafiz; and Baath Party 11–12; and Document of National Reconciliation 45–6; foreign policy dynamics of 117–22; Hezbollah as surrogate force of 31, 38–41; and influence in Lebanon 43–7, 153–55,

196, 198; and Iranian foreign policy cooperation 32–34, 38–41; and Islamic resurgence 11–12, 21; and 'land for peace' negotiations 184–5, 198, 201; policy 30, 118, 135, 186, 194; and Muslim-leftist coalition 31; and state-resistance two-track policy 129, 136, 190; and US support for Israel 30; and war against global terrorism 164–5, 185

Tacit understanding on rules of combat (1993) 117–19, 182
Taif Accord, see Document of National Reconciliation
Terrorism 65, 166, see Hamas, Hezbollah and terrorism 44, 195; Israel's position on 135, 141, 167–9, 186, 188, 194; Lebanon's position on 174, 179–82, 196; US position on 17, 164–5, 169–75, 193–95; see suicide-martyrdom attacks
Treaty of Brotherhood, Cooperation and Coordination 46
Tripartite Accord 44
Turabi, Hassan 13–5
Tufeili, Subhi 54–7, 59–60, 65, 108–10
TWA 847; hijacking x, 37–8, 169, 187
Twelver Shiism 9
Tyre, municipal elections in 105–7; parliamentary elections in 150

United Nations Disengagement Observation Force (UNDORF) 139–40;
Economic and Social Council for West Asia (ESCWA) 86–7, 90–4; Interim Force in Lebanon (UNIFIL) 140, 183; and Israeli-Lebanese Frontier in 1948 144; and line of withdrawal (in 2000) 140–3, 155, 157–9; Security Council Resolutions (242) 140, 184; (338) 184; (350) 141; (425–6) 113–5, 134, 141; (1373) 181
United States, anti-terrorism campaign, in Lebanon 175–6, 178–9, 197–8; in Syria 184–5, 198; and Iran, as sponsor of terrorism 27, 32–3, 36–7, 171–2 , 175, 191, 199–200; under Shah's regime 15, 31–2; under Khomeini's regime 32–4; and Iraq 33; and Israel 177; and Lebanon 178–9; and 'Most Wanted Terrorists List' 169; see terrorism; and war against global terrorism 163–4

Velayati, Ali Akbar 122

Wahhab, Mohammed Ibn Abdul 20
Waite, Terry 60
Water disputes 30–1, 49, 143–44, 159–60
Wazzani River 144, 159

Yassin, Ahmad 25, 71

Zionism 23